UP TO HEAVEN
AND
DOWN TO HELL

UP TO HEAVEN

AND

DOWN TO HELL

Fracking, Freedom, and Community
in an American Town

COLIN JEROLMACK

PRINCETON UNIVERSITY PRESS

PRINCETON AND OXFORD

Published by Princeton University Press
41 William Street, Princeton, New Jersey 08540
6 Oxford Street, Woodstock, Oxfordshire OX20 1TR

press.princeton.edu

All Rights Reserved

Library of Congress Cataloging-in-Publication Data

Names: Jerolmack, Colin, author.
Title: Up to heaven and down to hell : fracking, freedom, and community in
    an American town / Colin Jerolmack.
Description: Princeton : Princeton University Press, [2021] |
    Includes bibliographical references and index.
Identifiers: LCCN 2020045112 (print) | LCCN 2020045113 (ebook) |
    ISBN 9780691179032 (hardback ; alk. paper) | ISBN 9780691220260 (ebook)
Subjects: LCSH: Gas industry—Environmental aspects—Pennsylvania—
    Williamsport. | Hydraulic fracturing—Environmental aspects—Pennsylvania—
    Williamsport. | Oil and gas leases—Pennsylvania—Williamsport. | Landowners—
    Pennsylvania—Williamsport. | Environmentalism—Pennsylvania—Williamsport. |
    Williamsport (Pa.)—Environmental conditions.
Classification: LCC HD9581.U52 P445 2021 (print) | LCC HD9581.U52 (ebook) |
    DDC 338.2/7280974851--dc23
LC record available at https://lccn.loc.gov/2020045112
LC ebook record available at https://lccn.loc.gov/2020045113

British Library Cataloging-in-Publication Data is available

Editorial: Meagan Levinson and Jacqueline Delaney
Production Editorial: Ellen Foos
Text Design: Karl Spurzem
Jacket Design: Faceout Studio
Production: Erin Suydam
Publicity: Maria Whelan and Kathryn Stevens
Copyeditor: Stephen Twilley

Jacket images (front and back) courtesy of Colin Jerolmack

This book has been composed in Arno Pro and Trade Gothic

Printed on acid-free paper. ∞

Printed in the United States of America

10 9 8 7 6 5 4 3 2 1

To Shatima. For waiting. And for everything else, too.

Your rights extend under and above your claim
Without bound; you own land in Heaven and Hell

—WILLIAM EMPSON, "LEGAL FICTION" (1928)

CONTENTS

ILLUSTRATIONS

Land of the Freehold

"If I ever had to leave this property, I'd suck on a gun barrel."* George Hagemeyer was staring out the kitchen window of his modest farmhouse at the large swath of lawn once tended by his father. A fifty-eight-year-old retired school custodian and proud "country boy," he has lived on the seventy-seven-acre plot, tucked away in a secluded mountain hollow twenty minutes north of Williamsport in Lycoming County, Pennsylvania, his whole life.[1]

When George's parents bought the farmstead, in 1947, the house was rudimentary; a tornado destroyed the barn the next year. As the years went by, George's father patiently fixed the place up and rebuilt the barn. He finally got around to starting work on an indoor bathroom to replace the outhouse in the fall of 1957. But a few days before Christmas, just as the biting winter winds began to sweep across the Appalachian foothills, he fell off a ladder while hanging plastic over the kitchen windows. "Hit his head on a rock." George's glassy eyes meandered from a strip of peeling linoleum to the very window where his mother, cooking dinner at the time, watched his father die. "Mom had to put his body and the seven kids in the car and run him to the hospital." George was just two

---

* Throughout this book, double quotation marks signify that the utterance was audio-recorded and transcribed verbatim. Single quotation marks represent my reconstruction of dialogue based on handwritten notes. I make this distinction to signal that utterances inside single quotation marks may be less reliable than those inside double quotation marks, as it seems almost impossible to capture speech verbatim with notes, even if they are written contemporaneously.

years old. A bachelor to this day, he stayed home after all his siblings moved out, to help his mother raise a baby girl that his sister had planned to put up for adoption (a child whom he came to consider his), and then to care for his mother until her death, in 2008.

To be the steward of his dad's land, George beamed, was "all I ever wanted." He devoted most days to his estate. He paced the perimeter for hours each day ("I just love to walk my property"), religiously mowed the grass (which took the better part of a day), and tended to the lilac bushes his mother planted long ago. And he took hundreds of mundane photographs of his land with disposable film cameras, which he planned to compile as a book that will "stay with the property . . . after I'm dead and gone . . . [as] a record of what went on" here. George loved showing off his land and hated to leave the premises for even a few hours. He seldom did. In fact, he claimed it had been thirty years since he overnighted somewhere else. "My daughter *had* to see Disneyland," he chuckled.

I first met George in the spring of 2013. The Texas-based Anadarko Petroleum Corporation was in the midst of drilling six natural-gas wells on four acres of leased land it had cleared in a field 350 yards behind his house. It had long been rumored in these parts that vast reserves of methane lay frozen inside a stratum of shale buried a mile or so underground. Over the last century, ragtag "wildcatters" and a few more-established petroleum companies had periodically poked thousand-foot holes in the earth in the hopes of tapping into pockets of the gas that leaked out of the porous rock. In time, they threw everything but the kitchen sink down vertical wellbores to try to shatter the shale and increase the flow rate of escaped methane molecules. Some tried dynamite, and even napalm; the government once experimented with nuclear bombs.[2] It was mostly a fool's errand. Even when wildcatters began hydraulically fracturing—aka fracking—shale in the 1950s, by forcing water, lubricants, and sand down the well at pressure high enough to open up tiny fissures in the rock, the value of the amount of gas recouped from each well seldom exceeded the cost of drilling. Drilling vertically into shale is like taking a core sample— each well can only tap a tiny cross section of it.

In the 1980s and 1990s, petroleum companies began experimenting with remote-controlled drill bits that, during their approach to the rock layer, could gradually angle ninety degrees so that they tunneled along the methane-laced seam of shale—the equivalent of tapping the vein. It was only by marrying fracking with so-called horizontal drilling that the largest deposit of natural gas in the United States, the Marcellus shale "play" (industry parlance for a large shale mineral deposit), was finally opened up for development this century.

It is a cornerstone of American property law that estate ownership traditionally extends above and below the land's surface, excepting instances in which surface rights and mineral rights have been explicitly severed by a previous title holder. The idea descends from the medieval Roman jurist Accursius's dictum "Cuius est solum ejus est usque ad coelum et ad inferos" (Whoever owns the soil, it is theirs up to heaven and down to hell). This meant that energy companies could only extract the gas beneath George's and his neighbors' property if landowners gave them permission.[3] It also meant that energy companies had to pay them a leasing bonus, compensate them for any "surface disturbance" to the land, and share a portion of the royalties generated by selling the gas extracted from their estate. George was one of thousands across the poverty-stricken rust belt who eagerly leased their mineral rights in the ensuing land rush, inviting an energy company to drill under his beloved homestead in the hopes of winning the fracking lottery.

Wearing a threadbare Montoursville High School Basketball T-shirt, George excitedly led the way to the parking lot–sized gravel well pad. "I'm fascinated by what they're doing and how they're doing it and how much it takes to do it. It's really, really neat to watch it. I come down here every day." The trail of trammeled grass from his back door to the pad was testament to the retiree's preoccupation. As we scrambled atop the berm overlooking the giant industrial operation, a 150-foot-tall drilling rig loomed like a larger-than-life erector set, methodically driving three forty-foot segments of threaded steel drill pipes into a predrilled hole. George marveled at the engineering feat we were witnessing: ultimately, the threaded-together sections of steel pipe would plunge vertically for a mile, then gradually arc horizontally as they neared the shale layer, where they would then burrow parallel to the surface for another mile through the rock seam under George's and his neighbors' properties. After cement casing was poured as a protective lining, pipe-bomb-like depth charges placed along the horizontal portion of the wellbore would be detonated, unleashing a hail of ball bearings to perforate the shale. Finally, dozens of big rigs carting millions of gallons of water, sand, and chemical-laced lubricants would idle on the well pad as their contents were mixed and then injected at high pressure into the well to frack it, creating thousands of tiny fissures in the rock that allow the gas to escape. (The sand acts as a "proppant," holding the fractures open.)

George conceded that the rural serenity he held dear was shattered by the security guard shack and portable toilet stationed at the entrance to his unadorned gravel driveway, the caravan of big rigs inching by his house, the large earthmovers tearing up his meticulously mowed lawn, and the din of drilling equipment. "I might as well be in Williamsport," he grumbled, meaning that fracking brought the worst of the urbanized county seat to the pastoral landscape of Trout Run. Despite enduring months of near-nonstop disruption, however, George said he still felt good about having leased his land to Anadarko. "Anadarko's been great to me," he emphasized, noting that when they dug up "mom's lilacs" they carefully replanted them. If the gas firm caused any problems, George insisted, "I would be the first to tell you." His smile fading to a stone-faced stare, he vowed, "It's my dad's land. Excuse the phrase, but nobody's gonna fuck it up, or I'm going after 'em."

George had heard about problems with fracking in Dimock, a town to the north made infamous by the images of flaming faucets featured in the provocative 2010 documentary *Gasland*. But, a contrarian by nature, he was skeptical: "All the crap you hear on TV of this is bad, this is gonna happen, they're doing this, they're doing that . . . I just don't go for it." Perhaps George would have paid heed if he had known about the troubles experienced by a couple living just eighteen miles from Trout Run, in another rural hamlet outside Williamsport. Tom and Mary Crawley, childhood sweethearts who kept a tidy home on nine acres of ancestral farmland, only leased their land after consulting with other residents of Green Valley. They wanted to be good neighbors. In the end, the Crawleys and their neighbors decided to collectively bargain with gas companies as a landowner coalition in an effort to get fair leases for everyone. Strikingly, after a neighbor's gas well flooded their drinking water with methane, the Crawleys' neighborliness also kept them from "raising a stink" about it. Tom said he was determined to keep the incident out of the news. As he saw it, his friends benefited from fracking, and he worried that environmentalists might harass his neighbor if they found out how the neighbor's gas well had contaminated his water.

Environmentalists were not welcome around here. After many conversations with George, I could not help think that his skepticism about the risks posed by drilling was related to his disdain for a certain anti-fracking activist named Wendy Lee who taught philosophy at Bloomsburg University. A tattooed self-proclaimed Marxist, atheist, and feminist, Wendy was known for disrupting local town hall meetings, blocking gas trucks, and stalking lessors' properties to photograph how fracking "rapes" the land. What galled George the most was that she did not even live in the area. Wendy was, in the words of a local industry-funded pro-fracking advocacy group, a "professional protester," commuting from a college town located an hour and a half away—beyond the edge of the Marcellus shale   to stir up trouble.[4] George had yet to meet her, but he seemed to be almost spoiling for a fight should she dare trespass on his land.

Even more than by his dislike of Wendy, it seemed likely to me, George's confidence in the gas industry was influenced by the fact that Anadarko had provided him with a life-changing windfall before drilling even began: the pensioner received $60,000 for allowing a small-diameter pipeline to be buried along the perimeter of his field in 2012; the pipeline would transport the gas away from his wellheads to East Coast energy markets. He saved some of the money as a college fund for his adopted daughter's kids, and he proudly showed off a new Ford SUV, a zero-degree-radius mower, and a treadmill that he purchased with the remainder. Once the six gas wells in his backyard were hooked up to the pipeline, in 2014, George's first royalty check for the gas extracted from under his land was a whopping $34,880. George was on his way to becoming a *shaleionaire*.

* * *

Sociologist Kai Erikson notes that the Scotch-Irish and German immigrants who settled along the spine of the Appalachian mountain

range in the late 1700s and early-to-mid-1800s possessed a "keen independence of mind and a distrust of society." To this day, the rugged hol-
lows that stretch from Alabama to New York act as a "natural shelter from
the jurisdiction of state and Federal law."[5] Observers like J. D. Vance note
the perseverance of a "remarkably cohesive" Appalachian culture that
upholds the individualist spirit of its original settlers.[6] Life in Appalachia
is not easy. It has some of the highest unemployment and poverty rates
in the country, and many residents struggle with opioid and methamphetamine addiction. Locals can be notoriously hostile toward people
perceived to be racial and cultural outsiders. But where many outsiders
see a "white ghetto" marked by deprivation and pathology, many residents believe that their spatial and social isolation affords them "an almost perfect freedom," according to Erikson.[7] "To be free, unbeholden,
lord of himself and his surroundings," opined the documentarian of
Appalachia Horace Kephart, "is the wine of life to a mountaineer."[8]

George would agree. He was fiercely protective of his property, and
jealously guarded his sovereignty over it. He scoffed at the idea that his
community—or the government, for that matter—had any say in how he
used it. Live and let live, he figured. Many of his neighbors figured the
same. So when the traveling salespeople known as "landmen" stalked
country roads outside town, soliciting landowners to lease their minerals,
many potential lessors like George took for granted that the decision was
a private matter, even though development on their land could create spillover effects that harmed their neighbors' properties or degraded local environmental resources. In fact, there was no formal mechanism in place to
facilitate collective deliberation over leasing. Nor was there robust federal
oversight of land leasing or the industry itself. Most residents saw nothing
unusual or troublesome about the fact that landowners had near-total autonomy over this land use decision and bore responsibility for determining
the risk. Yet it struck me as odd, considering that many private decisions
that may impact the commonwealth, like constructing a cell phone tower
or a pond on one's property, required a greater degree of public consent.

Most of us can avoid acknowledging how our behaviors may hinder
others' ability to enjoy environmental goods. Carbon-intensive actions
like traveling by plane or eating meat are framed as personal lifestyle

choices that have no bearing on the public interest and therefore ought not be subject to oversight or restriction. The environmental impacts are diffuse and abstract. It is only when summed with countless others' individual acts that yours contribute to global warming, sea-level rise, droughts, wildfires, and hurricanes (which in turn jeopardize others' livelihoods). Though often described in the dispassionate language of behavioral science (e.g., "externalities"), the result is a political—and planetary—crisis: live and let live becomes a logical contradiction. It's impossible to freely live in a way that does not hinder others' ability to do so. I call this the *public/private paradox.*

Though few lessors thought about it on this scale, the decision to lease one's mineral rights for fracking can have significant planetary consequences. Every lease plays a small role in slowing America's transition to renewable energy. Methane itself is a potent greenhouse gas, and so the leakage of unburned methane from wells, pipelines, and other infrastructure contributes to global warming as well. But many of the spillover effects are felt much closer to home, on adjoining properties, in the form of air, water, and light pollution, damaged roads, the degradation of a community's rural character, and so on. Fracking is intimate. Shale communities are in the unenviable position of having to confront the public/private paradox face to face, at the fence post, the general store, Little League games, and town hall meetings. This book centers on how Williamsport area residents negotiated the conflict between their commitments to personal sovereignty and to letting others live free—a dilemma that the climate crisis will force all of us to reckon with, sooner or later.

My analysis of how the public/private paradox played out in greater Williamsport offers a pathway into a series of large and pressing questions about how and why natural-resource dilemmas arise and persist, and about how America's political traditions and the rural-urban divide contribute to them.

* * *

In the end, almost every landowner in greater Williamsport leased. The few who sounded alarm bells were, for the most part, dismissed as elitist outsiders with no skin in the game and a misguided faith in state regulation. Cindy Bower, a silver-haired environmentalist in her sixties, was one of those outsiders. She traveled the world, preferred the *New York Times* over the *Williamsport Sun-Gazette*, and drove a Toyota Prius hybrid. And she was considerably wealthier, more educated, and more liberal than most of her neighbors. (Donald Trump's populist message resonated with about 70 percent of Lycoming County voters in 2016 and 2020; the city of Williamsport, which is nearby but somewhat removed from the rest of the rural county, was Democrats' sole island of support.) Originally from Pittsburgh, Cindy moved to rural Pennsylvania with her first husband in 1973 to teach elementary school after getting a master's degree from Penn State. That made her a "rusticator"—someone of means who moved from a metropolitan area to the country—notwithstanding her decades of local residence. After getting divorced, she settled in town and remarried. In 1997, Cindy persuaded her second husband, a "city boy" and millionaire hotelier, to relocate from Williamsport to a 150-acre plot of dense forest and gently sloping fields adorned with a large man-made pond. "My husband said, I want water. If you can find some water, I'll move to the country." Cindy called the place her refuge from the world. The pond, the property's centerpiece, was rimmed by two handsome chalets that the Bowers had built (one for her parents) and a guest cottage reconstructed from the original nineteenth-century log farmhouse.

As we sipped coffee in her sunroom on an overcast April morning in 2013, watching raindrops send countless tiny ripples across the pond's surface, Cindy reminisced about carrying signs for the first Earth Day, in 1970, and lamented that the condition of the planet has only worsened since then. Most especially, she worried about the ecological damage wrought by what she described as America's century-long addiction to fossil fuels, of which the shale gas extraction around her was just the latest chapter.

The first time Cindy saw a well pad, she said, was on top of Bobst Mountain, in 2010. "It was a shock," she recalled. "It was a jaw-dropping shock." Five acres of century-old white pine trees had been ripped out and piled on the side of the road like matchsticks; dozens of belching big rigs overran the edges of steep gravel switchbacks. "I couldn't believe they were doing this here." She felt violated. Soon after, she joined the Responsible Drilling Alliance (RDA), an anti-fracking advocacy group cofounded by Jon Bogle, Ralph Kisberg, and six others, in 2009, and based in Williamsport. When the landman came knocking later that year, "I said, no thank you, we're not interested. I threw away the paperwork."

Over the next three years, Cindy watched fracking transform the tranquil, bucolic hamlet of Trout Run into a clamorous, gritty mining town. In the half dozen times I visited her, within just a quarter mile of her house I saw that earthmovers had leveled the side of a mountain to build a parking-lot-sized well pad; two huge drilling rigs manned by dozens of workers operated around the clock; tractor trailer caravans snarled traffic and pulverized the road; and a fifty-foot plume of fire shot from a flare stack for days. "We have a tendency to destroy what sustains us," Cindy rued, "and that's what I see happening here." But, unlike some RDA members, she also acknowledged that taking a stand against fracking was a privilege her land-poor neighbors could ill afford. She did not begrudge George, or the many other residents of Trout Run, for leasing. "Who am I to deny them the money? We don't have to make money off this land; we make money from hotels."

Cindy was doing her part to protect the region's natural heritage. Outraged that the governor had leased 102,679 acres of public forests for drilling between 2008 and 2010, she spent the next six years voluntarily assisting the Pennsylvania Environmental Defense Foundation in pursuing a lawsuit against the state. The suit alleged that auctioning and developing the mineral rights under public lands violates a clause in Pennsylvania's constitution that designates these areas "the common property of all people" and guarantees residents a "right to clean air, pure water, and to the preservation of natural, scenic, historic, and esthetic values of the environment."[9] Though Cindy had no say in what her neighbors did on their own private property, state forests are "our land." As a stakeholder, she felt she had both a right and a duty to stop the privatization of these commons.

Closer to home, Cindy and her husband obtained a conservation easement on their land in 2009 from the Western Pennsylvania Conservancy to enshrine its Arcadian character. She took comfort in knowing that her sliver of the dense second-growth forest ecosystem, which stretched from her front door up the side of a mountain a half mile away, would remain pristine in perpetuity. But Cindy was powerless to stop the "noise, the light pollution, and the smells" of industry—the aggregate result of George's and her other neighbors' decision to lease their land—from trespassing on her Eden. Her usual avenue of environmental advocacy—civic engagement in local land use public hearings—was effectively blocked. Although Pennsylvania is a "home rule" state, new industry-friendly laws enacted by the Republican-dominated government in Harrisburg neutered municipalities' ability to use zoning to control how fracking proceeded within their jurisdictions.

The acute sensory disturbances, like dynamite explosions and flames from a flare stack so bright and loud that they blotted out the stars and forced Cindy to sleep with ear plugs, were more than an annoyance: they produced a deep-seated feeling of anxiety and dislocation. Cindy lost sleep, stopped going for walks, and talked about moving to New York, where fracking is banned.

Of all the landowners I befriended during the eight months I lived in Williamsport, in 2013, and in my six years of follow-up research, Cindy was the last one I expected to lease her mineral rights to an energy company. But Cindy had a startling confession to make as we perused a new forest clearing for a gas well in her Prius one summer day—she and her husband had actually leased their land the year before I met her. Registering my stunned silence, Cindy quickly added that the lease did not violate their property's conservation easement. The gas company could only burrow 1,000 feet or more beneath the land. Not "a single fern or rock can be overturned" on the surface. The restrictions she put in place also meant that her lease would not contribute in any noticeable way to the industrialization of Trout Run. No well pads. No pipelines. No flaring. No trucks. No noise.

Cindy flatly admitted she did not need the $150,000 lease bonus. But she saw it as "the only possible compensation" for the deteriorating quality of life she had involuntarily endured for years because of her neighbors' decision to lease their land. Cindy's revelation shocked me, but I was sympathetic. Because of the state and federal governments' hands-off approach to regulating the industry, and because of the unique degree of control that American property law traditionally grants to mineral estate owners, she faced an impossible situation. In the end, she concluded that her principled holdout did nothing to allay the devastation caused by fracking in the area. "Everything around us is leased completely!" It was a lost cause. Cindy was entangled in a real-life *resource dilemma*, which is what decision scientists call a situation when noncooperation among individuals—that is, putting self-interest before the group—leads to the deterioration and possible collapse of a shared resource. In the end, she behaved seemingly just as economists would predict—selfishly.

George's relationship to fracking also changed over time. In April 2014, about a year after I first met him and soon after he got his first royalty check, for almost $35,000, I invited George to speak to my students at New York University (NYU) as a representative of lessors who benefit from and support fracking. He used a portion of his new-found wealth to make the four-hundred-mile round trip to my class in a stretch limousine—only to tell us that he now regretted leasing. George was not one of those well-documented lessors who became reluctant activists after their land or water was poisoned; his property suffered no environmental calamities.[10] His regret was the net effect of dozens of ostensibly minor indignities—a guard temporarily blocking his driveway to facilitate the removal of heavy equipment; a security camera installed by the gas company without his knowledge to monitor the well pad in his yard; the nonchalant manner in which truck drivers drove on his grass—that sapped George's enthusiasm for the industry. It was a profound lesson for my students, and for me. The essence of George's lament was that he had unknowingly surrendered his land sovereignty to a powerful industry that trades in misinformation. He was no longer lord of himself and his surroundings.

Cindy and George lived only two miles from one another, which qualified them as neighbors in the sparsely populated community of Trout Run. Though beginning with opposing views, over time, each of them became deeply ambivalent about fracking. Both second-guessed their decision to lease their land. Yet they never discussed their experiences with each other. In fact, they never met. One could say they occupied different worlds. Cindy was a member of the RDA, the small anti-fracking advocacy group comprised almost entirely of rusticators and townies that regularly gathered at a high-end restaurant in Williamsport's urban center. The group coordinated small protests in front of the courthouse and natural-gas installations, distributed leaflets in plazas and local businesses, sat down with local politicians and regulators, and organized local nature hikes and photography exhibits to raise awareness about gas drilling in state parks.

Few of the RDA's activities brought members face to face with residents in the surrounding rural parts of the county. Many nearby landowners like George avoided Williamsport. They felt more at home dining at Cohick's Trading Post, on Route 973, which advertised two items on its roadside letter sign: "Waffles and Chix" and Remington rifles; the woods were for hunting and fishing, not nature walks. They suspected that fracking skeptics like Cindy were liberal, elitist city slickers with no understanding of the local economy and no respect for rural values. Some saw fracking opponents as a threat, attempting to regulate away their livelihoods and land sovereignty (along with, perhaps, their guns).[11]

Over a period of seven years, I became intimately familiar with Lycoming County's urban and rural social worlds—and with the boundaries that often separate them. I hobnobbed with artists at city galleries, prayed with gas workers in backwoods churches, hiked with environmentalists and tailed along with hunters in state forests, huddled with farmers at the kitchen table, cheered with families at Little League games, and attended dozens of town hall meetings.

Yet in all my travels, I only came to know one person who regularly traversed the political, economic, and cultural divides that separated George and Cindy: Ralph Kisberg, the sixty-year-old cofounder and president of the RDA. Born and raised in Williamsport, this prodigal son returned in 2008 to care for his elderly mother after stints marketing oil-and-gas-drilling investments for a Wall Street firm, working in an offshore oil-and-gas-production field in the Gulf of Mexico, and managing a tribal-hunting preserve in New Mexico. Gas drilling was just picking up then, but his life experience led him to conclude that the idyllic outdoors of his childhood were endangered. At the same time, Ralph understood that many locals were desperate for the economic boon that fracking might provide and were not politically predisposed to see regulation of industry as a good thing. He also conceded that, from a planetary perspective, it could be worse—fracking was far less disruptive than mountaintop coal removal. And he was humble enough to recognize that he had spent far too long away from home (over thirty years) to swoop back in and tell people how to live.

From the beginning, Ralph sought common ground, a sentiment reflected in his support of the idea to name their organization the *Responsible* Drilling Alliance rather than, say, the *Anti*-drilling Alliance. He held out hope that many of the problems created by fracking could be solved with better technology and more oversight. And he sought understanding of the technology that underlies fracking and of the perspectives of landowners deciding whether or not to lease their land. Living mostly off unemployment insurance and the occasional housepainting job, Ralph dedicated his life to researching fracking from every possible angle. For five years, he went to almost every permit hearing and public comment forum that he heard about (his traveling expenses were offset by donations he helped secure for the RDA); spent several mornings a month at the regional Department of Environmental Protection (DEP) office scouring gas well inspection reports for violations; studied industry magazines and attended vocational workshops; and read peer-reviewed scientific articles to understand the properties of shale and methane. Perhaps most importantly, he spent hours each day traveling county backroads to document firsthand the impact of fracking and meet with landowners and hear their concerns. He routinely wrote up his findings for the RDA newsletter or used them to place stories with regional journalists. Even when Ralph encountered ardent supporters of drilling, he offered to help them figure out ways to mitigate the quality-of-life impacts.

Ralph took an interest in my research from the beginning and served as my informal community envoy after I moved to Williamsport in 2013.

He still sends me updates, minutes from meetings, and even his own field notes. A folk anthropologist in his own right, Ralph's research helps me stay abreast of local events in between my revisits to the area. I also count him as a friend.

Ralph's deep knowledge of all aspects of the issue, his preternatural capacity for empathy, and his low-key demeanor garnered him respect and goodwill from just about everyone he encountered, no matter their environmental politics. He mingled with buttoned-down petroleum engineers as easily as with anarchist Earth First! activists. He developed a network of professional experts whom he could call upon for advice. And he was often the only "citizen" invited to closed-door meetings with statewide environmental-policy leaders, state representatives, and industry stakeholders in Harrisburg. Despite his (measured) anti-fracking stance, it was through Ralph that I met many people on the other side of the issue. I befriended a landman named Russell Poole after Ralph invited us both out for a night of drinking and karaoke, and a pro-drilling state representative returned my phone calls after Ralph vouched for me. I am also indebted to Ralph for connecting me with George, whom Ralph befriended after he pulled over to look at a drilling rig in George's yard.

Ralph made real connections between the concerns of urbane, liberal environmentalists and provincial, conservative landowners. But it was a lonely mission. The more he rubbed shoulders with industry and Harrisburg power brokers, the more he lost stature among some of his activist peers. Most RDA members were not in the mood to compromise after the Republican legislature rolled back zoning regulations that restricted fracking. Yet here was Ralph, who, despite his personal disgust for the rollback, was saying that he thought a local pro-industry conservative state representative was someone they could work with and questioning whether the scientific evidence supported the RDA's alarmist claims about the link between fracking and cancer. As tensions mounted, Ralph decided to step away from the RDA in the fall of 2013 and embark on a road trip out West "to get back to landscapes that inspired me instead of depressed me." Williamsport lost its emissary between Cindy's and George's worlds.

* * *

Fracking is one of today's most consequential and contentious land uses. Many politicians, corporations, and ordinary people believe fracking offers a chance to return to America's postwar glory days: cheap fuel, energy independence, and a domestic manufacturing revival. But for many fearful environmentalists, fracking augurs poisoned groundwater and an indefinite extension of our dependence on carbon-intensive fossil fuels that will stunt the growth of renewable energy. The gas (and oil) boom enabled by "unconventional" drilling (the industry term for horizontal drilling and fracking) through shale is little more than a decade old, yet more than seventeen million Americans in eleven states now live within a mile of a fracked well. Millions more live within the blast or spill radius of the nation's 2.6 million miles of oil and gas pipelines.[12]

The federal government greased the skids for the boom, both by opening up millions of acres of federally protected land for drilling and by relinquishing its regulatory authority. The so-called Halliburton loophole that Vice President Dick Cheney, a former CEO of Halliburton (the world's largest provider of fracking services), slipped into the Energy Policy Act of 2005 exempted fracking from the Safe Drinking Water Act and effectively stripped the Environmental Protection Agency (EPA) of its jurisdiction over the process. Within this "federal policy vacuum," analysts observe, fracking is subject to "a patchwork of quite different governance systems from state to state."[13] A few states have banned fracking (e.g., New York, Maryland). But most states with lucrative shale deposits have facilitated development in one form or another, such as by preempting municipalities' autonomy to regulate or ban fracking locally (e.g., Pennsylvania, Colorado, Texas) and by leasing state public land. Pennsylvania does not even impose a severance tax on locally produced gas that is sold out of state. In 2020, a statewide grand jury investigation concluded that Pennsylvania regulators "did not do enough to properly protect the health, safety and welfare" of citizens. The state DEP was so loath to prosecute industry malfeasance that the jury suggested vesting that authority with Pennsylvania's attorney general.[14] Until recently, fracking enjoyed strong bipartisan support, including from President Barack Obama.

The status of fracking as the fulcrum of US energy policy was cemented after the 2016 election of President Trump, who vowed to ramp up domestic fossil fuel production and commanded the EPA to aggressively roll back oil and gas regulations. (Trump's original appointees to head the EPA, Department of the Interior, and Department of Energy were all climate change skeptics bullish on shale gas. Rex Tillerson, his first secretary of state, was previously the CEO of Exxon Mobil.) America's largest shale gas play is the Marcellus, which extends over 90,000 square miles from New York to West Virginia. Pennsylvania commands the lion's share of this mile-deep "super giant gas field," making it the epicenter of the gas boom. Over 12,600 unconventional wells have been drilled there since 2004, and over 9,000 additional permits for unconventional wells have been issued.[15]

As many energy analysts note, the frenetic pace and vast scale of the fracking boom constitutes an energy revolution that is transforming geopolitics and the world economy. "King Coal" has been dethroned. Mothballed factories have reopened to supply the steel for pipelines and drilling rigs. And the sudden glut of US natural-gas reserves available for export allows European countries to decrease their reliance on Russia's Gazprom, loosening Vladimir Putin's political stranglehold over his neighbors.[16] (In announcing plans in 2019 to build a liquefied-natural-gas facility to export America's newfound methane surplus to Europe, the Department of Energy called the fuel "molecules of U.S. freedom.")[17]

Yet the big picture overlooks how personal fracking is. Shale-gas and oil drilling in the US is peculiar insofar as the decision of whether to extract the resource is in large part an individual rather than a collective choice. To be sure, the federal government manages the mineral estate of about seven hundred million acres, almost one-third of the US, "for the benefit of the American public."[18] But the fracking boom depends on millions of private citizens, or companies, who own subsurface mineral rights privately agreeing to lease or sell their mineral estate to firms like Shell and Chevron. In most countries, decisions about subsurface oil and gas development aren't made by private citizens. Instead, the government retains mineral rights (only the surface can be privately owned) and decides whether developing them is in the public interest, often with input—if not votes—from its citizens.

The United States is in fact the only country in the world where private individuals own a majority of the subsurface estate.[19] Inspired by the philosopher John Locke's declaration of private property as a "natural right," eighteenth-century English common law—which governed property rights in the American colonies—adopted a "maximalist" definition of property ownership, called *freehold*, after the abolition of feudalism. "Land hath," the law stated, "an indefinite extent, upwards as well as downwards." This meant that a freehold title gave its holder control over not only the surface, but also the subsurface and the air above, "with freedom to dispose of it at will."[20]

In English common law, this freehold guarantee was accompanied by a huge asterisk: the Crown retained exclusive rights to all subsurface oil, gas, coal, gold, and silver. After throwing off the yoke of imperial oppression, America's founding fathers were determined to build a democracy that guaranteed freedom from government control over individuals' private actions and the fruits of industry.[21] Locke, whose classically liberal ideals—life, liberty, and property—undergird the US constitution, insisted that sovereignty resides solely within individuals, and that the state can "never have a power to take to themselves the whole or any part of the subject's property, without their own consent."[22] American property law embodies this tenet in a concrete and consequential way.

It was only in America, the true land of the freehold, that it became possible for "whoever owns the soil" to own it "up to Heaven and down to Hell." (The advent of air travel, however, restricted air rights.)[23] Freehold titles are still the most common form of property ownership in America. But another distinctive dimension of American property law has resulted in a situation whereby millions of landowners—especially in the American West—do not own the minerals underneath their estate: the title to the mineral estate and the surface can "vest in different owners," meaning that a freehold property owner can convey the mineral estate separate from the surface. This is known as split estate.[24] One reason why split estate is common west of the Mississippi is that the federal government retained the mineral rights to most of the land it granted to Western settlers from 1909 onward. Another reason is that the long history of conventional gas and oil drilling in states like Texas and Colorado means that the mineral estate may have been severed from the surface during a previous era of development by the original freehold title holder.[25] In split-estate scenarios, the surface owner can't prohibit the mineral estate owner from developing the subsurface, even if the surface is impacted. Nor does the former share in any profits that result.[26]

Lest we get bogged down in the details of split estate and public versus private subsurface ownership, the upshot is this: it is only in America that private citizens own the majority of the mineral estate and are granted the exclusive right to enter into private negotiations with a third party to extract subsurface gas and oil—and profit from it.[27] This reality goes a long way in sealing the fate of shale-gas and oil extraction in the US as a seemingly unavoidable resource dilemma. There was little room for collective deliberation. And rather than mediate land use decisions in the name of the public interest, the government mostly stepped aside—or got in on the action itself.

It is estimated that over three-quarters of producing oil and gas mineral estate acreage in the continental US is privately held.[28] It just so happens that most of these mineral estates sit under the socially and geographically isolated heartland communities most decimated by the postindustrial service and tech economy. What this means is that, especially east of the Mississippi, where split estates are far less common, this incredibly momentous and far-reaching decision about the planet— to frack or not to frack—is largely in the hands of conservative, working-class whites residing in rural America—precisely the communities that purportedly feel forsaken by beltway politicians and coastal elites. This book tells the story of one such place: greater Williamsport, Pennsylvania, a down-on-its-luck Appalachian rust-belt community known for hosting the Little League World Series that tried to reinvent itself as "The Energy Capital of Pennsylvania."

Williamsport, a city of 28,000, is the gateway to North-Central Pennsylvania. Served by several interstate highways and proximate to the

FIG. 0.1. Williamsport. Photograph by Tristan Spinski.

Susquehanna River and East Coast energy markets, this faded former lumber town affectionately nicknamed "Billtown" became ground zero of the gas boom. Its tiny downtown added new hotels and restaurants to cater to an influx of itinerant gas workers; its office buildings and industrial parks enticed oil and gas companies like Halliburton; and the gas companies met many of their servicing needs through subcontracting with myriad local businesses. White pickup trucks—the company car of the oil and gas industry—were everywhere.

The surrounding area saw more new gas wells drilled in 2012, the year before I moved to Williamsport, than any other county in Pennsylvania.[29] For a time, Billtown was boomtown. These days, however, a glut of natural gas has led to a massive industry slowdown. White gas trucks have disappeared from the Holiday Inn parking lot; a Texas barbeque restaurant popular with gas workers closed; the local Halliburton facility went from six hundred to forty employees.

When I first moved into a former lumber baron's subdivided mansion in Williamsport, in January 2013, with a trusty old Toyota Camry I bought with 178,000 miles on it, I worried that my outsider status (and maybe even my Japanese car) might hinder my ability to integrate into the community. Although some were quick to ask if I was a "liberal" biased against fracking when I told them I was a professor at a university in New York, few objected to me asking questions and hanging around. It is plausible that other aspects of my biography—in particular, that I am white and was born and raised in Pennsylvania—may have helped facilitate rapport. Parochialism worked for me in other ways too: the quirks of small-town living created surprising social networks, with the result that one acquaintance could often introduce me to a broad array of people. Many locals were involved in civic groups that cut across social class and occupational lines. Even George, who was mostly a loner, sat on the school board of Montoursville Area High School, where he was a janitor for thirty years, which connected him to some of the town scions. I eventually became so well-known in certain social circles that it became socially awkward to stonewall me. One petroleum engineer politely refused to meet with me for months, but after running into me repeatedly at public gatherings and seeing that I knew many of his acquaintances, he graciously relented to my request for an interview.

My move to Billtown was inspired by my NYU students. I had just finished teaching a course called "Environment and Society" for the third year in a row. The course coincided with the release of the incendiary anti-fracking film *Gasland* and the drilling explosion that heralded the so-called Shale Revolution. The flaming faucets and brown water featured in *Gasland* prompted fierce debates among environmental scientists and in the media about whether drilling can cause methane to migrate into drinking water (it has) and to what extent the millions of gallons of frac fluid (0.5 percent to 2 percent chemical additives; the rest is water) injected deep underground to stimulate each gas well can contaminate groundwater (there is less evidence of this).[30] Against this backdrop, my students and I watched President Obama's 2012 State of the Union address, in which he declared that fracking could unlock enough natural gas from under America's soil to supply cheap domestic energy for a hundred years and support more than 600,000 jobs by the end of the decade. In addition to the economic benefits, he added, it could reduce greenhouse gas emissions by making "dirty" coal obsolete. Tapping into the mood of an increasingly war-weary and isolationist populace, Obama also held out the tantalizing prospect that fracking could finally allow the US to free itself from dependence on Middle Eastern oil.

Amid the euphoria over the game-changing economic potential of fracking, my home state of Pennsylvania was suddenly being called the "Saudi Arabia of Natural Gas." Governor Ed Rendell (D) moved quickly to auction the mineral rights to over 100,000 acres of public land, raking in $413 million for state coffers.[31] In my adopted state of New York, Governor Andrew Cuomo (D) could not decide whether to lift a moratorium on fracking installed by his cautious interim predecessor or ban it. Fired up by *Gasland* and the star-studded protest anthem "Don't Frack My Mother" (penned by Sean Lennon and Yoko Ono), many of my NYU students became fractivists, organizing protests in Washington Square Park and chartering buses to Albany to push for a ban. Opposing fracking suddenly became chic. After years of public equivocation, Cuomo enacted a ban in 2014, citing health and safety risks. Poor upstate rural residents, who lost the ability to develop their mineral rights, accused Cuomo of spurning them; one online headline read: "Gentry Class Elites Tell Rural America to Drop Dead."[32]

I admired my students' passion, but I felt ill-equipped to lead a discussion about an environmental issue so new that I had trouble locating scholarly research on the topic. I had no idea if fracking posed a significant threat to drinking water. And I did not know enough to deliberate the complicated question of whether the costs outweighed the benefits for impacted communities. One day in class, several students launched into a diatribe against the oil and gas industry—and against the landowners who had leased to them—and urged their classmates to attend an anti-fracking rally. I asked the class of eighty whether anyone had ever seen a gas well or met anyone who leased their land. No one had, including me. This made sense: almost all of the country's shale deposits are located in flyover country, while almost all of the epicenters of

fractivism are coastal cities. I realized that this reality spoke to the political and cultural distance between rural and urban America. And I
worried that my students and I were enveloped in a cosmopolitan "filter
bubble" that isolated us from information and viewpoints that might
tell a different story about fracking.[33]

I wanted to hear directly from rural landowners who leased and, in
some cases, refused to lease their properties to gas companies. I would
adopt the mission and methods of the anthropologist by moving to a
shale gas community and doing my best to understand things from locals'
perspective. Yet, as a trained sociologist, I had absorbed the key lesson
from the classical sociologist Émile Durkheim's book *Suicide*: even the
most seemingly personal or selfish actions, like taking one's life, are often
impelled by broader social and cultural trends. So I was skeptical from the
outset about claims that lessors were acting out of purely economic self-
interest. In my class, we talked a lot about "environmental inequality," by
which we meant that poor and politically marginalized communities are
least able to escape environmental problems: they are more likely to live
near a toxic-waste facility and to suffer from asthma, lead poisoning, and
other maladies.[34] In light of studies that show that these populations often
have no other choice as to where they live, it was tempting to think of
many lessors as helpless casualties: because they struggled financially and
had few other economic opportunities, they had no real choice but to
allow industry in their backyards. But most lessors bristled at the suggestion that they were victims. "Nobody held a gun to my head," a retired
truck driver named Doyle Bodle insisted, even as he showed me how gas
drilling had blackened his water.

The story of fracking is often told as a parable of Main Street versus
Wall Street: rapacious corporations threaten to crush Middle America's
soul (the journalist Seamus McGraw's *The End of Country* falls squarely
in this genre). Otherwise, fracking is presented as a "wedge issue" that
tears towns in half or leads communities to rise up in solidarity, as in the
Matt Damon–starring film *Promised Land*. But most shale communities
do not easily fit into either of these narratives. Greater Williamsport is
one of them. I was surprised at how uncontroversial fracking was here.
Very few people mobilized against it. And almost everybody leased, so

I did not find a community divided between lessors and holdouts. I now know that more shale communities responded like greater Williamsport than not.[35]

Surveys indicate that the majority of people residing over shale plays do not merely condone fracking. They endorse it. What was it, I wondered, about rural political and community life that led communities like greater Williamsport to enthusiastically support what armchair analysts categorize as a "locally unwanted land use"?[36] Certainly, locals had concerns. But they were much more likely to complain about truck traffic and noise, which to them made the country feel like the loathsome city, than they were to worry aloud about pollution and health. Was fracking less disruptive to the land and local communities than fractivists believed? Did locals simply have other priorities? And what happened to generations-deep bonds among neighbors, I wondered, when one struck it rich while the other struck out in the fracking lottery?

It was only after getting to know lessors like George and Cindy that I began to understand the social dynamic set in motion by land leasing as a rare opportunity to observe the unfolding in real time of a resource dilemma. A resource dilemma arises when the pursuit of self-interest results in the degradation of a shared resource, harming the common good. An oft-cited example is the abrupt collapse of the codfish population off the Atlantic coast of Canada in the 1990s after decades of unchecked overfishing, which crippled the marine ecosystem and put as many as forty thousand people out of work.

In the absence of external regulation or mechanisms that promote collective decision-making, understanding how people choose between self-interest and the community is critical for preventing resource dilemmas that endanger the planet. Yet researchers are usually forced to simulate resource dilemmas in a lab: they present subjects with a tangible and mutually exclusive choice set—hoard money or contribute to a collective pool—that forces them to deliberately choose between putting themselves or the group first. Such behavioral games can reveal important insights: for example, that the prospect of being shamed can make people more likely to act altruistically.[37] But knowing whether or not someone in a lab setting will donate a dollar that a scientist gave them to a group of strangers hardly seems like an adequate way of predicting how they would respond to a community resource dilemma. Though nobody talked about fracking this way, I began to see it as a quasi-natural experiment: the "exogenous shock" of fracking forced people to choose between themselves and their neighbors. The stakes were palpable and high, and the fracking lottery created winners and losers largely based on geology and geography. The lived experience of the people of Lycoming County offered important real-world lessons that behavioral games could not uncover.

* * *

Behavioral scientists would explain lessors' decision to lease their land (or not) as a rational strategy aimed at maximizing their utility: many locals leased because they needed the money. On the one hand, it's important not to treat such a verdict, if correct, as indicative of human nature: if lessors had some say in how fracking transpired in their communities, or if the government took a more active role in regulating mineral leasing and the process of fracking itself, local landowners may have responded to fracking differently. On the other hand, much like classical sociologist Max Weber observed that the "Protestant ethic" of asceticism and capitalism's logic of accumulation mutually reinforced each other, my research in and around Billtown convinced me that certain so-called American values played a distinctive role in enabling the resource dilemma associated with fracking.

Echoing nationalist public discourse about energy independence and the vaunted conservative principle of minimal governmental interference in the private sector, people like George firmly believed they had not only the God-given *right* to total autonomy over how they used their land but also a *duty* to realize its productive potential. They saw no conflict between gas drilling and so-called traditional values; fracking dovetailed with their ideals. After all, while citizens consent under the Rousseauian social contract to cede some independence to a higher authority in exchange for protection of their remaining rights, the US constitution enshrines personal liberty and property rights as inalienable. Exercising these rights and retaining any benefits that accrue from them is more than permissible—it is moral, perhaps even patriotic.

The moral language that lessors like George used to defend private land-use decisions that have planetary consequences reflects the libertarian ideology that, according to cultural observers like Colin Woodard and Kai Erikson, reaches its apex in Appalachia: government distrust is rampant, individual sovereignty and private property are exalted (and protected, if need be, with guns), and privacy and self-reliance are prized. Yet it is worth bearing in mind that this worldview isn't a fringe political position. It is the product of a distinctively American mindset that has deep roots in our country's pervasive cultural veneration of individualism.

In his landmark study *Democracy in America*, written over 185 years ago, the French intellectual Alexis de Tocqueville noted Americans' peculiar "habit of always considering themselves in isolation" and "fancy[ing] that their whole destiny is in their hands." Americans feel that they "owe no man anything and hardly expect anything from anybody." (One need only imagine the archetypal homesteader, forty-niner, or entrepreneur.) This sentiment, Tocqueville observed, "disposes each citizen to . . . withdraw to one side with his family and friends, so that after having thus created a little society for his own use, he willingly abandons society at large to itself."[38] American property rights are a tangible and distinctive manifestation of this bootstrapping sensibility: one's land is her fiefdom; a freehold title holder is free to dispose of the soil and subsurface at will, and to hoard the fruits of her labor. Woodard credits Thomas Jefferson, the principal author of the Declaration of Independence, as the founding father most responsible for the abiding libertarian vision of America as a "republic of free and self-sufficient individuals whose economic and civic decisions would, in aggregate, produce a thriving economy [and] an ideal society."[39]

Yet Tocqueville also observed that Americans' fear of government tyranny led citizens of all stations in life to display an unusual zest for self-governance and volunteerism. He perceived his subjects to be "forever forming associations"—from service organizations like the Rotary Club to school boards and civic groups—to foster local self-reliance.[40]

Such participation, Tocqueville deduced, created a civic-minded citizenry committed to the common good. Citing Jefferson's nemesis Alexander Hamilton, who rejected the doctrine of laissez-faire and persuaded his colleagues that "the accomplishment of great purposes" required that individuals cede some sovereignty to a centralized federal government, Woodard claims that communitarianism is also a cornerstone of America's political heritage. The US remains "an individualistic outlier among liberal democracies." However, there are notable times and places in its history where cooperation aimed at advancing the general welfare and ensuring equality of opportunity triumphed over private interests.[41]

From the Constitutional Convention to the present day, political life in America has hinged on the problem of how to balance individual freedom and the *commonwealth*, which, in the words of constitutional and environmental-law scholar Jedediah Purdy, can be understood as "the general good or the well-being of the whole community."[42] The question of independence versus community is an existential as much as an ethical question. And, despite the fact that conservatives are seen as prioritizing personal liberty while liberals are viewed as favoring the common good, it sometimes transcends traditional left-right politics. It is at the heart of debates about whether parents have the right to exempt their children from vaccines when doing so endangers population health, whether the invasion of privacy is justified in the name of national security, or whether citizens should be able to own assault rifles. And it explains why physical distancing and wearing a mask during the COVID-19 pandemic became such an explosive political issue in the US.

The advent of fracking imposed this political dilemma on rural communities in an acute form. Almost all residents felt they should be free to do what they wanted with their own property. On this principle, private leasing was nobody else's business. But they also believed others were equally entitled to that same right and in being a responsible community member. On these grounds, neighbors' interests warranted consideration since private leasing often impacted their quality of life.

Many prominent public intellectuals have concluded that Americans' emphasis on self-reliance and privacy has eroded citizens' involvement in the public sphere and isolated them from one another. According to the well-known political scientist Robert Putnam, membership in voluntary associations, from the Lions Club to bowling leagues, has declined precipitously, as has voting, attendance at town hall meetings and public hearings, and churchgoing.[43] If "the ultimate ethical rule is simply that individuals should be able to pursue whatever they find rewarding, constrained only by the requirement that they not interfere with the 'value systems' of others," sociologist Robert Bellah and his colleagues lament, there is no common purpose that unites us as a polity.[44]

Concerns about excessive individualism and the apparent decline of associational life have become a recurring theme in our national public discourse. Yet missing from the conversation entirely, at least until President Trump exited the Paris Climate Accord, in 2017, is how the trend toward what could be called *civic dissociation* may impact Americans' commitment to protecting the commons—the finite natural resources that equally belong to all, like air and water. In the pages that follow, I ask how American individualism and property law color people's stance toward resource management on both private and public (i.e., state) land. I explore how environmentalism's failure to craft a message that resonates with Middle America relates to the movement's generalized antipathy toward self-governance. And I conclude by considering how our nation's reverence for liberty and independence is implicated in America's halting response to climate change.

* * *

When I moved to Billtown, I worried most about whether fracking tainted groundwater. By the time I left the area, my biggest concern was whether the liberty granted to citizens to lease their land, or to otherwise act in ways that limits others' access to environmental goods, taints democracy.

CHAPTER 1

Billtown

On a frigid and snowy morning two days after New Year's 2013, I moved into an apartment at 829 West Fourth Street in Williamsport. I rented it, sight unseen, through a local property management company. Even in the gray of January, with the trees stripped of their leaves and the snow drifts blackened with soot, my block radiated an aura of grandeur in an otherwise nondescript if not scruffy townscape: the towering English Gothic stone spire of Trinity Episcopal Church, built in 1876 at a cost of nearly $80,000 ($2 million in today's dollars) and adorned with a nine-bell chime that was reputedly the first in America to mark the quarter hours, overlooked three opulent mansions fronted by mature oak groves. Each house evinced a distinctive Victorian or Neoclassical style and was set back dozens of feet from the sidewalk to "ensure a fine perspective for viewing" from the street.[1]

Serendipitously, I had taken up residence on one of the most historically significant city blocks in all of central and northern Pennsylvania. It just so happens that this small stretch of State Route 2014 was the epicenter of Billtown's brief and unlikely rise to national prominence as "the lumber capital of the world." It is alleged that, in the second half of the nineteenth century, timber made Williamsport one of the wealthiest cities in the country. More millionaires lived on West Fourth Street, it is said, than on any other street in the world.[2] And the 800 block, where I lived, was the heart of Millionaires' Row. Though it long ago became déclassé (the mansions are subdivided rentals today), this seven-hundred-foot strip of the boulevard feels like a Gilded Age time capsule.

Local historians assert that it was the "boundless energy and ruthless determination" of one man, Peter Herdic, that conjured Millionaires' Row from a literal backwater and put Williamsport on the map.[3] The youngest of seven children born on a modest farmstead in upstate New York, this Horatio Alger figure arrived in 1846, at the age of twenty-three, in Lycoming County, rich in white pine and hemlock, to seek his fortune in lumber. Using proceeds saved from working at a sawmill outside Ithaca, New York, Herdic opened a sawmill with a business partner along Lycoming Creek, just north of Williamsport. In 1853, Herdic liquidated his assets and moved with his farmer wife, Amanda Taylor (who died in 1856), from their homestead to Billtown, where he contracted the locally renowned architect Eber Culver to design a sumptuous Italianate villa amid swampland and a few modest farmhouses at the edge of town (407 West Fourth Street). At the time, Williamsport was little more than a riverside trading post of 1,700 or so denizens bordered by mountains, dense forests, and a few hardscrabble homesteads.

Herdic "sensed that a boom was around the corner" in this placid outpost and snatched up "building lots, woodlots, sites for sawmills . . . [and] enormous tracts of timberlands."[4] His optimism was well founded. Just two years before he moved to town, the Susquehanna Boom was opened. A seven-mile-long system of 352 massive sunken stone "cribs" and chained logs stretched diagonally across the West Branch of the Susquehanna River (at a cost of $1 million), the Boom functioned like a massive floating warehouse. It could corral and store nearly one million logs that lumberjacks had floated downstream until they were ready to be processed, enabling the sawmills to stay busy long after the harsh winters shut down the harvesting season. By the 1860s, the boom had revolutionized Lycoming County's timber industry, leading to an explosion of sawmills—more than sixty—in and around Billtown and spawning a thriving local furniture-making business. The West Susquehanna Branch of the Pennsylvania Canal, completed in 1834, allowed sawmill owners and furniture makers to efficiently transport their finished wood products to markets as far away as Baltimore. It also allowed Daniel Hughes, a "mulatto" (according to the census) barge owner who shipped lumber down the river, to return with runaway slaves from the South.

He hid them in caves near his home just above town until Quakers guided them north on the "Freedom Road" to Elmira, New York.[5] Inadvertently, timber had made Lycoming County a pivotal stop on the Underground Railroad, which in turn spurred the growth of Williamsport's nascent African American community (today, Billtown is 13 percent Black).

In 1857, Herdic and two other local businessmen purchased the Susquehanna Boom Company. He then leveraged his considerable political influence to convince the state legislature to raise the boom tolls by 150 percent, helping make Herdic one of the richest people in Pennsylvania. Given his newfound status, when it came time to remarry, Herdic sought a bride with refined tastes. Concerned that his vestigial plebeian mannerisms might repulse the local debutantes, he "engaged a dance teacher and tutors to polish his social skills." His efforts seemed to pay off handsomely. In 1860, Herdic married Encie Maynard, "the belle of the ball," who came from a "well-established and respected Williamsport family" (Maynard Street is named after her father, Judge John W. Maynard). Known for her intelligence and grace, and also a fine pianist and occasional composer, Encie was "the center of the social scene" in town and "entertained in a style befitting the wife of a lumber baron." She also filled Peter's house with rare books and other artifacts that evinced gentility.[6]

Having secured a fortune, built a palace, and wooed a trophy wife, Herdic was eager to surround himself with other nouveau riche burghers who shared his proclivity for ostentation. And he resolved to make the scrappy town of Williamsport into something grand. To this end, he drained and filled the land west of his estate and planned the development of an exclusive enclave along with a cluster of businesses to cater to it. The centerpiece of his efforts was the Herdic House (now called Park Place), located right across the street from my apartment, which when finished, in 1865, was considered one of the finest hotels on the Eastern Seaboard. The mammoth four-story Italianate edifice could "accommodate 700 guests in luxurious comfort."[7] Set amid five well-manicured acres shaded by oaks and dotted with flower gardens, a fountain, and a fenced deer park that "never contained less than 3 or 4 deer," the hotel featured "sumptuously furnished rooms," gas fixtures, crystal

FIG. 1.1. The original Herdic House (now called Park Place). Photograph by Tristan Spinski.

chandeliers, a telegraph office, a barbershop, several fine restaurants, a ballroom, and marble-tile-lined halls.[8] It was a "very pretentious struc-ture at the time," to say the least.[9] Herdic's audacity to build something so palatial in such an isolated area brings to mind the luxurious opera house that rubber barons plopped down in the heart of the Brazilian Amazon in the 1880s.

Legend has it that Herdic asked Culver to survey the best hotels around the country and then submit a design and estimate for the Her-dic House; when Culver turned to leave, though, Herdic amended his request and said not to provide a budget, because he might balk at the price. It cost $225,000. Many thought Herdic's decision to locate the ritzy hotel more than a mile from the town's center and train station was harebrained, but Herdic induced the Pennsylvania Railroad Company to relocate the train station so that it abutted the Herdic House. Trains traveling to and from Erie and Philadelphia stopped at the hotel's north portico at mealtimes, where passengers were greeted by the "beating of a large gong and a foghorn voice announcing that meals were ready for serving at the hotel dining room." The specialty of the house was planked shad, "as prepared in local lumber camps."[10] The hotel quickly became a popular summer resort, attracting people from as far away as New York and Washington, DC.

The Herdic House was only the first step in Herdic's master plan. The opening of the hotel coincided with the inauguration of Billtown's first streetcar line, which he commissioned to connect the Herdic House and the center of town. The horse-drawn carriages even had wood stoves to keep passengers warm in the winter, and later models of the so-called Herdic—considered the forerunner of the modern taxi—had side seats and a back entrance and were painted yellow to make them easily identifiable. With West Fourth Street well situated between the new train station and downtown along the town's only streetcar line, Herdic made a killing selling building lots and handsome mansions that Culver had designed along the route. In an effort to shift the commercial center of Williamsport from Market Square to the area around the Herdic House, in 1870 he constructed the "Herdic Block" just across Campbell Street from his hotel. This dignified four-story brick behemoth, now called the Weightman building, takes up an entire block; each floor has eighteen-foot ceilings, concrete floors, and sixteen-inch plaster walls. Early tenants included Lumberman's National Bank (which had walk-in, lead-lined safes), Lycoming Gas and Water Company, and the Williamsport Manufacturing Company—all owned by Herdic. It was also his hope that the Herdic Block would eventually host an opera house, a public market, the town's post office, and the Western District Court of Pennsylvania.[11]

By hook or by crook, over the course of the 1860s and '70s, Herdic "awaken[ed] the sleepy little country town . . . and transform[ed] it into a thriving city."[12] He was instrumental in having Williamsport chartered as a city in 1866 and was "the power behind the throne" in having the neighboring area of Newberry annexed to Williamsport against the will of many of its inhabitants (allegedly by forging their signatures on the incorporation document).[13] He became mayor in 1869, after a campaign against the esteemed lawyer Henry C. Parsons that allegedly cost him $20,000—$15 per vote; it is said that his minions stashed $10 and $20 bills among the bottles at saloons to buy voters' support.[14] During the peak of his influence, Herdic either owned or controlled through patronage almost every political, economic, and civic enterprise in the city, including the newspaper (the *West Branch Gazette and Bulletin*) and all the principal financial and religious institutions. Yet his philanthropy was almost as legendary as his avarice. He donated the land upon which many churches, including Trinity Episcopal, were built. On the day that the costly Trinity Church, adjacent to his hotel, was consecrated, Herdic surprised the parish by announcing that he would foot the entire bill for its construction as well, so long as the pews remained free (it was common in that era for parishioners to purchase their pews). After the financial panic of 1873, Herdic helped relieve local unemployment by constructing eight hundred houses, which he then donated to workers. Under his patronage, it seemed as if "blocks of buildings sprung up like magic, street railways, paving jobs, political jobs, manufactures, newspapers, gas companies, water works, banks, and stores grew up at once."[15]

Billtown was booming. Between 1862 and 1891, more than 31.5 million trees were processed by Williamsport mills into more than 5.5 billion board feet of lumber.[16] Over those same thirty years, Billtown's population jumped from 5,664 to 27,132, as its national reputation as a boomtown spurred an influx of entrepreneurs and itinerant workers. By 1886, six major rail lines connected Billtown to Eastern cities, and sixteen passenger trains stopped there daily. Electric lights illuminated the streets, and five miles of underground pipe delivered steam heat to downtown. Williamsport became just the second city in Pennsylvania to establish a telephone exchange, in 1879 (the first was Erie), and it was the first city in Pennsylvania to establish electric streetcars, in 1891 (a year ahead of Philadelphia).[17] By that time, the city boasted "six hotels capable of housing more than 1,000 guests, 25 dry goods and millinery stores, 95 grocery stores, 13 boot and shoe stores, eight hardware and cutlery stores, 14 drug stores, eight bookstores, seven jewelry stores, and 13 livery stables."[18] In 1892, it welcomed the elegant four-story, 1,600 seat Lycoming Opera House.

Those most responsible for the boom reaped the least rewards. Life was harsh for laborers in the mills, where occupational hazards like projectile wooden splinters and broken saws abounded. In exchange for working twelve-hour shifts six days a week, millworkers were paid only $1.50 per day ($28 today). When they shut down the mills during what became known as the 1872 "Sawdust War" and demanded a ten-hour workday, the governor sent in four hundred to five hundred militiamen, including the all Black division known as the Taylor Guards, with fixed bayonets, to crush the strike and arrest the organizers. (The governor later pardoned the ringleaders, apparently at the urging of Herdic, who supported the ten-hour workday.)[19]

The ruthless exploitation of millworkers created fabulous wealth for the cartel of owners—known as the Lumbermen's Exchange—that controlled the industry in Lycoming County. And when the lumber barons "made a buck, they wanted their neighbors to know it." There was no better way to telegraph one's status than by occupying a swanky mansion designed by Eber Culver on land along West Fourth Street purveyed by Peter Herdic. Here, "lumber magnates competed fiercely for the distinction of owning, maintaining, and entertaining in the most extravagant and expensive home." It was also fashionable to bequeath a mansion to one's children on their wedding day.[20] Mahlon Fisher, president of the Susquehanna Boom Company, epitomized the cutthroat decadence of Millionaire's Row. After the completion of the Herdic House, Fisher contracted Culver to design an even more ostentatious structure in plain view of the hotel (815 West Fourth Street). Fisher imported stonemasons and woodcutters from Europe to construct the immense stone villa, complete with "towers fore and aft," balustrades, a carriage house, a large reception hall with a rotunda, steam heating, and an English garden ornamented by fountains and statues. Completed in 1867, the "Million Dollar Mansion"—aka the Fisher Home—indeed costed over $1 million.[21]

Sandwiched in between the "Million Dollar Mansion" and the handsome Queen Anne–style Emery House stood a mansion owned by the lumberman Benjamin Taylor. When it burned to the ground, the jurist Henry C. Parsons—Herdic's erstwhile rival for mayor—bought the lot and muscled his way onto the most exclusive block of Millionaire's Row. As other parts of West Fourth Street began to look more urban, with newer constructions crowding closer to the sidewalk, the 800 block preserved its bucolic splendor: there were only four residences on the block, in addition to the Herdic House and Trinity Episcopal Church, and each was set back from the street and surrounded by generous amounts of green space and shaded by canopies of oak trees (it looks almost exactly the same today).

Parsons is considered among the most "distinguished dead of the city" and was, in many ways, the antithesis of Herdic. Educated at Brown University and descended from a "highly respected New England family," he served in his father's Philadelphia law firm before returning to his hometown to open a practice in 1857. When the American Civil War erupted, he enlisted for two campaigns, serving as sergeant and then captain in Pennsylvania's Volunteer Infantry. Though Herdic's election chicanery denied Parsons the mayor's office in 1869, Parsons later served as a state representative and, in 1881, won his own mayoral term. His administration "was marked by the business-like conduct of the city's affairs and its perfect cleanness"; when he left office, he reportedly received "the thanks and best wishes of his fellow citizens irrespective of party."[22] Parsons was also president of two prominent local banks. When it came time for the decorous lawyer to design a home on Millionaire's Row for himself, his wife, and five children, he chose a style—Queen Anne—and materials—wood—that were simple and elegant rather than showy. The two-and-a-half-story shingled "Parsons House," fronted by a graceful wraparound porch, was embellished with stained-glass windows and cherry mantels above every fireplace. It also featured modern touches like a copper-lined bathtub and an intercom that allowed residents to communicate throughout the twenty-seven rooms via a network of tin tubes.[23]

At the time I moved into apartment 2R of the Parsons House, it was obvious that the exterior of the home had retained its regal appearance. It was handsomely bedecked in yellow paint with green trimming on the eaves and window frames, and the original oversize cherry front door and stained-glass windows were intact. Although the interiors of its apartment units were up to date and rather unremarkable, the owners

FIG. 1.2. The Parsons House. Photograph by Colin Jerolmack.

had preserved the grand hallways and carved-wood stairways as they were over a century ago (residents were told not to use these areas; each unit had a private entry). The hall on my floor was hung with faded but resplendent heirloom red wallpaper decorated with tigers. A Victorian sofa at the far end of the hall was bookended by antique end tables and lamps. The downstairs spilled into an immaculate hall featuring a decorative cherry desk nestled in the corner. Upon the desk was a small brass lamp illuminating a framed portrait of Mr. Parsons, giving the impression that he had just stepped away from penning a letter and might return at any moment.

* * *

By the time Parsons settled into 829 West Fourth Street, in the late 1880s, the regional lumber industry was well past its zenith. Although it once seemed as if the area's supply of timber was limitless, it only took three decades of rapacious clear-cutting to rob Lycoming County of all its old-growth forest. Catastrophic floods in 1889 and 1894 sounded the death knell of the lumber era. Many sawmills, and the Boom itself, were washed away, along with millions of logs. The golden goose had been killed. Billtown had suffered the classic postboom crash that typifies resource-dependent communities that overspecialize in extractive industries at the expense of more stable forms of development.[24]

Peter Herdic died in 1888, after slipping on ice and fracturing his skull. He was sixty-three. It is perhaps fitting that the man eulogized for making a world-class city out of this former frontier village did not live to witness Williamsport's swift fall from grace. With the demise of the lumber industry, "most of the population who lived in small towns and rural areas returned to farming."[25] Lumber barons fled Millionaires' Row. Although many "Old Line" families like the Parsons continued to occupy West Fourth Street after the turn of the century, a pattern of migration to Grampian Hills and Vallamont—newly constructed posh suburbs located in the foothills above town—was apparent.[26] The wealthy chased new amenities, but also higher ground: West Fourth Street sat on the floodplain and was often waterlogged after heavy rains and spring thaws.

Before long, many of the glittering mansions along the 800 block of West Fourth Street, and elsewhere, fell into disrepair. The imposing "White's Castle" (so nicknamed because it was owned by lumberman John White and had two spiraling towers), which anchored the southwestern corner of the block, sat vacant by the early 1900s. The philanthropist J. Roman Way, who lived across the street, bought the castle and razed it to prevent its rumored conversion into a boarding house. (In 1913, Way donated the land to the city; it remains a charming park, named Way's Garden.) While he was able to temporarily block the incursion of the hoi polloi into his front yard, Way was powerless to check the area's decline. Millionaires' Row had lost its luster. In 1929, Mahlon Fisher's storied Million Dollar Mansion, which bookended the eastern end of the block, was razed to make room for the construction of the YWCA. Its lavish furnishings, many imported from Europe and built by master craftsmen, were unceremoniously disposed of at a public auction.

The Parsons House, located next door, was sold around that time and turned into a funeral home. The Emery House, which abuts Ways Garden, was subdivided into apartments and used by the Army as a reserve center in the 1940s (it is said that soldiers shot up the plaster walls for target practice). The legendary Herdic House, across the street, was damaged by a fire in the late 1930s (it was known then as the Park Hotel). The building was salvaged, but the top two floors had to be removed. In 1939, all the furnishings were liquidated and the edifice was repurposed as a women's retirement home.[27]

By the 1940s, most of the surviving mansions along West Fourth Street had been converted into multifamily apartments. They were simply too large and costly to be kept up as single-family homes. Also, the establishment of the Williamsport Technical Institute (now the Pennsylvania College of Technology, or Penn College) on nearby West Third Street created new demand for affordable rental units. Area historians lament that this trend hastened the deterioration of these once-proud homes. In addition, fires, demolitions, and "modern infill construction" in the form of squat, utilitarian brick or concrete commercial buildings diluted the Victorian atmosphere that marked Billtown's golden era.[28] The only "Millionaires" left on West Fourth Street were the eponymous sports teams of Williamsport High.

Billtown was down, but not out. The local Board of Trade campaigned to rebrand Williamsport as a manufacturing center, raising hundreds of thousands of dollars to entice new industries to set up shop in town. The initiative was credited with attracting a dye works, a steel mill, a glue company, a glass and mirror factory, and a shoe manufacturer, among others. By the end of the 1920s, it is estimated that there were eighty-four industrial institutions in town, employing almost ten thousand workers and making everything from automobile motors to woodworking machinery, cement blocks, candy, shirts, paint, tiles, wire rope, caskets, carpets, mattresses, and carriages.[29] The unglamorous but steady new jobs provided by the area's budding manufacturing sector caused the city's population to grow from 36,198 to 45,729 between 1920 and 1930. Billtown had reinvented itself as a blue-collar city. Although its "hopes for continued growth were cruelly dashed by the Great

Depression"—the loss of the US Rubber Company alone cost the city almost two thousand jobs—the material demands of the US military (e.g., plane engines, wire rope, cots) during World War II resuscitated local businesses like the Lycoming Manufacturing Company, the Bethlehem Steel plant, and the Williamsport Furniture Company.[30]

The first half of the twentieth century also witnessed the rise of the legendary small-town newspaper *Grit*, which was printed every Sunday for over a hundred years in Billtown. "America's greatest family newspaper" began as a Saturday supplement to the *Daily Sun and Banner*, with a circulation of no more than four thousand. By 1950, thirty thousand boys—many recruited from comic-book ads—"knocked at the doors of more than 700,000 American small-town homes and were welcomed with a smile and a dime as they delivered the weekly edition." One of the first papers in the nation to feature color pictures, *Grit* highlighted news and stories that "celebrated family and community"; it was also known for its fiction and comics. At its peak, *Grit* reached 1.2 million subscribers, most of whom resided in whistle-stop towns of fewer than ten thousand residents that had no newspapers of their own. *Grit* was—and remains—beloved for its documentation, and valorization, of rural American life.[31]

The postwar period in Williamsport also nurtured the growth of an even more iconic small-town institution: Little League Baseball. Legend has it that on one fateful day in 1938, Carl "Uncle Tuck" Stotz was playing catch with his nephews "when he stepped on a cut-back lilac bush at the rear of his house." As he tended to his scraped ankle, he envisaged a baseball field just for kids, and recalled asking his nephews, "How would you like to play on a regular team with uniforms, a new ball for every game, and bats you could really swing?"[32] He spent the next year lining up sponsors to purchase equipment; he and his sister stitched the bases. In 1939, Little League was launched, with three teams. Stotz toured the state and later the country, promoting organized youth baseball as a vehicle for promoting the "attributes of fair play, good sportsmanship, and a desire to excel through friendly competition." By 1946, there were twelve programs across towns in Pennsylvania. The following year, Stotz organized the first Little League World Series. Just two years later, Little League consisted of 198 local leagues spread across thirteen states. In the 1950s, the World Series began featuring teams from other countries (Monterrey, Mexico, was the first foreign winner, in 1957; Japan is dominant today). With the aid of corporate sponsorship, in 1959 the World Series was moved from West Fourth Street to a seventy-two-acre site across the river in the neighboring borough of South Williamsport. Today, the Little League International Complex houses a modern museum, two baseball diamonds—complete with grandstands, stadium lights, and concessions—and a players-only village, International Grove, where sixteen teams live for the ten-day event in August. Like the Olympic Village, International Grove is a temporary community designed to promote interactions that "transcend cultural and language barriers." These days, almost three million kids from 105 countries—boys *and* girls (Mo'ne Davis captured America's heart in 2014 with her smile and her blistering, seventy-miles-per-hour fastball)—play Little League Baseball. The World Series finale, free to the public and broadcast on ESPN, draws forty thousand fans to Howard J. Lamade Stadium.[33]

The Little League World Series is certainly Billtown's claim to fame these days. But this halcyon image belies the everyday problems of a rust-belt city with outsize rates of drug abuse and violent crime that has seen its population decline by over one-third in the past sixty years. In many ways, Williamsport exemplifies the seemingly permanent decline of Appalachia and other parts of Middle America.[34] Even on my genteel block, the signs were everywhere. The fabled Herdic House barely escaped demolition and sat vacant in the early 2000s, though by the time I arrived it was limping along as Park Place, an underutilized professional office building. The YWCA (on the site of the Million Dollar Mansion, and next to where I lived) served as a group home for recovering addicts and domestic-abuse survivors and their children. The stately Weightman (née the Herdic Block), just across the street, was a Low-Income Housing Tax Credit apartment building; several of its storefronts were empty. My market-rate apartment house struggled to attract renters (my unit cost $750 a month). The former mansion was eerily deserted during my time there; the first- and third-floor units sat vacant, and some tenants stayed for only a month. No wonder: in my neighborhood, the poverty rate surpassed 50 percent; unemployment exceeded 20 percent.[35] Just a week after moving in, I heard the pop of gunfire and saw the haze of blue and red police lights through my bedroom window for the first—but not the last—time. Terrell Henderson-Littles, twenty-one, had been killed in a drug robbery two blocks east of where I lived (the killers were two alleged Bloods gang members from Easton, PA).

Most of the troubles buffeting Billtown reflect broader national trends. The desire for lower taxes, more space, and new homes sparked an exodus from the urban core to the suburbs in the 1960s. The advent of malls and superstores decimated the city's downtown retail district in the 1970s. As lamented on a diner's back-of-the-menu history of downtown, the city's attempts at urban renewal mostly meant "tearing down everything in sight." Everything "south of the main stores on Third Street including Little Italy and the historic train station was leveled and left fallow for many, many years without any development or purpose" (the area now hosts several hotels, a Kohl's department store, a Wegmans supermarket, and a massive parking lot).[36] Many of the region's manufacturers began moving to China or Mexico, a trend hastened by the passing of NAFTA (1994). Although a few, like Lycoming Engines, Shop-Vac, and Bethlehem Wire Rope, managed to stay in the area, automation dramatically reduced their labor force.[37] By the mid-1990s, local sociologist Carl Milofsky observed, most "all of the area's traditional industries were dead or dying," except for farming, and "the rural working-class culture they supported declined into poverty."[38]

More recently, the relatively cheap cost of, and easy access to, methamphetamines, painkillers, and heroin incited an epidemic that has been hitting rural America especially hard.[39] Locally, this trend is aggravated by the legacy of "recovery migration." As Milofsky explains, a 1982 state welfare law allowed people in recovery to collect general assistance for nine months if they were certified as "in treatment" for drug addiction or alcoholism. Coming at a time of "underutilized housing stock and low rents" in Lycoming County, entrepreneurs began opening unlicensed sobriety houses to capture these new general-assistance dollars. They advertised "the healing powers of the countryside" to overburdened probation officers and drug court personnel in the New York City–Philadelphia corridor, who were often all too eager to offload their cases. Milofsky estimates that by the end of the 1980s, about two thousand "recovery migrants"—many of whom were homeless—had become permanent residents of greater Williamsport. He speculates that thousands more cycled through, and that many of their friends and families came with them.[40] Although it is plausible that a large proportion of these folks succeeded at recovering and integrating into society, it appears that the so-called influx put Williamsport on the map as a place to buy and sell narcotics. Violence and drug sales are routinely linked to perpetrators from other cities, like Philadelphia, who have a local connection and are passing through town to do business.[41]

Despite its difficulties, greater Williamsport has managed to maintain "a degree of growth and prosperity that is rare in the Appalachian region."[42] Not coincidentally, the area is less isolated than most of Appalachia; it is proximate to two major highways. The presence of the biggest hospital network in North-Central Pennsylvania (which employs over 2,500 people) and several small colleges nurtures a sizable educated and white-collar workforce. Also, the Middle District of Pennsylvania federal court and the Lycoming County court, both located on West Third Street in Williamsport, support a veritable cottage industry of lawyers, paralegals, and related professionals. Billtown also boasts a surprisingly vibrant arts scene, anchored by the Community Arts Center, a gorgeously restored theater; and the Pajama Factory, a rabbit warren of artists' lofts. On the first Friday of every month, restaurants, the hip coffee shop (Alabaster), and goldsmith and pottery studios stay open late to showcase local artwork and musicians. On a pleasant evening, Converge Gallery may be so full of patrons that they spill out onto the often-desolate downtown sidewalks. And, of course, there is the Little League World Series, an annual community celebration and "economic homerun for Williamsport and Lycoming County." During its ten-day run, every hotel, motel, and bed-and-breakfast in the region, and most restaurants and other ancillary businesses, are flooded with tens of thousands of out-of-towners. The Grand Slam parade draws 45,000 onlookers, and West Fourth Street in downtown is closed to traffic for "Williamsport Welcomes the World," an evening street festival. It is estimated that the World Series brought over $30 million in "direct sales activity" to the region in 2011.[43] The city is also home to the Williamsport Crosscutters, a minor-league affiliate of the Philadelphia Phillies.

As the biggest county, and one of the most rural, in the state, Lycoming County also abounds with natural amenities. Approximately 90 percent of the county's 116,000 residents live on just 3 percent of the land—all along the valley floor; only 10 percent of its 796,000 acres has been developed.[44] After the lumber boom went bust, the Commonwealth of Pennsylvania bought hundreds of thousands of acres of denuded timberland from the lumber barons and "set about reforesting the land." Most landowners were happy to be rid of their abandoned barren plots in exchange for forgiveness of the back taxes that had accrued to them.[45] Two of Pennsylvania's twenty state forests, the Tiadaghton and the Loyalsock (which comprise over 250,000 acres), are located mostly in Lycoming County. Featuring a wealth of accessible creeks, lakes, waterfalls, trails, mountaintop vistas, and campsites, they annually attract thousands of anglers, kayakers, hikers, hunters, campers, ATV riders, and other recreational tourists. Additionally, between 1997 and 2002 the county witnessed an unexpected 19 percent increase in small family farms—the traditional economic mainstay of the countryside—after decades of decline in the face of commercial agriculture. (There are now about 1,200 such farms; the average size is 130 acres.) Fueled by a revived back-to-the-land movement, many of the newer farms have diversified beyond corn and dairy—the customary staples of the region—and revitalized the county seat's primary farmers' market, the Williamsport Growers Market.[46]

The dawn of the twenty-first century found Lycoming County lurching toward the future, unsure of the best way forward. Lumber had been overexploited. The short supply of tillable land stifled agricultural expansion. "Any gas or oil that might be present," local historians concluded, seemed destined to remain "unmolested," because it was simply too difficult and costly to mine.[47] The retail and manufacturing sectors seemed to be in a death spiral. The recovery migration brought more trouble than jobs. And, like in so many other Appalachian towns, successful young people often left for college and didn't return."[48] Yet many civic leaders in the new millennium adopted an optimistic vision of the area as a budding destination for the arts, education, health care, and nature tourism. This feeling of uncertainty mixed with hope is captured in Billtown's slogan: "A proud past, a promising future."

* * *

Before leaving the history of greater Williamsport behind, some additional words about the demographics, culture, and politics of the region are in order. Lycoming County sits squarely in the middle of "the T," the largely rural, working-class, white, conservative swath of Pennsylvania that excludes the southwestern (Pittsburgh) and southeastern (Philadelphia) corners of the state. (Lycoming County is 92 percent white; the remainder is mostly African American. Almost all Black residents are clustered in Billtown, which is poorer and more liberal than the backcountry.)[49] Perhaps nowhere better illustrates America's stark urban-rural social divide than the T's contrast to Philadelphia. Philadelphia is a thriving, majority-minority East Coast "sanctuary city" where Joe Biden garnered 81 percent of the 2020 presidential vote. The T, which delivered the state to Donald Trump in 2016, is called—sometimes proudly, often pejoratively—Pennsyltucky, a label meant to highlight the region's racial, political, and cultural affinities with its southern Appalachian neighbor. It is not uncommon to see a Confederate flag here, and Democratic operative James Carville memorably called the region "Alabama without the Blacks." Indeed, it was primarily Appalachian farmers in Pennsylvania and Kentucky who took up arms against President George Washington in the Whiskey Rebellion to fight the nation's first domestic sales tax.

Rebelliousness and individualism are at the heart of Lycoming County's origin story. After the Treaty of Fort Stanwix of 1768 settled land disputes between the Iroquois nation and the Penn family, the area between present-day Pine Creek and Lycoming Creek—the heart of Lycoming County—was recognized by Pennsylvania's provincial government as

"Indian land." The government forbid settlers to enter the area under penalty of a heavy fine and imprisonment. Nevertheless, "a number of fearless Scotch-Irish settlers from the lower counties and from New Jersey had come up the river and squatted near the mouth of Pine Creek." Unable to appeal to any external authority for physical or legal protection, for a twelve-year period the squatters organized a simple form of self-governance they called the Fair Play System. Three commissioners elected each year by the group were responsible for ensuring that each settler received fair treatment, and for meting out punishment to those who violated group norms. All decisions by the commissioners were final, and those who did not respect their verdict were set adrift in a canoe at the mouth of Lycoming Creek and banished.[50] Most astonishing, it is reported, a coincidence "without a parallel in the annals of history" occurred here in 1776: with rumors of revolution swirling, the Fair Play Men held a mass meeting under a giant elm tree and signed their own declaration of independence "on the same day and at approximately the same hour as the better-known document was signed" in Philadelphia" (both copies of the declaration vanished).[51] After the Iroquois ceded the territory to Pennsylvania, in 1784, the Fair Play squatters successfully petitioned the state to grant them deeds by invoking the Lockean principle of natural law: by applying their labor to common property and "improving" it "at the risk of our lives," they had converted it into their private property.[52]

To this day, the vast mountainous region stretching from Pennsylvania to Kentucky retains traces of this heterodox ethos. Political writer Colin Woodard describes Appalachians as unruly and populist.[53] "Faith in government" is considered an oxymoron here, though many locals depend on unemployment benefits and Supplemental Security Income.[54] In the 2016 Republican presidential primary, Trump captured 295 of the 311 counties (arguably) within Appalachia. His dominance here is attributed to his antiestablishment message (Bernie Sanders did better here than nationally as well), and to his pledge to give pride of place to downtrodden white communities ravaged by free trade and rural brain drain and spurned by urban elites.[55] Many folks in Lycoming County, who, the local chamber of commerce CEO told me, adhere to "core traditional conservative values," have not forgotten that then

Senator Obama described small-town Pennsylvanians as "bitter" at being left behind by the new economy and in turn "cling[ing] to guns or religion or antipathy" toward outsiders. With Obama ensconced in the White House, many Lycoming County residents adopted what political scientist Katherine Cramer calls "the politics of resentment."[56] But then along came a tantalizing new prospect, one that had the potential to restore the political and economic might of the rust belt.

CHAPTER 2

Boomtown

In the spring of 2012, a plainspoken landman named Steve arrived in a quaint Pennsylvania town nestled amid rolling fields and horse farms. His mission: to persuade landowners to sign over the mineral rights beneath their beloved heirloom farms. With a cornhusker's brawny build and boyish good looks, Steve delivered an earnest pitch to would-be lessors. He too grew up on a family farm that struggled to survive, in an Iowa town that lived for Friday night football, and he too knew the pain of rust-belt decline. His hometown became a depopulated waste-land after its only manufacturer, a Caterpillar plant, closed. Steve offered something in short supply in this beleaguered rural town: hope. Though many locals were eager to lease, a sizable minority worried about the risks. Over a series of town hall meetings, which drew almost everyone in town, residents carefully debated the merits and the hazards and tried as best they could to coordinate a response to fracking that the entire community could live with. In the spirit of democracy, they decided to vote on whether to allow it. In the interim, an environmental group began sounding alarms about tainted water. By the time the moment of truth arrived, the landman's idyllic narrative about fracking had given way to local disillusionment, as the energy firm's false promises and bullying tactics were exposed. For many, fracking came to be seen as antithetical to their rural values; the town was poised to reject it.

And then the credits rolled. As my eyes adjusted to the lights, I took stock of how many people had joined me on this Saturday night to watch the just-released film *Promised Land*, cowritten by and starring

Matt Damon. The parking lot for the Great Escape multiplex had been mobbed when I arrived, and snaking lines formed at the box office and concessions. Because *Promised Land* had been released just the day before, and because I was attending a screening at the most popular day and time (Saturday at 7:00 p.m.), I was in my seat by 6:25—something I routinely did in New York City but was probably overkill at the Lycoming Mall. I especially anticipated a packed house because the film dramatized tensions around fracking that I presumed hit home for many locals. But it was only my second day living in the area, and I had a lot to learn. No more than three dozen people trickled in to see *Promised Land*. A casual scan at the masses of patrons spilling out from the other screening rooms left me with the impression that *Promised Land* was the one film that locals were *avoiding*.

A few weeks later, I mentioned my surprise at the lackluster turnout to Russell Poole, a Mississippi-born landman who had been living in town for three years, over dinner at Joy Thai. Russ shook his head and tried to stifle a knowing smile. To him, the reason was obvious. Williamsport, he explained, "is a recession-proof town in the middle of a [nationwide] recession." Though only thirty-one, Russ's Barry White bass-baritone voice, gray-tipped sideburns, and salesman's confidence endowed his statements with an air of finality. "I fly back to Mississippi and see boarded-up buildings and get calls from friends who are looking for work. But Williamsport couldn't spell the word *recession*, much less know what one looked like, . . . because of natural gas." With everybody "winning" and the "mockumentary" *Gasland* debunked (in his view), why would locals want to indulge in a contrived dystopian film?

Russ, whom I met through Ralph Kisberg, president of the Responsible Drilling Alliance (RDA), was well aware of the stereotype of landmen as snake-oil salesmen. A self-described "karaoke-holic" and partier, he once shouted across the street to me as I headed home just two stops into one of his all-night pub crawls, 'Life is the fruit and I am the juicer. I just want to mix it up as much as I can!' On another occasion, Ralph and I watched him sing self-deprecating lyrics to the tune of Radiohead's "Creep" in front of bar patrons at Ozzie and Mae's Hacienda:

FIG. 2.1. A ramp by Lycoming Mall, where the Marcellus shale breaches the surface.
Photograph by Tristan Spinski.

You signed a lease, I looked you in the eye.
Felt kinda guilty, but I still made you sign.
You ask me some questions, but I just deny.
I wish I was local, but instead I'm just a yokel.
Cause I'm a creep, I'm a gashole.

I asked Russ what he thought of Matt Damon's portrayal of an honorable landman in *Promised Land*, and he quipped in his subtle Southern drawl, "I prefer the portrayal in *There Will Be Blood*." Russ practically choked on his curry chicken as he laughingly repeated the money-grubbing taunt of the ruthless oilman played by Daniel Day-Lewis, "I drink your milkshake!" Jokes and karaoke aside, Russ liked to believe that lessors trusted him to be "sincere and informative." But in the end, he implied, whether or not landowners had faith in him was largely irrelevant. Money talks. And unlike other door-to-door salesmen, the landman's job is to "pay them money" rather than to take it. Russ credited this simple fact as the reason "I haven't gotten any flat-out no's, don't call me again." He remembered how one suspicious man answered the door "in his tighty-whities" and holding a gun. But after "I spoke my piece" while the man sat in a La-Z-Boy with his gun on the table, he signed.

Russ went so far as to describe the work of "getting that ink" as fun. "I feel like the Ed McMahon of the oil and gas business," he said earnestly. In his telling, most landowners were thrilled to get that knock at the door. Some, he said, did not even know that they owned the mineral rights or that they were worth anything, while others saw the lease as a lifeline. His eyes misting, Russ recounted the story of an old man who lived atop a mountain with his dog and was straining to live within his meager means. The man had to cease his favorite daily ritual—walking up and down the mountainside with his dog—because his trusted companion's cataracts got so bad that it was walking into furniture around the house. He didn't have the money to pay for surgery. Russ knew what the man was going through: he recently had to cough up $6,500, when his dog broke its leg. Russ said he was able to convince the energy firm to forgo the typical obligatory ninety-day waiting period between lease signing and bonus payment so that the old-timer could make an appointment to fix his dog's eyes. Russ beamed, 'That's like a life changer for this guy, and that's what I get to do in this job. I love it.' Though it was hard for me to gauge how representative (or true) stories like this were, I watched Russ constantly field phone calls from lessors seeking to extend their contracts; their friends and relatives also called him, asking how they could sign. Most people's biggest concern, according to him, was not getting a smaller bonus than their neighbors. (By the time I moved to town, the land rush was over. Most of the county's prime acreage was leased. Russ, the last landman standing, was mainly scooping up small residual parcels and renewing expired leases over the phone. He spent a lot of his time at the courthouse and online, researching land titles all the way back to 1850 to make sure that the current claimants of the properties that he wanted to lease had "clean" ownership of the mineral rights. It was a lot of paperwork; I once saw him compile a five-hundred-page dossier for 0.34 acres).

"I *love* negotiating," Russ declared. I wondered if part of the thrill came in seeing how much he could lowball potential lessors. After all, Russ seemingly always had the upper hand in his dealings with landowners: he knew more than they did about the risks, how much money the petroleum company that contracted him was willing to pay per acre, which restrictive addendums could be added to a lease, and so on. And it was in his client's interest to obtain leases with the fewest land use restrictions at the lowest price possible. In Russ's world, unlike in *Promised Land*, whether and how to proceed with leasing and drilling was not up for public discussion and a vote. In most cases, it was a private matter brokered at the kitchen table; it was up to landowners to fend for themselves. (The central conceit of the movie, that a town could ban fracking, is unconstitutional in Pennsylvania.)

It seemed obvious to me that it was virtually impossible for lessors to be on equal footing with landmen when it came to negotiating the terms of their lease. But Russ didn't see unfairness in leasing. He saw two rational agents freely brokering a contract and consenting to terms that were mutually beneficial. Lessors could hire a lawyer; Russ was happy to recommend one. It was not his fault if they chose an incompetent lawyer, or no representation. (Russ estimated that two-thirds of owners of large properties hired a lawyer, but that only a third of those with plots of less than fifty acres did, presumably because attorney's fees would eat up most of the lease bonus. I couldn't verify this.)[1] And he was quick to emphasize that a fair number of lessors got "something for nothing," because gas companies paid leasing bonuses on properties that they subsequently decided not to develop.

Russ called himself "libertarian at heart." When the National Football League announced a $765 million settlement with 4,500 players who had sued the league for hiding the risks of concussions, Russell told me it was "so fucked up" that the NFL was held responsible. The majority of players wound up being cut or injured before making enough to retire and were left with few marketable skills and no long-term benefits.[2] While I sympathized with the players, Russ argued that their salaries already included hazard pay and that they voluntarily chose to play an inherently risky game in exchange for a good paycheck. To him, the NFL and players were equal parties that negotiated their respective rights and responsibilities in a free market. Players shouldn't be able to ask for more just because things didn't turn out as they'd hoped. The lessors Russ signed deals with were no different from the players, and he suspected that part of the reason he "related to 'em" so well is that they shared his worldview.

Russ didn't see a whole lot of what sociologists call "structural inequality" in the world. He saw opportunities; it was up to individuals to recognize and seize them. As we sat in his apartment one afternoon drinking our third carafe of French-press coffee that hour, I mentioned the "recovery migration" to Billtown and its concomitant social problems. Lighting a new cigarette with the butt in his mouth, Russ immediately looked at it "through the eyes of a drug dealer from Philly or New York." To come to "a town like this with no competition and a recent influx of opportunity, it's a no-brainer. Sign me up!" He then pulled a board game off the shelf, Cash Flow 101, created by the author of *Rich Dad, Poor Dad: What the Rich Teach Their Kids about Money—That the Poor and Middle Class Do Not!*, which he said changed his life. In the middle of the board, Russ explained, is a circle that represents the "rat race." You pull a card that assigns you a hypothetical profession (e.g., police officer), income, and liabilities (e.g., a mortgage). Outside the rat race are dreams that you can select to pursue, such as a vacation home. The game teaches you how to practice investing so that you can jump out of the rat race and onto "the fast track," building up assets and living off passive income rather than a salary. Unlike Monopoly, Russ pointed out, 'It's not the case that you win by making others lose. Everybody can win.' In his view, this made the game 'a lot more like real life.'

Russ recalled that he bought his first piece of real estate at age twenty-one, a month after learning Cash Flow 101. "I had no business buying a house!" he chuckled. Soon he was "obsessed, buying houses left and right." Russ called real estate one of the best investments, because mortgages allow you to 'make money without using very much of your own—you use somebody else's.' He half joked that he was on his way to 'becoming the Donald Trump of Mississippi,' until he was seduced by the business of brokering mineral rights, which is 'just another kind of real estate.' Over the next seven years, Russ said, he led a suitcase existence chasing the oil-and-gas-leasing wave—first to Williston, North Dakota, now the oil capital of America, and then on to Plenty-wood, Montana; Accident, Maryland ("true story!"); Shreveport, Louisiana; Eutaw, Alabama; a couple of towns in Mississippi ("It was nice to be able to sleep in my own bed"); Somerset, Pennsylvania; and, finally, Williamsport.

Like Damon's character in *Promised Land*, Russ wholeheartedly believed that fracking was the antidote to the heartland's slumping economy. He had seen it with his own eyes, from Williston to Williamsport. It wasn't just the happy faces of land-poor farmers cashing their bonus checks; it was also the revitalization of Main Street and the reopening of shuttered factories. From where he stood, everywhere Russ looked he saw the invisible hand of shale gas uplifting Billtown. When he first came here in 2010, Russ lived in the 123-room Holiday Inn Express & Suites, an addition to the Holiday Inn constructed in 2009 to accommodate the gas industry's need for short-term housing. It came to be known as the "White Truck Inn," because so many oil and gas workers driving company trucks—many with Texas and North Dakota plates—stayed there. Its bar broadcast Dallas Cowboys games. Since then, Russ watched Marriott construct both a TownePlace Suites and a Residence Inn within view of Interstate 180 and the Holiday Inn, which itself splurged on extensive renovations in 2012. Russ next lived at the Genetti, a sagging historic hotel in the center of town that undertook what he called "gorgeous" restorations of its suites, ballroom, and conference rooms in 2012. "There's no way they would have done that without [fracking]. Little League World Series is only once a year."

In less than five years, six new hotels (by my count) were built to cater to migrant gas workers. Amenities included "boot washing stations for their dirty footwear, staggered housekeeping and multiple breakfast shifts for their round-the-clock schedules and Internet fast enough to accommodate dozens of PlayStation games played in tandem."[3] When I stayed at the Hampton Inn in September 2012, a lobby message welcomed MBI Energy, whose executives were holding meetings in a suite next to my room. The breakfast buffet was jammed with young, gruff men with Midwestern accents wearing Halliburton shirts and Shell baseball caps stitched with the slogan, "Drill the Limit." Landlords also got in on the action. When I looked for an apartment, some listings were for fully furnished units—"even towels!"—available on month-to-month leases and mentioned that gas workers were welcome.

Perhaps nowhere epitomized shale gas's role in rejuvenating downtown Williamsport more than Russ's apartment, which was part of a "live, work, play" development completed in 2012, after the partial demolition of three run-down buildings that once anchored a thriving garment district. The middle lot was turned into Pine Square, a cozy landscaped courtyard bedecked with a fountain, murals, and string lights. The Brickyard, a popular "up-scale pub" (according to the establishment's website), was installed on the ground floor of the gut-renovated building next door. In the summers, Pine Square hosted a beer garden for the Brickyard and live music. Russ called it "an idea as cool as can be" and said he could not imagine another town with fewer than 30,000 people "having something that neat in it." Above the Brickyard were four floors of high-end loft-style apartments, which when opened were explicitly pitched toward "workers in the natural gas industry who can afford it."[4] That would be Russ. He lived (and worked) in the penthouse, a full-floor two-bedroom, two-bath suite accessed via a private elevator that opened into an open-plan living and dining area with exposed brick walls, commercial-grade kitchen appliances, and a bank of windows offering some of the best views of

FIG. 2.2. Signs put up by landlords and businesses catering to gas workers.
Photographs by Colin Jerolmack.

the city to the north and east. (A patron of the arts, Russ also crammed the walls with a rotating sample of paintings by contemporary Bill-town artists; known for making purchases in cash, he amassed more than a hundred works in his time in town.)[5] The unit came completely furnished; a maid service, utilities, and Wi-Fi were included in the rent, which was $3,500 a month—the average cost of a two-bedroom apartment in New York City. (Russ paid extra to park his Audi coupe, 'a very impractical car for the country,' in the nearby garage.) Russ loved overlooking Pine Square and other nearby recently opened side-walk venues: 'I can literally check out up to three bands playing out-side and decide if I want to join them.' He recognized that the rent was "outrageous in comparison to what locals pay," but to him it was "a no-brainer" to live here, because it was no costlier than a hotel and his client reimbursed him for living expenses up to $3,000 per month. Indeed, rent that high seemed impossible here without petroleum dollars.

Pine Square was one of a number of chic retail and residential refur-bishments that took off downtown after the advent of fracking. Nearby was 135 Flats, "executive" lofts featuring hardwood floors, tin ceilings, and room service from the ground-floor bistro (which sourced its in-gredients locally and billed itself as "the city's most popular martini bar").[6] Patrick Marty, whose (Re)Imagination Group developed the project, proudly told me that "there was nothing like that in town" be-fore, and conceded that he would not be able to do fun projects like that "if it wasn't for the gas companies." He recalled, back in 2007, showing the first apartment he completed to a "very nice young guy" who "frankly looked like he was a pro motocross guy." Pat said that the tat-tooed man, who turned out to be a landman for Range Resources, did not blink when he learned that the rent was $1,600, and responded, "I want a year lease, and your rent's too cheap, and let me know when the two [units] below it are done." (Landmen were the first to arrive in town. Civic leaders recalled learning of the impending "gas rush" when hordes of them, many wearing cowboy hats and boots, began lining up outside the courthouse each morning to research land titles.) Since then, Pat transformed two more vacant buildings ripe for "demolition by neglect" into the (Re)Imagination Group's office and furnished loft-style live/work spaces whose occupants included Anadarko Petroleum, Schlumberger Oilfield Services, and Precision Drilling. Pat said he even began attracting young professionals affiliated with the hospital and the courts. Though he saw himself as a liberal and believed that fracking should be heavily regulated, Pat credited "Big Oil" with instigating "ass kickin' change" downtown that saved old buildings from becoming parking lots and imported a new "level of sophistication." The streets were livelier, so much so that it was hard to get a table on a Saturday night at Bullfrog Brewery.

Lots of developers and property managers got in on the action. Pat's good friend Dan Klingerman, whose Liberty Group was the largest commercial real estate holder in the county, realized the potential of build-to-suit warehouses for the gas industry. Teaming up with Brent Fish, the largest residential real estate holder around, he told me, he provided the equity for a 165-acre industrial park about fifteen miles east of Williamsport that is convenient to several rail spurs and the interstate and features a water withdrawal site (to frack one well one time takes millions of gallons of water). At the time I spoke with Dan, Marcellus Energy Park hosted six different companies involved in various phases of natural-gas extraction (e.g., drilling, cementing, and well completion). The anchor tenant was the "complete oilfield service" behemoth Weatherford. Dan also entered the water transport business, founding a trucking company called Infinity Oilfield Services.[7] Dan estimated that the gas industry boosted Liberty's revenue 12–13 percent, which he claimed enabled him to create "450 family-sustaining jobs" for locals.

Stories like this abounded. Allison Crane & Rigging, a family-owned company, reportedly almost tripled its stockpile of cranes and added a water- and equipment-hauling business that employed a hundred new workers.[8] The local division of Stallion Oilfield Services became a magnet for underemployed local young men without college degrees, who suddenly were able to pick up all the overtime hours they wanted and potentially earn more than Lycoming College's professors. Travis Foster, a burly, bearded, and tattooed twenty-six-year old, was one of them. Over drinks at Rumrunners, a kitschy Jamaican-by-way-of-Jersey-Shore-themed bar in town, he recalled how he struggled for years to find steady manual labor, including an ill-fated move to Cleveland to pursue auto mechanics. Travis returned to Billtown, but said he was barely paying the bills doing seasonal construction jobs. His girlfriend's uncle convinced him to invest $5,000 for the three weeks' training required to get his commercial driver's license, and he immediately found work at Stallion transporting "flow-back" wastewater to underground disposal wells in Ohio. Travis normally worked fourteen-hour shifts for four days and then had two days off, though he told me he often chose to work on one of his off days to secure more time and a half.

Justin Campbell, who grew up on a dairy farm in nearby Liberty, Pennsylvania, also secured long-sought steady work at Stallion, laboring in a subdivision that refurbished modular homes and offices for the workers who lived in "man camps" (temporary trailer parks) on-site during drilling and fracking operations. A fit, clean-cut father of two toddlers, Justin said he joined the army at age nineteen, after being laid off from a welding job. "I just got out of basic training when 9/11 hit"; about a week later, "I was on a plane and heading over to Afghanistan." After serving seventeen months there and then ten months in Kosovo, Justin wound up back in Pennsylvania, working in construction, hustling to make ends meet for the next six years. In 2009, he recalled, he simply showed up at the newly opened Stallion branch office and asked for a job. He got much better pay and benefits for the same kind of work, he said, and he felt that there were more opportunities for rapid career advancement. Sure, he had to work long hours and regretted missing substantial portions of his children's development, but that is a sacrifice he felt blessed to be able to make. Now he never worried about the bills, and "It's like, yeah, let's get the plane tickets . . . [and] go to Disney World." As we walked around Stallion's buzzing gravel lot inspecting trailers that were being remodeled into deluxe mobile homes with new kitchen appliances, memory foam beds, and satellite TV, Justin recounted his rapid advancement through the ranks at Stallion, from service technician "in the field" to operations manager in the office. Allowing himself a bit of pride, he grinned, "I was always a blue-collar-type worker; I never thought I'd have an office job."

Justin's story was not unique. Billtown was gaining a national reputation as an economic and administrative axis of fracking. Halliburton built a twenty-four-acre facility southeast of town to serve as its hub for all of North-Central Pennsylvania. When Republican presidential hopeful Ted Cruz toured the area in 2016, he stopped at NuWeld—which expanded from 60 to a peak of 290 workers to meet the industry's need for pipes and wellhead components—to highlight how shale gas extraction could bring "millions and millions of new, high-paying jobs . . . back to America."[9] Penn College began offering specialized vocational training, from roustabout (unskilled laborer) to mechatronics, to prepare locals for industry jobs through its Shale Training and Education Center. It even had a simulated well pad and drilling rig, along with its own white pickup, some of the costs of which were underwritten by the gas industry.

Penn College was hardly alone in jumping at the chance to increase enrollments and program funding by forming teaching and research partnerships with the gas industry. Penn State's Marcellus Center for Outreach and Research has published industry-funded research for well over a decade (a widely touted study predicting that gas firms would shun the state if legislators enacted a severance tax was clandestinely funded by a gas-lobbying group). I served as a counselor for Mansfield University's "Marcellus Shale Camp," in which high school students from around the state spent a week learning from industry representatives about careers in the petroleum industry. Colleges invariably refuted charges of bias. Yet the coursework and scholarship that resulted from their partnerships with petroleum companies, critics contend, likely played a role in legitimating the industry narrative that fracking is a safe, environmentally friendly engine of economic growth.[10]

Greater Williamsport's civic leaders were just as eager to hitch their wagon to the Marcellus. Early on, they formed a Community Gas Exploration Task Force consisting of prominent executives from the private sector, public servants from the city and county, educators, and the county Planning Commission. The task force's mission was to identify and promote "the positive economic impact of gas exploration" and to "propose public policy" that would help facilitate the industry's growth in the region.[11] Its chairman, Vince Matteo, president of the county's Chamber of Commerce, told me that fracking was a "game changer" that created "economic hope in bleak times."[12]

It is hard to overstate Matteo's fracking boosterism. I saw him toss out the first pitch at a Crosscutters minor-league baseball game, to which his Chamber had given out free tickets as part of its "Marcellus Shale Pack the Park" promotion. And there he was at the ribbon-cutting for the new Marriott Residence Inn, boasting of the synergy between the gas industry and the local business community. He was also a key eyewitness at the Congressional Natural Gas Caucus "field hearing" at Penn College, testifying to lawmakers that he had never seen anything like the gas boom in his thirty-three years working on economic development, and that 115 or so businesses opened or located in Lycoming County as a direct result of the industry. One would have to go back to the lumber era, he added, to find comparable growth. Vince told me that his conservative estimate of local jobs created by fracking was two to three thousand, and that there was no question that the county's unemployment rate would be more than five percent higher without shale gas. He claimed that "it's pretty much true" that anyone who wants a job can get one, suggesting that the roughly eight percent of the local adult population that was unemployed was only held back by criminality or an unwillingness to work. And he dismissed concerns voiced by others about decreasing quality of life and unaffordable rents, asserting, "I haven't seen any real problem yet."

Notably, I could not find reliable numbers on the amount of local jobs created by fracking. But it is clear that gas drilling was no silver bullet. Billtown's median household income of $33,147 in 2012 was no different than its preboom median, and its poverty rate remained twice as high as the state's. Also, although Pennsylvania's gas boom peaked between 2011 and 2012, its unemployment rate actually increased almost a full percentage point in that time and was about a half point above the 7.8 percent national average. A common perception, impossible to verify, was that many jobs went to Texans and Dakotans. Additionally, a 2011 study found that Section 8 units were getting hard to find in Billtown, as landlords rented to itinerant gas workers at a premium.[13] Relatedly, researchers have found that local officials may tout the economic

gains from mineral extraction even in regions where it is barely occurring. The implication is that the presence of landmen, white pickups,
and other markers of industry activity may be enough to convince civic
leaders that the local economy is taking off even if key economic indicators do not provide objective support for the boomtown narrative. This
type of thinking can create blinders to the risks of betting everything on
such a volatile industry.[14] Indeed, it sure seemed to me that local boosters ignored the historical lessons of the timber bust.

If Matteo had a rival for chief cheerleader of natural gas, it was Billtown's flamboyant, thrice-elected mayor Gabe Campana. Eager to
upend the "negative perception of Williamsport because of the drug
activity and crime," he officially declared the city "the energy capital of
Pennsylvania" and drove to City Hall in a methane-powered Honda
Civic with "Say Goodbye to Gasoline Forever" emblazoned on the
doors in neon green (he even installed a fueling station at his house).
"I bought the car," the boyish mayor emphasized to me. "I went and got
a loan for it"—it was not given to him by the gas industry—because "I
believe in [natural gas] that much, that it's clean, it benefits our economy, and it creates jobs here in the US." He credited the gas boom—and
"my leadership"—with helping foster a "renaissance for the city," especially the commercial strip sandwiched between downtown and the
interstate that hosted a cluster of hotels, restaurants, a Wegmans market,
and "the only Kohl's in the United States built in the downtown." Campana readily told the *New York Times* that "We're wrapping our arms
around the industry" and invoked Sarah Palin's energy maxim, "Drill,
baby, drill!"[15] (Although the mayor identified with the political movement that adopted the motto—the Tea Party—and had a framed picture of Sarah Palin hanging in his office, he told me that his recitation of
"Drill, baby, drill" was tongue in cheek.)

* * *

And drill they have. Lycoming County had the most new wells "spudded" in 2012 (207) of all the forty-plus counties located over the Marcellus shale play (to spud a well is to begin drilling operations).[16] In the

FIG. 2.3. Gabe Campana, Williamsport mayor (2008–2020). Photograph by Tristan Spinski.

words of Lycoming County commissioner Jeff Wheeland, the greater Williamsport area emerged as a "gas producing Mecca." Signs of the boom were evident in the countryside as well, though they were some-times subtler than downtown's new luxury lofts and the sprawling in-dustrial parks that ringed the city. Most apparent was the truck traffic; I routinely got stuck behind convoys of big rigs as they clumsily navi-gated gravel roads and hairpin turns to deliver water, sand, and equip-ment to well pads. Roving drilling rigs, which loomed over treetops and could often be seen from miles away, also dotted the landscape and were surrounded by temporary trailer-park-like cities complete with maid services and food trucks. While residents routinely complained about traffic and other disturbances associated with gas drilling, many minimized them as inconveniences worth the rewards and opportunities afforded by fracking. And telltale signs of the benefits were everywhere: a new roof for the ramshackle barn; a gleaming pickup truck in the driveway; a remodeled kitchen for the missus.

Old-fashioned general stores, still the de facto social hubs of the backcountry but fighting for survival in the age of big-box stores and Amazon, received a much-needed boost from fracking. I learned to avoid McConnell's Country Store, in Waterville, around lunch time, after being forced to wait twenty–thirty minutes to pay for gasoline at the counter (the gas pump was analog), behind as many as a dozen greasy "roughnecks" whose sandwich orders overwhelmed the store's two employees. (I always looked forward to the rotating pro-gun message on McConnell's letter-board sign out front; one example: "Till Death Do Us Part: My Wife and My Guns.")

The employees and owners of another general store, the storied Cohick's Trading Post, in Salladasburg (population: 260), which I made a point of visiting each week to hear the latest gossip, credited the gas workers with keeping the store in business. The quaint but dumpy wood-paneled interior—still heated by a wood stove—was like a museum celebrating its former glory days. A stool at the lunch counter read, "Katharine Hepburn sat here"; two others marked where James Cagney and Red Grange used to partake of the famous Cohick's homemade ice cream. The grungy old store, which was also the town post office, held as many relics as it did guns and groceries for sale: rusty cola signs; taxidermic deer heads; two conjoined tree trunks, labeled "Nature's Oddity"; countless tchotchkes, like star-spangled birdhouses; a small library of cracked-spine books; and several off-color signs (my favorite: "I'm somewhat of a bullshitter myself, but occasionally I enjoy listening to an expert. PLEASE CARRY ON!"). Watching over it all was a pigtailed American Indian mannequin in an Adirondack chair holding a sign: "You ask credit, we no give, YOU MAD! You ask credit, we give . . . you no pay . . . WE MAD! Better you mad!"

Founded in 1924 as an ice-cream and soft-drink stand, over the years the 8,750-square-foot barn-like structure had housed an inn, an ice house, a cider house, a pool hall, and an appliance showroom. The original Cohick, Jim, even dammed the creek and trucked in sand to make a beach. For decades, hundreds of hunters would crowd the store to buy permits and ammunition at the opening of deer season. Lines of cars formed at its gas pump, Salladasburg's only one. By the 2000s, though, the general store was a shell of its former self. A modern six-pump gas station and convenience store opened a block away (on the highway), siphoning so many customers from Main Street that Cohick's closed its single pump. The only remnant of the halcyon beach days was the crumbling stone bathhouse. And the store's inability to compete with Lycoming Mall and the Lowe's in Montoursville led it to stop selling home appliances. Although it still purveyed hardware and some foodstuffs, nobody was doing one-stop shopping here. For the most part, Cohick's limped along as a greasy-spoon diner distinguished by its "famous homemade ice cream" (the signature sundae was called the Katharine Hepburn), soups, and apple dumplings. It was an especially popular place for old-timers, some of whom spent hours at the simple wooden tables taking potshots at each other and flirting with the waitresses as they sipped on bottomless cups of coffee. Regulars were even entitled to their own special mug, which the servers would wordlessly remove from its wall hook and bring to them as they sat down at their usual spot, and were greeted on their birthday with handwritten signs and a specially made cake.

When gas drilling and pipeline construction ramped up, the breakfast and lunch crowds swelled, providing much-needed additional business in between the shifts of old-timers. Though few regulars would mistake the gas workers for locals, the new arrivals were not unwelcome in Salladasburg. The gas workers were reportedly always courteous, and they wore the same rural workingman's uniform (Carhartt jacket, camouflage cap, flannel shirt, jeans, and steel-toed boots) and had the same parlance, complaining about "big government," discussing how to best prepare smokehouse turkey, and debating gun- versus bowhunting. And, most importantly, the roughnecks had big appetites, tipped generously, and would routinely order more breakfast sandwiches to go, for their coworkers on site. Sometimes they even bought gear. Gas workers like to say, when they need a particular tool or piece of equipment, that they "need it yesterday." Because many roughnecks worked long hours and could get reimbursed for business expenses, they were often willing to pay a premium to avoid the one-hour round-trip drive to Walmart. Cohick's, which was convenient to many of the mountainside "man camps" where roughnecks lived, responded in kind, stocking items like flame-resistant outerwear. For a time, it felt like a real general store again. (Cohick's closed in 2015 and was reborn as the Waltz Creamery and Farm House Café, after a court-ordered sale to settle a family feud over ownership.)

According to state representative Garth Everett, who was first elected to the district that encompasses Salladasburg in 2006, the gas industry jibed with "small-town, rural Pennsylvania culture." Seated in his modest office, in a strip mall just off I-180, the self-described libertarian told me that, in his estimation, most of those who were against development—like members of the RDA—were "not part of our indigenous population." They were rusticators who "moved here from downstate or Jersey, cause it's so beautiful here," and now they were upset, because "the industry's caught up with them again." To the ruddy-faced assemblyman, it all came down to personal liberty and land sovereignty. "We've got a lot of—oh, I would say, Charlie Daniels Band long-haired country boys that enjoy being left alone . . . [and] don't want the government interceding in their lives." It was Garth's duty to ensure that they "have the right to do what they want with their property, and develop it." Outfitted in moccasins and a red fleece vest, Garth took issue with those who might characterize him and his constituents as anti-environment. "So many of us are outdoor people. Hunting, fishing, and kayaking . . . There's so many people that belong to the Muncy Creek [Watershed] Association, the Loyalsock Creek Preservation Association." What separated them from environmentalists was that "we're more conservationists. We're used to harvesting natural resources and don't see [fracking] differently," whereas they "don't like the fact that there's economic development" at all and want to "overregulate what doesn't need to be overregulated."

"When I grew up, in the late fifties and early sixties," Garth reminisced, his hometown of Montoursville (five miles east of Williamsport) "was classic, like TV-show, small-town America. It was in the day when you could jump on your bike and ride up the road and jump off the bridge and go swimming." The postwar economy was humming, and "everything seemed to be good." You could "graduate from high school and go to work at the mill, and have a lifetime of stability." After spending twenty years away in the Air Force, followed by three years in law school, Garth said he returned to the area to find that the Norman Rockwell way of life he so cherished had vanished. "There wasn't any jobs. Nothing. We had, across the river was a big plant that's now empty where they made all the Bali miniblinds—they're in Mexico now. From three shifts to an empty plant just in the time—since 2000, when I moved home." Because of the lack of opportunity, many kids graduating high school wanted to "get the hell outta here." Montoursville's population declined 25 percent in Garth's absence, sapping voluntary associations like the Rotary Club and draining the community of vital social capital. His hometown had become just another rust-belt town.

All most people around here wanted, Garth claimed, was to "have a blue-collar job and still [be able to] live here." They "don't wanna get rich. They wanna go to work, go home, be left alone." Natural gas, from all he had seen, made that possible for the first time in a generation. Chuckling, Garth added, "We thank the state of New York every day for their moratorium [on gas drilling]," which allowed the Williamsport area to enjoy all the economic benefits of hosting the "Halliburtons and Weatherfords," instead of having to share with towns like Elmira or Binghamton. Garth also credited the gas industry with providing a lifeline to dying family farms. He said he knew "tons of people who are still on their old family farms, but they're not really full-time farmers." They needed another job to support their families and worried that their children would see the ancestral homestead as nothing more than a millstone. But gas drilling, he said, changed that. Garth recounted the story of Barry Farnsworth, a local dairy farmer who, thanks to a lease bonus and royalties from Exco, didn't "have to get up at four in the morning and milk cows anymore." Rather than get out of farming, Garth recalled Barry saying, he was freed up to double down on it: "I sold my dairy herd. I raise beef now. I have new machines. I don't have to work as hard as I used to, and my family's gonna be able to farm forever." Garth said that, for farmers like Barry, their whole lives had been "scratching away just trying to keep the farm." Now, the farms—or the shale rock buried beneath them, anyway—were cash cows.

I heard more stories like Barry's while hanging out at a butchery—which was just a concrete garage next to a barn—outside of Hughesville. Over the course of a Saturday morning, overalled men arrived with a freshly killed cow or two, their glistening-red slit throats agape, in the back of their pickup. The bulbous-nosed and bespectacled patriarch of the shop, Ralph, and his middle-aged son Fred hung the cows on meat hooks and dismembered them while "shooting the shit" with their customers. Some regulars said they inherited the family business but could no longer make a living from their cows' milk or flesh. They had other jobs, but were loath to give up the lifestyle they knew and the land they grew up on. Natural gas, the butcher opined as he sawed some fat from the cow carcass dangling before him (which caused blood to dribble down his unprotected face and hands), brought in some money that helped these farmers ride out the recession and purchase new equipment, so that they could "farm better." Keith Shaner, a semiretired farmer and butchery regular, added with a snicker, "And your wife gets to go to the [Philadelphia] flower show!" "Yeah, mum gets the flower show," Ralph huffed. "But that's mum! What do I got?" Sipping a can of Busch beer (at 10:00 a.m., at Ralph's insistence), Keith reckoned, "Life hasn't really changed [with fracking]. We still farm, we still butcher. We just get a little bit of royalties to help us out. It certainly improved the economic environment . . . around here, with all the people getting royalties."

Keith would know. Within a half mile of his house at the time were six wide dirt scars in the landscape, including one cut into a steep hillside, where pipelines were being installed. A drilling rig lorded over the mountaintop. Graded gravel lots amid manicured fields, topped with green-painted wellheads (the industry refers to them as "Christmas trees"), indicated the presence of well pads. The erstwhile pastoral valley had come to resemble an industrial park. Dozens of white trucks, diggers, and construction vehicles inched along narrow gravel roads, their roaring diesel engines and backup beepers echoing off the valley floor. Flaggers directed traffic. Orange-vested work crews swarmed like an ant colony around infrastructure projects. This is what it looked like to farm the cash crop that was breathing new life into beleaguered family farms like the Shaners': methane.

Keith pointed to benefits beyond his and other farmers' enrichment. His son, who graduated college with a degree in fine art, faced dim job prospects unless he was willing to leave home. But now he worked for Halliburton, reportedly earning $120,000—almost three times the starting salary of the only other job he was offered: art teacher in the East Lycoming School District. And tiny Penn Township (population: 960), of which Keith was an elected (unpaid) supervisor, was able to capture a sizable chunk of "impact fees"—tariffs imposed on unconventional gas wells by the state (in lieu of taxes) and distributed directly to municipal governments to mitigate the local impacts of drilling. In 2011, Penn Township received the maximum allowance—$500,000, which the supervisors used to replace road graders and dump trucks that were more than thirty years old.[17] It was slated to receive close to the maximum again in 2013 (it got $495,867), which Keith planned to put toward grading—and finally paving—some vital local roads. It was an unheard-of sum of money in the township. Historically, supervisors and their electors quibbled over expenditures of $1,000, or even $100. "We certainly can use it," Keith said of the impact fee money, before adding with a laugh, "Everybody wants a piece of it!"

Fracking offered the promise of escaping the seeming inevitability of rust-belt decline. At the same time, it portended an age of energy independence that would finally make it possible for America, in Garth Everett's words, to avoid "fighting in the sand with people that don't like us." It was mostly only the gentry, Garth opined, "who don't like the fact that there's economic development" based on harnessing natural resources. Ralph Kisberg countered that many of the area's wealthiest residents made money from the gas industry and supported it, and that most RDA members were middle-class rather than rich. But he didn't dispute other aspects of Garth's characterization of them. Ralph once mused about everyone getting "thrown out of here," so that the area could become a national wilderness park. And he conceded that the

RDA's small group of supporters were mostly "well-educated profes-sional people" who loved nature and didn't hunt.

Ralph recalled the RDA putting a traditional broadside in the news-paper in 2009 that listed all the potential harms that could befall the county from fracking. Though it resulted in close to a thousand people signing up for the RDA's e-mail newsletter, the group only heard from a few civic leaders or landowners interested in meeting with them. Four years later, their e-mail list hadn't grown. "We have no credibility in the community . . . We're perceived as a bunch of hysterical panicking luna-tics," Ralph lamented. Almost everyone else rejected NIMBYism. If anything, they engaged in "please-in-my-backyard" advocacy, inviting gas companies to drill on their land and working to ensure that the area's hotels, restaurants, offices, colleges, and workforce accommodated the gas companies' needs. "They're just, it's gas mania. It's the panacea to them," Ralph said of his neighbors and politicians. "You don't even need to tax it, it's so wonderful," he derisively chuckled, referring to Garth Everett's and state senator Gene Yaw's ongoing efforts—in concert with the Republican majority—to ensure that Pennsylvania remained one of the only states not to levy a severance tax on its gas production.

More than 120 years after the collapse of the timber industry, Bill-town found itself another golden goose. Sometimes, it seemed as if the community embraced the goose so tightly the creature might suffocate.

CHAPTER 3

The Fracking Lottery

"Mary and I grew up right next door to each other," Tom Crawley recounted as he playfully elbowed his wife, who sat beside him in a matching Adirondack chair on the lawn in front of their tidy colonial home outside Hughesville (about twenty minutes east of Billtown). "Here we are, almost thirty-five years [of marriage] later. We're still plugging along," he observed dryly. The gray-haired empty nesters momentarily shared a knowing smile, before Mary laconically added in her boisterous voice, "Still here!"

It almost seemed preordained that Tom, who labored at a nearby machine shop, and Mary, who worked at a social-service agency in Billtown, would still be *here*. After all, Crawleys have lived in the area for generations. The couple's nine-acre wooded lot, tucked away atop a steep gravel driveway leading up the hillside from a small creek named Sugar Run, is a remnant of Tom's great-grandfather's 444-acre farm, which encompassed most of the valley. Tom and Mary's front porch, furnished with wooden rockers they seldom found the time to enjoy, overlooks Crawley Road.

Hidden beneath the surface of what was once the Crawley family farm are two natural-gas pipelines. Tom could vividly recall a black-and-white photograph of his mother, pregnant with his sister, smiling as she stood atop the first pipeline before it was buried in 1958. "We've had pipelines coming through here forever," Mary remarked as she puzzled over why environmentalists were suddenly protesting oil and gas pipelines like the Keystone XL. Tom said that his grandfather was able to settle all his debts with the money he made granting a right-of-way for the first pipeline; the second pipeline put a new John Deere tractor in the old man's barn. So when landmen began poking around Hughesville last decade, Tom allowed himself to fantasize about obtaining a leasing bonus big enough to buy himself a new pickup—or maybe even a Ford Mustang.

"It was November 2007 they started talking gas leases," Tom recalled in his gentle monotone as he patted the head of his dog Ollie, who was parked at his feet. "Our neighbor down here heard about it. At that time, they were talking $35, $40 an acre. Then it was up to $80." Although Tom and Mary were personally interested in leasing, they said, they wanted to be good neighbors. So, before agreeing to a sit-down with the landman, they decided to hold a meeting to sound out others on Green Valley Road. Almost everyone was reportedly enthusiastic about the prospect, though some were worried about being lowballed. Tom was one of them: "I'm just nine acres among everybody else." Nearby farms consisting of a hundred acres or more were the real prizes. So "by my-self, I'm not worth anything." The landman's usual pitch, especially to smaller landowners like the Crawleys, I was told, insinuated that gas companies would get along just fine without your signature. They would simply drill around you. It was, Tom and Mary believed, a pressure tactic designed to convince them that they had no leverage to negotiate the terms of their lease. "So we talked about it," Tom said, "and we decided that our best bet was to stick together."

In the ensuing months, the Crawleys and their neighbors attended information sessions with gas companies, researched leases, consulted lawyers, and talked to people who had already leased. In the end, they devised a strategy that significantly amplified their negotiating power, forming a landowner coalition consisting of seventy-five community members committed to collectively bargaining with gas companies as a block.[1] Raymond Gregoire, a salesman who served as the coalition's reluctant spokesman, estimated that the group represented about four thousand acres. 'That's over three million dollars,' Ray pointed out, valuable enough to be a plum trophy in the gas rush that was then unfolding. (Ray's lease bonus was $62,000.) Midwestern petroleum companies like Anadarko and Chesapeake were competing for acreage township by township, and door to door, across northern Pennsylvania.

The Crawleys and Ray saw the landowner coalition as a vehicle for maximizing their personal leasing bonuses and potential royalties. Yet they were adamant that being "all in this together" was also driven by altruism—especially a desire to reduce or eliminate leasing disparities within their little community in the valley. Tom didn't consider it fair if, for instance, he secured $1,000 an acre for himself while his next-door neighbor received only $400 an acre. The landowner coalition tried to help ensure that fracking would raise all boats. Ray recounted how, as the group's representative, he fielded offers from several gas companies. The most generous offer, from Chesapeake, came with a caveat that Ray could not in good conscience accept: the company was not interested in leasing a seven-hundred-acre portion of the coalition's land on the other side of Route 118, so the owners within that tract would be excluded from the deal. The coalition said no, thank you.

Eventually, the coalition agreed in principle to a deal with a Texas-based petroleum company for $450 an acre for a standard five-year lease.[2] In what Mary described as a "wild scene," the two hundred or so landowners and their relatives descended on the Lairdsville volunteer fire hall en masse to sign. "Mary and I have grown up in this area and know a lot of people," Tom marveled. But "there was people"—before he could finish his thought, his wife interrupted, "We'd never seen!" The drama was just beginning. When Ray arrived at the fire hall, he shouted over the din, 'Don't sign those papers!' Recalling the moment, at a barbeque on the Crawleys' front lawn, Ray chuckled, 'They all wanted to kill me for telling 'em not to sign, but when they heard why, they wanted to hug me.' As it turned out, on his way to the fire hall Ray had taken a phone call from a rival gas company that was prepared to offer $600 per acre. The crowd roared its approval. "It was total chaos," Tom sighed as he brushed back his chin-length silver bangs. Even some people "having only one or two acres" began imagining they "were gonna become rich." Some reportedly goaded the energy company executives who sat before them, unsigned leases in hand, and urged Ray to escalate the bidding war by calling back the other energy company. The suits from Texas upped their offer to $800. Though the rival firm told Ray over the phone that it would match that offer, the coalition agreed to stick with its original partner. In the span of just two hours, the landowners had almost doubled their payout. As far as Tom and Ray knew, no one else in the area had received such a generous leasing bonus at that time. 'Of course,' Ray smirked, 'the next day an acre was going for a thousand.'

The bonus only amounted to about $7,000 for the Crawleys, given their relatively small parcel; farmers in the coalition who owned hundreds of acres got six-figure checks. But the Crawleys stood to make more from royalties—perhaps a thousand dollars per month—if gas was extracted from their property. Also, Tom and Mary knew that it was highly unlikely that a gas well would ever be drilled on their land. Gas companies preferred to place well pads, which require clearing and leveling as many as five acres, on large tracts. Their next-door neighbors Doyle Bodle, a retired truck driver, and his wife, Peggy, who used to make Pop-Tarts at the nearby Kellogg's factory, made the same calculation. "We knew they were not going to drill on our land," Doyle said of their 2.5-acre plot. "They'd just come beneath us," Peggy added. In fact, the Bodles and the Crawleys faced little threat of any kind of surface disturbance. Should a company be interested in a pipeline right-of-way, that would require a separate negotiation and bonus payment. In the eyes of Russ the landman, lessors of small plots like the Crawleys and the Bodles got "something for nothing," receiving a bonus and a chance for royalties while not having to host a gas well or any other development.

* * *

I have come to think of land leasing as akin to a lottery. Like some economists have observed of state-sponsored lotteries, leasing was particularly attractive to people of modest means as a "convenient and otherwise rare opportunity for rapidly improving their standard of living."[3] It was certainly a narrative that gas industry representatives embraced. Scott McClain, a semiretired former game warden who lived in a modest ranch house situated on a five-acre mountainside homestead, shook his head as he recounted the landman's pitch. Wearing a cowboy hat and gifting turkeys from the trunk of his shiny black Cadillac Escalade (it was the holidays), the landman suggested that gas drilling could make Scott "richer than Jed Clampett" (of the Beverly Hillbillies). Few of the twenty-six lessors I befriended believed all the hype. In fact, most walked into leasing with their eyes wide open: none reported signing a lease on the spot, and everyone consulted either with neighbors who had already leased or with a lawyer. Yet their distrust of the landman did not dampen their hope that they might be fortunate enough to walk away with an unexpected windfall. Almost every time I hung out with Russ, who recounted stories of lessors responding like sweepstakes winners after he secured their signatures, he was constantly fielding phone calls from their friends and relatives asking how they too could obtain a lease. For some, the lease was a lifeline—a way to secure the family farm for the next generation, or to prevent the car from getting repossessed. There were some lessors willing to leave some money on the table in exchange for greater control over drilling and fracking operations on their property, such as a stipulation that the lessor must approve the location of any permanent structure (e.g., a gas well). However, by far and away, the most common lease alteration that landowners sought was a bigger leasing bonus and greater share of gas royalties.

Geography and geology contributed to the lottery-like randomness of leasing. Many of the factors that determined which landowners were the biggest economic winners were not known in advance and were beyond lessors' control, such as the thickness and depth of the shale layer beneath their properties and the productivity of the wells (the greater the production, the greater the royalties). Companies typically placed gas wells, pipelines, and other infrastructure on only a fraction of the acreage they leased, which resulted in some landowners receiving just the one-time lease bonus, while their neighbors reaped much more through royalties, pipeline rights-of-way, and so on. This meant that residents who owned just a few acres could theoretically reap a bonanza greater than nearby large landholders if they happened to sit in a key location. For instance, one retired marine named Merril, known as "The

FIG. 3.1. A pipeline right-of-way. Photograph by Tristan Spinski.

Colonel," who was a regular at Cohick's Trading Post, crowed about his "little pipeline deal." 'That landman spent two years securing the rights to thirteen miles for the pipeline, and then there's little old Merril with just a few acres who hasn't agreed yet,' he giggled. Because the pipeline could not be completed without crossing the corner of Merril's property, he said he was able to obtain a payment of over $60,000, which was more than some nearby farmers received for leasing dozens of acres. 'Bought me a new roof and siding for the house!'

Although property ownership is commonly associated with privilege, in the country many people are land-poor. Folks of modest means may own tens or even hundreds of acres that they inherited, but in the era of Big Agriculture and rural brain drain, that land may be an encumbrance. For many, their homestead's value is more sentimental than monetary. They sometimes face difficult decisions about whether it still makes sense to hold onto the family farm—especially when it is time to pay the property tax bill. But the advent of fracking changed the equation. Each acre was like a lottery ticket: the more one had, the greater one's odds of winning the jackpot—that is, of earning monthly royalties from gas extracted from underneath one's property, or securing a pipeline right-of-way. And it paid to play no matter what, because per-acre leasing bonuses were disbursed in full after signing. It was only in this new financial reality, Tom said, that it made sense for an "outsider" to buy eighty-three acres behind the Crawley's house, for $530,000, that did not even have access to a public road.

It was this new financial reality that preserved the Shaner family farm, located just over the hill from the Crawleys. After hearing about my research from a mutual acquaintance, Amy Rogers, an energetic mother of four in her early forties with shoulder-length amber hair, was eager to show me the 150-acre estate that she and her nine siblings inherited. On an overcast late September afternoon, we met up on the leafy campus of Lycoming College, where Amy had earned her bachelor's degree and was now a professor and chair of the education department. (Fittingly, she sported a blue Lycoming College hoodie that day.) As I followed Amy in my car out of Billtown and along Route 220, which cut a meandering path through cornfields dotted by the occasional antique store and faded red barn, white tanker trucks labeled "Residual Brine Waste" and oversized cherry red transporter trucks emblazoned with the Halliburton logo lumbered in front of and behind us. The truck convoys, indicators of gas-drilling activity, created a bottleneck at the stop sign where 220 intersects with Main Street in Hughesville, slowing traffic to a crawl. It took nearly ten minutes to make the left turn and park at the Sunoco gas

station, where I climbed into Amy's SUV for the rest of the journey.
I now understood firsthand why locals were clamoring for a traffic light
on the outskirts of this small town (population: 2,000). 'You *never* had
to wait like that before,' Amy groused as we ascended Beaver Lake Road.
But, she was quick to add, 'We should be happy with what we get,
because before we had nothing.' Upon cresting the hill, we were rewarded
with a stunning 360-degree view. Rolling mountains resplendent in the
early fall foliage, occasionally interrupted by tidy rectangular swatches of
hay fields studded with stacked bales, extended miles to the horizon.
Presiding over it all was the modest vinyl-sided Mt. Zion Lutheran
Church. Amy's parents were buried in the cemetery out back, which now
overlooked an incongruous industrial site emitting some kind of vapor—
the newly built Barto compressor station, which purified and pressurized
the methane pulled out of local gas wells so that it could be transported
via a pipeline to the East Coast.

Continuing on Beaver Lake Road, Amy pointed to the porched colonial house nestled among golden fields that belonged to her brother
Keith Shaner, the man who had taken me to the local butchery and
bragged about his son drawing a six-figure salary working for Halliburton. Next door was her brother Chris's place, and across the street was
the new "McMansion" owned by Keith's son. All of it once comprised
her parents' farm, which itself was at one time part of her grandfather's
estate. As their children reached maturity, Amy's parents carved off
twenty- to thirty-acre lots for them. (Amy, the youngest of ten, lived on
the other side of town; by the time she came of age her parents had
stopped dividing their property.) Their last will and testament stipulated that nothing more could be built on the remaining 150 acres, Amy
told me. By the time the children's mother died, in 2009 (their father
having predeceased her), and bequeathed the 150 acres in equal shares
to all ten of them, each had established their own households, and none
were interested in farming as a vocation. With the fields fallow and the
house vacant, the farm threatened to become an albatross unless the
clan could find a new way to make it productive.

As we turned onto Dr. Poust Road, which bordered the eastern edge
of the present border of the Shaner family property, we confronted a

five-acre impoundment pond (aka "frac pond") surrounded by dirt berms. Lined with thick plastic and enclosed by chain-link fences affixed with signs warning people to keep out (and with life preservers, in case they didn't), the pond served two purposes: to store fresh (i.e., chemically untreated) water for subsequent use in fracking operations, or to hold wastewater that came back out of gas wells after they were fracked until it could be hauled away to be disposed of or reused (the industry was moving toward reusing frac fluid). In exchange for hosting the frac pond for a renewable four-year term, the Shaner estate—now organized as Penn Brook Farm, LLC (incorporated in 2009)—received $24,000, paid up front. Every time trucks withdrew water from the pond to frack a gas well offsite, which was twenty-two times in 2012, Penn Brook Farm received an additional $500. Turning onto Election House Hill Road, a 1,300-foot-long and forty-five-foot-wide ribbon of dirt through the middle of a cornfield indicated a pipeline right-of-way, for which Penn Brook Farm received a bonus of $10,400 from Exco, plus a one-time payment of $1,253 for crop loss. Although Amy and her siblings were annoyed that pipeline construction disturbed more acreage than their lease had stipulated, Amy acknowledged that "they did a good job putting it right back the way it was before"—and that the farm got an extra $10,000 as recompense.[4] Penn Brook Farm was also slated to be paid $16,000 for hosting eight fire-hydrant-like valves (for pipeline maintenance) that would be hemmed in by a fifty-by-fifty-foot fence.[5]

We parked in front of the estate's handsome gray Victorian home, which regularly hosted family gatherings in warmer months. Then we crossed the road and entered a slumping red barn to visit horses that Amy kept on the property. As we fed half-rotten baby carrots to a bedraggled thirty-three-year-old brown pony that Amy rode as a child, she told me that the farm received royalties from underground horizontal wellbores whose wellheads originated on three different neighbors' properties. In 2010, when the price of natural gas averaged more than $4 per thousand cubic feet (MCF), and the wells were at their peak productivity, Chesapeake Energy sent Penn Brook Farm over $40,000 in monthly royalties, which the siblings split equally among themselves.[6] It was enough to bump Amy's family up to a higher tax bracket, and to

FIG. 3.2. Amy Rogers feeds her horses on the family farm.
Photograph by Colin Jerolmack.

allow them to set up a scholarship fund that put her oldest daughter through college. She claimed to know another family that drew $90,000 a month. "I saw the receipts," she insisted. Repeating an oft-heard refrain, Amy said she always knew when someone around here got a big royalty check, because she'd see a new pickup truck in the driveway or a new roof on the barn. But with the national glut of natural gas causing the price to tumble as low as $2.26 per MCF, and given a natural decline in productivity of the wells from which she drew royalties, Amy was presently getting only $1,500 per month. Her brief window of being able to hire a maid appeared to be closed. "Not that I'm complaining, but don't quit your day job." Betraying a hint of envy toward her older brother Keith, who in addition to drawing royalties from Penn Brook Farm also received income from leasing his inherited land, Amy liked to joke that he was "double-dipping."

Keith seemed much more in his element on the family farm than his kid sister, giving Amy instructions on how to tend to the horses and showing little patience when she had difficulty turning on the water supply. And, unlike Amy and me, he was immune to the charms of six kittens wrestling on a nearby hay bale. Just another litter of barn cats.

Sporting a gray mustache, trucker cap, and a T-shirt that clung to his large stomach, Keith was in his late fifties at the time but looked older. His life had had a very different trajectory than Amy's, and his body paid the price. His face was crisscrossed by creases. His skin was leathery. And when I reached out for a handshake upon meeting him for the first time I was met with a stump; as a child, Keith had lost all four fingers and part of the thumb of his right hand to a piece of heavy equipment while performing his farm chores. (Like the recent death of his daughter, from cancer, the accident was one of those things that the stoic man kept silent about.) Although he eventually left the farm for the Air Force, upon retirement Keith returned to agriculture on a part-time basis. For the past four years, he had also been a township supervisor.

Not one to dally, Keith was willing to entertain more of my questions on the condition that I not interfere with his farm chores. So I followed him around the barn as he filled grain bins and tinkered with the tractor. Keith began with a jibe at "liberal New Yorkers," who at the time were lobbying (successfully) for a ban on fracking in that state. "Where do they think their energy comes from? It has to come from someplace. Right now, there's no natural unlimited supply of energy."

On Keith's own property, he said, "I got a water line and then the gas line across the corner of it." Although he lamented that "we were dumb around here," meaning he and many of his neighbors leased for relatively paltry amounts (e.g., $5 an acre) and accepted the state-mandated minimum royalty percentage (12.5 percent), he expressed gratitude that leasing had provided "more than we ever had before." The money didn't make him rich, Keith said, but it meant that "We don't have the skimping from paycheck to paycheck to pay the bills." He recalled the first royalty check making it possible to finally take his family on an honest-to-goodness vacation (to Virginia Beach). He was proud that he could now afford to enroll his youngest daughter in more sports activities and camps and to loan his older children money when they had financial shortfalls. And yes, he chuckled, "the wife has bought more things." The time I visited Keith in his home, he emphatically smacked the patent leather sofa and exclaimed, "This is gas money!" As he pointed to a loveseat and other furniture around his living room, Keith chanted: "Gas money! Gas money! Gas money!"

* * *

Like state-run lotteries (and unlike most of real life), the fracking lottery was also rather random from a sociological perspective, in that lessors' socioeconomic status had little bearing on their chances of coming out a winner.[7] In fact, some of the biggest winners were land-poor folks like George Hagemeyer, whose inherited properties were millstones before fracking. Not long before I met George, he was barely getting by on his custodian's pension. Duct tape traversed his linoleum kitchen floor. The cabinets sagged. A faded wallpaper mural of a fall landscape that had enjoyed pride of place on his living room wall for forty years was peeling. A tarp had been hastily draped over the leaking roof of a ramshackle trailer parked in his front yard that George used as a shed. He drove a jalopy.

Not that George was one to complain. "If you wanna look at the bad things all the time, that's all you're ever gonna see. You hafta look at the good side, too." The good side was that, out of seven siblings, he was the one who had been gifted his dad's land. He planned to die here, but he worried about what would happen to the property afterward. The natural order of things, according to George, is for a father to entrust his son to be the land's next steward. But George didn't have a son, and neither his adopted daughter nor his teenage granddaughter showed interest in living on the estate. His brother, who used to live next door, on a sliver of the family farm, had already sold out.

George's fortunes did not change overnight. Like the Shaners, he leased in the mid-2000s, before anyone in the region had even heard the word *fracking*. The going rate at the time was only $5 per acre, roughly the amount that wildcatters had been paying for decades for the right—which they almost never exercised—to probe for trapped pockets of underground methane. Given the region's historic experience with vertical gas wells, which were low impact, few in number, and almost never put into production, a visit from the landman didn't set off alarm bells for George. (Some lessors complained that gas companies intentionally glossed over how horizontal drilling would be different—i.e., far more disruptive for lessors and far more lucrative for the industry.) George ran the lease, which offered $12 per acre for the first year and $4.50 per acre for the remaining four years (for a total payout of $2,360), by his lawyer. He was told it was a good deal. George smirked. "How many times do you think I'm ever gonna hire that lawyer to do anything for me again? It's between zero and none."

Sociologist Stephanie Malin and colleagues argue that leasing disempowered lessors like George, "precisely because negotiations occurred privately between industry representatives and individual landowners."[8] Most lessors, including people with counsel, lacked full information on what they could bargain for. The structure of private land leasing played into the industry's hands. In most instances, gas company representatives were able to convince landowners to lease through one-on-one negotiations—situations in which the industry held all the cards. It never occurred to George that he could have collectively bargained with his neighbors, as the Crawleys did; as a result, he arguably got fleeced.

When I asked George if he felt cheated, though, he responded, "I can't holler." He noted that he "made a nice chunk of money" for the pipeline under his field. More than the gleaming Ford Explorer SUV and the $8,000 Scag riding mower, what mattered most to him about the windfall was being able to start a college fund for his granddaughter Maddie. Her portrait—knees tucked close to her chest, her blond hair framing a shy teenager smile—was the only tabletop adornment in his living room. Tearfully glancing at her photo, George managed to blurt out, "I love that girl to pieces," before momentarily going silent to collect himself. "She deserves everything."

George hoped to be able to give his granddaughter everything in the near future. I stood with him on a scorching July afternoon in 2013 as he supervised the workers preparing to bring his moneymakers—that is, the six gas wells in his backyard—online (i.e., connected to the pipeline). Despite the heat, the roughnecks were required to wear thick fire-retardant suits. "Ugh," George commented, "I'd rather go pick shit with the chickens than wear one of those damned things!" As was his wont,

George chatted up the nearest hard hat, who happened to be a field analyst who told us he recently migrated here from the oilfields in Wyoming. "We're hopin' for some pretty good wells here," the man remarked nonchalantly. "You are?" George asked excitedly, rubbing his hands together as if caressing an imaginary stack of royalty checks. "I am too!" he exclaimed, before becoming overwhelmed by belly laughs. The worker readily indulged George's fantasy. Based on the wellheads' high-pressure-gauge readings, he had "a feeling they're gonna be some pretty good ones."

Once the man walked away, George began chuckling as he imagined life as a "shaleionaire." He told me he would be the lousiest rich person alive, because he would give it all away. In addition to planning to pick up the tab for his granddaughter's college tuition and buy her a car for graduation, he wanted, he said, "to be able to take care of my brothers and sisters that were born and raised here." On second thought, George conceded that he didn't plan to give *all* the royalty money away. "I wanna protect my home as much as possible." Materially, that meant remodeling his careworn kitchen and installing a new roof—ideally, a metal one. Legally, that meant rewriting his will so that part of his new-found fortune stayed with the property, meaning that his daughter would forfeit any claim to her inheritance if she attempted to sell or transfer ownership of the estate. George also entertained more fanciful visions, like constructing a pond in his field "big enough to put two islands in," with "an arch bridge going from one to the other with a flowering cherry [tree] in the middle of each one," and like buying out his neighbor and bulldozing the house, so he didn't have to look at it.

When the money, such as it was, began rolling in, George had some fun. He purchased a kayak and a large passenger van to transport it, so that he didn't have to bother attaching a trailer to his SUV. On one visit, I found his table littered with ads torn out of magazines for resorts in the Poconos, casinos in Atlantic City, and even a fourteen-day cruise in Alaska. He had taken to purchasing decorative plates painted with American flags and animals like deer and eagles—which he displayed on counters, sills, and almost any other flat surface he could find throughout the house—and to collecting limited-edition Monopoly board games (the crown jewel, which he said he picked up on a day trip to Corning, New York, with his granddaughter, was gold-foil-stamped and constructed of mahogany). And he sported a fancy new watch that he had seen on TV and had to have. 'They said the list price was $1,500, but I got it for a little more than $500.'

It took some time to get his kitchen remodeled, in part because George acted like a self-described "pain in the ass." Seeming to relish a rare opportunity to play the part of a bigwig, George gleefully recounted how he fired two contractors for not following his detailed specifications (he said one bought the wrong sink; another "hung the cabinets too darn high!"). The kitchen was finally completed in the fall of 2016, and it was such a total transformation that it could have been featured on *Extreme Home Makeover*: all stainless-steel appliances, including (finally) a dishwasher; wraparound stained solid-wood cabinets; marble countertops; an embossed ceiling that imitated the tin ceilings of old; and, of course, a new tiled floor to replace the duct-taped linoleum. The bathroom, whose origin as an outhouse attached to the kitchen meant that it was perennially dank, was also gut renovated. Its newly installed cedar paneling (including on the tub), wall-to-wall carpet, and insulated walls emanated both figurative and literal warmth. The showpiece, which George couldn't wait to present to me, was a walnut bay window installed in the laundry room, off the back of the kitchen. Previously, he had no view of his backyard from the kitchen. Its three panes now framed an archetypal rustic scene: the lush green expanse of his lawn extending toward distant tree stands, with the misty mountains looming in the background. (He shrugged off the occasional odor of industrial chemicals like benzene that wafted in from the well pad through his window, noting that the problem was easily solved by jamming rags between the window and the sill.) 'They were gonna do that window with pine,' George said with disgust. He went on, 'Now, pine would've only set me back $800, and this cost ten times that. But you ain't doing my window with pine! Over my dead body!'

Though the living room was relatively unchanged, George did make one significant alteration as an ode to his mother: he replaced her faded, flaking wallpaper mural. The new mural, also a fall scene that took up

FIG. 3.3. George Hagemeyer in front of his new living-room wall mural.
Photograph by Tristan Spinski.

the entire wall, consisted of dozens of painted vinyl squares glued together. George had actually purchased it four years earlier with his pipeline bonus money, but it sat rolled up behind his loveseat for want of the
additional funds required for a professional installation. Knowing that
I used to rib him about the unfinished job, George proudly sat for a
portrait session with the mural as a backdrop when I visited him in the
fall of 2017 with a photographer.

Although the declining productivity of his wells, along with the
bottoming-out of natural-gas prices, reduced George's monthly royalties from five figures to four figures in less than a year, he fulfilled his
dream of surprising his granddaughter with a new Ford Escape for her
high school graduation, in 2017. He joyfully recounted the story of driving Maddie to the dealership under the pretense that his own car needed
repairs, and then parking by the white SUV and announcing, "It's
yours!" George sold his two-year-old passenger van to finance the

$28,000 cash purchase, which was a reminder that his newfound wealth was finite. Yet the fact that George had grown accustomed to paying in full up front for big-ticket items was an indicator of how privileged fracking had made him. One way he expressed his gratitude was by donating $500 worth of food and new clothes to a shelter on Thanksgiving; he said he made his granddaughters tag along, 'to show them how to be charitable.'

Thanks to land leasing, George had finally broken free of a lifetime of relative deprivation. Though he was hardly alone in turning to the fracking lottery in an effort to escape hardship, George certainly made out better than most. Of course, those who didn't own any mineral estate couldn't participate in the fracking lottery. What's more, in some places—especially Billtown—tenants faced rising rents, and in 2012 residents of the Riverdale Mobile Home Park were forced out after a company bought the land in order to construct a water withdrawal site. In the rural places of Lycoming County where most drilling occurred, though, almost everyone owned rather than rented (in Gamble Township, where George lived, only 10 percent of the population were renters).[9] And, unlike in parts of the Midwest, almost all the landowners here held the mineral rights. Everyone who leased got something, but it's a minority, it seems, who wound up with life-changing money.[10]

The fact that few lessors hit the jackpot, while most of them experienced some degradation in their quality of life, has led some analysts to conclude that petroleum companies exploited the vulnerability of marginalized small-scale farmers and homeowners. Like the disproportionately impoverished group of people who buy lottery tickets, the thinking goes, many lessors felt they had little choice but to sign, because leasing was their only potential escape from economic insecurity. Some scholars call scenarios like this "environmental blackmail," because, they argue, residents must choose between their health and their livelihood.[11] In addition, fracking introduced new inequalities among neighbors: members of the Shaner clan earned enough royalties to endow college funds and hire maids; the Crawleys, just down the hill, received just a $7,000 one-time bonus, which came at the expense of their freshwater supply (now laced with methane from a neighbor's gas well). The

Department of Environmental Protection shut in the faulty well, fore-closing the possibility of it generating royalties for the Crawleys.

As for his own misfortune, Tom Crawley resignedly concluded that "accidents happen" and optimistically pointed to the Shaners, implying that he could just as easily have been in their shoes. His neighbor Doyle Bodle, whose water was also impacted by drilling, reiterated that most lessors "are not having any problems," and that even people not impacted by drilling can wind up with bad water, suggesting that geology itself shouldered much of the blame. "Losers" like Tom and Doyle saw themselves primarily as victims of bad luck—in particular, of an unfortunate location—rather than of bad actors or systemic inequity. And the fact that topography and luck largely determined the winners appealed to residents' egalitarian sensibilities. *Anyone* could win, regardless of occupation, education, or wealth. In this way, private mineral ownership, a peculiarly American idea, made fracking compatible with the American Dream—even as it created new socioeconomic disparities, exposed landowners to significant environmental risks, and oftentimes left lessors holding the bag.

CHAPTER 4

My Land

If you follow Route 973 north out of Billtown, after several monotonous miles of strip malls offering fast food, propane, and auto parts, you'll find a Revolutionary War–era log cabin. Beyond that, the road crosses Lycoming Creek, sneaks under Route 15, then cuts a meandering path west as it traces the Appalachian foothills. Civilization almost vanishes; you could drive the road at night for twenty minutes without encountering headlights. The few lonesome houses to be found on this stretch of Route 973 all huddle by the road, as if trying to resist being swallowed up by the surrounding forested State Game Lands. The closest thing to a town is Quiggleville, a bend in the road marked by a couple simple homes and a squat brick church. Just past a haphazard apiary consisting of a few dozen hive boxes stacked on a strip of grass, a small "no outlet" road defiantly juts off the main route, cutting a half-mile path through the woods as it ascends straight up the lower slope of Coal Mountain. This is Stony Gap Road. Several hundred feet before Stony Gap dead-ends, the asphalt gives way to gravel. Should anyone miss the not-so-subtle signal emanating from their car's wheel wells to retreat to the safety of the main road, two posted signs reinforce the message: "Mc-Clain Home-stead: Private Drive"; "Private Property: No Trespassing." Only one residence stood between those signs and Coal Mountain's peak. Scott McClain liked it that way.

Scott's estate consisted of a simple red ranch house (wooden, with a painted red cinderblock annex) and a shed plopped on five rocky acres, bisected by a small stream that fed a manmade koi pond and an old-fashioned water well, complete with hand crank and wooden bucket. Patches of grass, whose primary function was to satiate the appetite of a wooly brown bull that wandered the property, resisted the surrounding forest's efforts to reclaim the clearing. Black bears, deer, and hummingbirds were among the animals that frequented the yard, and the chirping of crickets provided the evening soundtrack.

During the time I lived in the area, Scott shared his home with his new wife Betty (née McCall), who taught sociology at Lycoming College. Having raised a family with his first wife (the fifty-six-year-old had seven grandchildren), Scott seemed intent on having fun this time around. Married in the fall of 2012, he and Betty marked the occasion in a small ceremony in Loyalsock State Forest; after exchanging vows, they plunged into Rock Run's frigid late October waters. During my visits in the warmer months, I often found the newlyweds hand in hand, lazing on a porch swing as their dogs jealously guarded them. In the colder months, they'd snuggle by the woodstove while sipping on bottomless cups of coffee poured from an industrial-sized urn, or they would hit the slopes for some snow tubing. The bond between the short, barrel-chested, and goateed former game warden and his taller, heavyset professor wife with the Texas twang was forged in the summer of 2011, when Betty helped her then friend safeguard his property by sitting in a lawn chair in the driveway to prevent oversized gas trucks from using it to access mountaintop well pads.

The driveway protest, which brought the couple a flash of local notoriety, was in keeping with Scott's individualist persona. He called his property a homestead in part because he liked to believe that his lifestyle of (relative) self-sufficiency carried on the legacy of his Scotch-Irish pioneer ancestors who settled this small corner of Appalachia. Indeed, Scott possessed the skills of an old-fashioned mountain man, identifying and tracking animals by the feces they left behind, wrangling rattlesnakes with a stick, and harvesting berries from the forest (he loved teaberries, the texture and taste of which reminded me of Necco Wafers). He didn't mind at all when a cold snap iced over his driveway, making it impossible for anyone to enter or leave the property by car, and brought subzero temperatures that the weather service warned were deadly. Scott went into survivalist mode. He had plenty of fire-wood, which he harvested from the hillside, to keep him warm. He dined on venison from hunting season that he stored in a freezer, and also on beaver meat that he acquired from a friend who only wanted the pelts. (I drove with Scott to Cohick's to pick up the black trash bag full of beaver flesh; it stunk up his red Jeep Cherokee for days, and Betty refused to eat it.) To get around, Scott strapped on cross-country skis; he even reportedly summited Coal Mountain on his skis on a day when it was minus seven degrees Fahrenheit, *before* taking into account the wind chill, at the base of the mountain. 'I was fine,' Scott told me non-chalantly; 'I felt toasty in my military arctic gear.'

Scott fancied himself a woodsman who, like the Appalachians de-scribed by Horace Kephart, "cheerfully put aside all that society can offer" in exchange for "freedom and air and elbow-room."[1] He claimed to have walked away from the military after clashing with his superiors, even though that meant giving up pitching on one of the best military baseball teams and a shot at playing on a Houston Astros farm team ('I had a wicked curve ball'). Although chronically underemployed, Scott proudly recounted how he resigned from the only job he ever loved—and a steady paycheck—with the Pennsylvania Game Commission, because he could not in good conscience work for such a corrupt bu-reaucracy. The tipping point came when the state allegedly undermined Scott's and other wardens' efforts to reintroduce elk to the county by selling off hunting permits for millions of dollars before the animals had a chance to repopulate. In his mind, most social institutions were crooked: corporations, the government agencies charged with regulat-ing them, the police, nongovernmental organizations, his township su-pervisors, and so on. Scott also trafficked in conspiracy theories. I had a difficult time discerning whether Scott actually believed all the outra-geous allegations he recounted (e.g., that the US government is covering up the fact that the West Nile virus outbreak was a terrorist attack), or whether all the details of his personal biography were accurate. I think their truthfulness was less important to Scott than their utility as para-bles. The lesson was Rousseauian: civilization corrupts; living an iso-lated, self-reliant existence close to nature was noble and liberating.

Jean-Jacques Rousseau called property rights "the most sacred of all the rights of citizenship," the implication being that sovereignty over one's land is a requisite of individual liberty.[2] Tocqueville, for his part, believed Americans zealously defended in principle the right of property precisely because the young republic's democratization of land ownership endowed commoners with political rights that European peasants could only dream of.[3] Thomas Jefferson shared this view. His utopian vision of a free (white) society was "a nation of small farmers," or yeomen, each "owning enough land to guarantee economic self-sufficiency and personal independence."[4] The Jeffersonian ideal, historian Steve Gillon argues, "dominated American thinking from the Revolution thru the Civil War."[5] It justified the Louisiana Purchase, the war with Mexico, and the extermination of American Indians. As Jedediah Purdy poignantly observes, "The country began as both a world-historical land grab and a world-historical experiment in republican self-rule."[6] For millions of predominately white plebeians, westward expansion was a means of securing the American Dream: in exchange for settling and cultivating so-called empty land, they secured hearth and home—and the right to self-determination. For Black people in the postbellum South, the state's rescinded promise of forty-acre plots to former slaves was proof they were still in bondage.

As Gillon notes, "Jefferson's vision of the American Dream was based on the idea of limitless land." As late as 1860, over 80 percent of workers were self-employed, most as farmers, and 75 percent of Americans lived in rural areas. But the frontier closed by 1890, a time during which the US was rapidly transforming from an agrarian nation to an urbanized, industrial one.[7] Despite the near disappearance of the yeoman and the hollowing out of Middle America over the last century, it is revealing that rural residents like Scott still thought of their properties as *homesteads*. Bundled into this conception is the idea that one's humble parcel is one's dominion. Private property was the font from which Scott's sense of autonomy flowed. Like Jefferson, he believed freeholds were citizens' best defense against government overreach and the debasing influences of the city. Scott had no qualms about intercepting trespassers with a holstered gun. The notion of needing a township permit to alter his land was, to him, unconstitutional; he laughed at the fact that the berm he built in his backyard to channel runoff violated local ordinances. On his land, he was king.

Scott's feeling of connection to the land was not merely proprietary; it was flesh and blood. His first wife was a Paulhamus, a legendary local family whose time-honored farm still stood sentry near Paulhamus Road. (Scott's older brother also married a Paulhamus—his ex-wife's sister.) The surrounding landscape was a topography of memories that forged Scott's identity: the creek where he learned to fish, the hollow where he killed his first deer, the branch upon which his dad built him a treehouse. He knew the mountains' secrets—that the whitewashed Red Fox Hunting Club, now a nondescript cabin in the boondocks, was once a hotel that hosted Abraham Lincoln and the centerpiece of a small but thriving town called Steuben; and that the crumbling masonry poking out of the hillside along a narrow gravel road (Roaring Run) hid munitions during the French and Indian War and runaway slaves during the Civil War.[8] It was also in these backwoods, locals whispered, that the husband of Hazel Craig, Scott's eccentric elderly neighbor who reportedly married at age twelve, was mysteriously found dead, with his hand poking through the fall foliage; she promptly began an affair with her father-in-law, whom she married after he survived being shot by Hazel's mother-in-law.

Around here, local history haunts the present. The land is *kindred*. Dividing up homesteads among family and passing them down through generations is commonplace, as is the experience of driving on country lanes or plowing the sides of mountains named after one's forbears. Living in the company of these ancestral ghosts gives locals a heightened sense of entitlement, if not dispensation, over the land. George believed that "the man upstairs" was responsible for him being gifted his dad's land rather than his six siblings, because God "knows I'm gonna take care of it." When I asked George if he discussed his leasing decision with neighbors who might be impacted, he replied with a decisive "nope." After some prodding, he added, "It's my land. I'll do as I damn well please." At the time, I chalked up his "to each his own" attitude to selfishness. But it eventually became clear that this fiery individualism was a defining ethos in George's and Scott's neck of the woods, even a point of pride. Most folks kept to themselves, neighborly obligations were minimal, and the right of personal sovereignty over one's land was sacrosanct. Live and let live, as the old saying goes.

Writing a century ago, the Appalachian documentarian Kephart considered this live-and-let-live spirit to be the heritage of the Appalachian "mountain man" (and woman), who was fiercely attached to place and family and yet "immune to the spirit of cooperation."[9] Many a mountaineer, Kephart contended, "would hold up one hand to testify his respect for the law while the other hand hovered over his pistol"; each man was a "law unto himself."[10] Although the mountain man has been tamed by indoor plumbing, television, and other creature comforts, some say this legacy manifests today in Appalachians' highly libertarian political attitudes and suspicion toward "ordering institutions of any kind."[11] That pretty much summed up George, though when I asked him how he identified politically he refused to be boxed in. 'I would say I'm an American,' he insisted. 'I identify as American. I think people just use all these labels to make themselves feel important. Why can't people just be humans and treat each other with decency?'

George had no use for politics because he didn't see himself as part of a polity. His notion of community extended only as far as kin. He liked to half-jokingly say that if he had all the money in the world, he would buy out all his neighbors so that he wouldn't have to deal with anyone else. But then George would face a new problem: 'I'd have to buy out the next circle of neighbors around my new property boundary.' He'd have to keep doing this 'until I owned the entire US of A!' The allure of geographic seclusion was that it facilitated the avoidance of social entanglements and their attendant constraints on personal liberty. He hated the idea of being tethered to a phone, and so he was perpetually delighted that his yard remained a cellular dead zone. Even having to drive through Billtown felt like an assault on George's independence. "I don't like stop signs or red lights or traffic or anything like that. All the people. I'm a country boy. I like the openness and freedom." He added that, although he didn't drive a motorcycle and couldn't fathom "why anybody would wanna drive a bike without a helmet," Pennsylvania's

2003 repeal of its helmet law was the right move. "I don't think the states should have the right to say you have to have it. It's your bike. It's your life."

George did his best to make his seventy-seven acres a sovereign island of splendid isolation, where he was beholden to no one and free to do as he pleased. He put frosted film on the living-room windows to block the view of the "stranger's" (i.e., nonkin) house next door (which his brother sold years ago). And the retiree went days or even weeks at a time without leaving his grounds or having any social contact aside from the occasional phone call or fencepost chat with his sister, whose house was on the other side of a line of trees that marked the edge of his property. On one of my many afternoon walkabouts with George through his back field and down to the wooded creek, I asked him if he ever felt bored. 'Some people,' George scoffed, 'need to get away to be happy.' For him, it was quite the opposite. 'Every day on this land feels to me like a vacation. There's nowhere else I want to be.' Indeed, George decided not to go on the Alaska cruise he promised his family when he got his first royalty check, after realizing that the misery of being away from home outweighed the thrill of voyaging the famed Inside Passage. He also worried about who would safeguard the land in his absence. George was known to walk the perimeter of his property with a shotgun, spoiling for a confrontation with hunters, anglers, or others who dared to trespass in his woods. And it annoyed him so much that his neighbor's dog traipsed through his fields that "I finally got my gun and shot it into the ground." Because there was a security guard stationed in his driveway at the time to monitor the well pad, George said, the police told him he could be issued a citation (he wasn't). He was incredulous. "I wanna tell you something. I have every right to protect me and my home any way I see fit."

The way George saw it, the fact that he leased his land was nobody's business. In turn, though George speculated about who among his neighbors had leased and the sums of money they made, he avoided talking directly to them about these matters, because it was "none of my damn business." For George, conversations of this sort were as taboo as talking about how much money you made. Yet the reason for privacy went beyond propriety; it was about preserving property rights.

* * *

In contemplating on what grounds individuals could legitimately claim ownership over land "in the state of nature" (i.e., in the absence of law or government), John Locke began from the so-called natural law of self-ownership. It is self-evident, he observed, that we own our bodies and, therefore, can claim ownership of any goods produced from the work of our hands. Although God gave land to humanity in common, when man mixed his self-owned labor into it he removed it from the state of nature and annexed it to himself. Through labor, free individuals secured the right to "enclose [land] from the common" and make it an *excludable*, or private, possession. This right included both the earth itself and the fruits of the earth. After all, it is only through "the improvement of labour" that "land lying in common" attains value at all. And "labour being the unquestionable property of the labourer, no man but he can have a right to what that is joined to" (i.e., land).[12]

"Land improved," the geographer Gary Fields writes, had two key attributes. First and foremost, it was cultivated. Second, it was enclosed with a fence or other marker to "separate it from plots owned by other improvers, and from unimproved land surrounding it" and still held in common. In late seventeenth-century England, owners of large estates began relying on the Locke-inspired "improvement doctrine" to justify terminating the age-old right of tenant farmers to use portions of the land collectively (mostly for grazing cattle).[13] The enclosure of the commons was hastened by a series of "Inclosure Acts" that codified manor owners' exclusive right to usership, under the guise of increasing agricultural productivity. The quaint stone walls, wood fences, and hedgerows that zigzag across the English countryside embody this historical process of privatization through "lawfare."[14]

Locke's labor theory of property has long been considered "the cornerstone of classical liberalism," the political ideology that exerted the greatest influence on the American constitution.[15] (Locke advocated for a limited government whose raison d'être was to protect individuals' property.) The improvement doctrine also became the principal justification for homesteading, whereby US common law recognized that westward "settlers" gained exclusive and permanent ownership over "empty" land (indigenous people didn't count) on the condition that they continually inhabited it and "improved" it through their own labor. This legal edict was established by English colonizers as early as 1630, when John Winthrop, the first governor of the Massachusetts Bay Colony, infamously endorsed dispossessing the land from "the Natives in New England," on the grounds that they "enclose no land" and neither had the skills nor the inclination to "improve the Land."[16] The first white yeomen in Lycoming County successfully petitioned the state of Pennsylvania in 1784 to recognize their claim to Iroquois-occupied territories precisely by invoking Winthrop's logic: the squatters had continually inhabited the land "at the risk of our lives" and improved it through cultivation.[17] An 1823 Supreme Court case affirmed that "Amerindians did not possess rights to the land they occupied and used." In turn, the Indian Removal Act, of 1830, empowered the government to expel Indian "tenants" and set the land aside "for settlement by white American colonists."[18] Homesteaders erected "seemingly endless miles of fences" around their newly settled land to prevent incursions, and they were authorized to defend it from usurpation with deadly force if necessary.[19] (Notably, after the 1909 Coal Lands Act, the federal government granted only the surface estate to homesteaders.)[20]

These days, of course, there is little to no extant unclaimed land in America. Property is a commodity; most people acquire the rights to it through purchase or inheritance, not homesteading. Yet what has not changed in American common law is that owners are, for the most part, entitled to dispose of their property as they see fit and to enjoy exclusive rights to any "fruits" it produces—unless those rights have been expressly circumscribed by a previous titleholder (e.g., via a lien, or split estate). There is greater constitutional protection of freehold rights in America, law scholar Stuart Banner writes, than anywhere in Europe. And, despite the fact that the advent of air travel limited property owners' air rights, American freehold law still comes the closest of any legal system in the world to recognizing the common-law maxim "Whoever owns the soil, it is theirs up to heaven and down to hell." Although "some version" of this phrase is "ensconced in the law as a verbal formula" in many European countries, Banner observes, it is "hardly consistent with European historical practice, in which mines and treasures located underground were owned by monarchs rather than the owners of the land."[21] To wit: in the UK, whose common laws regarding property the United States inherited, the legal force of the axiom is blunted by the reality that oil, gas, gold, and silver are held by the Crown. In most countries, landowners have little to no claim, or control over access, to the subsurface. In the US, however, he who "digs into my soil a thousand feet below the surface . . . is guilty of trespass"—except, of course, if the mineral estate has been severed from the surface; she who appropriates *any* fruits (e.g., gas, gold, zinc) that my soil may hold is guilty of theft.[22]

Dominion over one's property, and sole ownership over any benefits derived from it, is not just a legal guarantee. It is, for many, an ethical principle. Following Locke, Founding Fathers like Jefferson saw freehold rights as a means of "limiting the moral authority of the state," thereby shoring up citizens' other natural rights—to life (i.e., self-sufficiency) and liberty (i.e., personal sovereignty).[23] As political theorist Isaiah Berlin noted, this individualist ideology presupposes the virtue of "negative liberty"—that is, the *absence* of constraints that limit a person's ability to "do or be what he is able to do or be."[24] (Conversely, the communitarian-leaning conception of "positive liberty" emphasizes the *presence* of mechanisms that enable everyone to flourish—e.g., political guarantees of welfare, equality, and collective governance.) In this view, people are considered free when they possess the sovereignty "to order their actions . . . as they think fit . . . without asking leave, or depending on the will of any other man."[25] The only constraint that ought to be placed on people's ability to privately pursue their own ends is that such pursuit does not limit others' autonomy. For classical liberalists, the sole mandate of government is to prevent and remedy violations of personal sovereignty.[26] (Karl Polanyi, among others, famously argued that a self-adjusting market paired with a small, decentralized government "could not exist for any length of time without annihilating the human and natural substance of society"; in predicting that the result would be "a state of wilderness," Polanyi turned Locke on his head.)[27]

For both classical liberals and contemporary libertarians, freedom is, essentially, *being left alone* and *leaving others alone*. The landowners I met didn't bother justifying their politics by quoting ideologists like John Stuart Mill (or ideologues like Senator Rand Paul, for that matter). But in practice, they tacitly abided by the liberal social contract: live and let live. When it came to leasing their mineral rights, this is not to say that everyone made the decision entirely on their own—some, like Tom, consulted with their neighbors before leasing. But few, if any, thought others had a right to veto their decision. The very idea of needing others' consent to improve the use value of one's land, or of being required to share the spoils generated by freehold property ownership, was almost unthinkable—if not immoral—because it entailed a restriction of personal and economic freedom. It was a happy coincidence, from their perspective, that petroleum companies shared this view.

Even Locke, however, recognized that there ought to be limits to someone's private right to enjoy her property. "No man but he" (the landowner) can determine how his property is used, "*at least where there is enough, and as good, left in common for others*" (my emphasis). The libertarian thinker Karen Vaughn interprets this caveat to mean that one's "right to property is only clear and exclusive so long as it doesn't jeopardize anyone else's ability to create equivalent kinds of property for themselves."[28] The libertarian political theorist Robert Nozick considers the "Lockean proviso" a justifiable restriction of liberty, even within a negative-rights/minimal-state framework, because it is consistent with the idea that one's "natural rights" do not include the right to infringe on others' personal sovereignty. American property law ratifies the Lockean proviso: zoning ordinances, building permits, restrictive covenants, and easements all place restrictions on individuals' land sovereignty. The rationale is that "the position of others" ought not be "worsened" by private land use decisions.[29]

* * *

Private land leasing, as it turned out, routinely violated the Lockean proviso by creating spillover effects that worsened the well-being of others in the community and infringed on their freedom to benefit from their own property. Just ask Scott McClain, who created a Facebook page to document how his "beautiful parcel of land" was being damaged by petroleum companies operating on land leased by Poor Shot Hunting Camp. In 2002, Scott recalled, he gave Poor Shot permission to use his driveway to access its mountaintop cabin. It was, he said, the neighborly thing to do. Scott even made the covenant permanent through an easement to ensure that, should he ever move, the new occupant could not deny access to Poor Shot. With ingress guaranteed, Poor Shot constructed a gravel road all the way up Coal Mountain, picking up where Scott's driveway left off. Years later, when the landman came knocking, both Scott and Poor Shot leased. It promised to be mutually beneficial: Poor Shot's thousand-plus acres would host the gas wells and bear the brunt of disruption in exchange for large royalties; Scott's five-acre plot would earn modest royalties with no surface disturbance. But then the hunting camp acceded to the gas company's request to use the existing gravel driveway. (It claimed that building a new road might be too expensive to warrant drilling.) As a result, hundreds of big rigs and earthmovers began rumbling through the middle of the McClain homestead just a few yards from Scott's house. A culvert under the driveway collapsed, prompting Scott to ask Poor Shot to deny the gas trucks access to the road on the grounds that it damaged his property and was against the spirit of the easement. The camp members, who were on their way to becoming shaleionaires, reportedly maintained that it was their legal right to use the driveway as they saw fit.[30]

Things went downhill from there. Betty, his girlfriend at the time, was issued a restraining order in 2011, after she sat in a beach chair in the middle of the driveway for three days to prevent truck traffic from traversing the mountain. Eventually, Scott's chimney collapsed from the reverberations of the big rigs. Gas workers reportedly told the police that Scott menaced them with a gun when they drove by his house, which led to Scott's arrest and loss of the right to wear his licensed firearm on his own property. After winning a small settlement from the gas companies for damages to the property, which required Scott to sign a nondisclosure agreement, he and his wife were also forbidden to talk to the workers (who sometimes idled right in front of their porch).[31] On my first visit to Scott's house, a ladder still leaned against the new cinderblock chimney he had just finished building. Truck caravans continued to roll by, occasionally wreaking havoc. On two occasions, I arrived to find that a decorative stone wall bordering the driveway had been toppled. We jokingly placed bets on how long the metal culvert would last before being crushed anew under the weight of the oversized vehicles. When that occurred, its metal pins would jut out of the gravel, threatening to puncture car tires.

The sight of tractor trailer convoys inching along the steep, narrow mountain pass certainly struck me as incongruous. It was impossible for their dual tires to avoid trampling the grass, which violated the gas companies' road use agreement. "It's *our* driveway," Scott fumed. The biggest vehicles overhung the gravel road so much that they were mere inches from Scott's shed and house. The concrete speedbump atop the culvert crumbled more and more with each passing truck. "This road," Betty complained bitterly, "is not built for these kinds of trucks." She alleged in an e-mail complaint to her state representative that the gas company "is endangering our lives as well as our property." Scott and Betty were incensed that Poor Shot—whose members "don't even live here" (the cabin was only occupied during hunting season)—was "the one making money hand over fist" while "we are the ones with the little parcel" having "our constitutional rights" violated. Their anxieties were hardly assuaged when state representative Rick Mirabito paid them a courtesy visit in response to Betty's e-mail. He acknowledged that Scott's ability to enjoy and exercise sovereignty over his property had been debased—perhaps permanently—by Poor Shot's land use decisions. But he wasn't sure there was a remedy. "Life's too short," Rick mused as we sipped sweating glasses of iced tea on Scott's front porch. He gently suggested that they consider moving.

FIG. 4.1. An industry truck rumbles by Scott McClain's home.
Photograph by Colin Jerolmack.

Moving was something that the Crawleys, who lived on the opposite side of the county from Scott, were considering. By the time I met them, it had already been two years since they stopped drinking their tap water. After a natural-gas well was drilled up the hill about two thousand feet from their house, the spigot hissed, and the water—which became as cloudy as "a cup of skim milk," in Tom's words—fizzed like soda. These were telltale signs of methane gas. Before drilling had commenced, the Crawleys invested $350 in a certified, independent lab test that measured the concentration of methane in their well water. It was 4.45 milligrams per liter in July 2010, which, Tom rightly noted, "is quite acceptable under EPA and DEP standards." (Trace amounts of naturally occurring methane were a common feature of water wells in the area.) Soon after the neighbor's gas well was drilled, the DEP cited the energy company for "failure to report defective, insufficient, or improperly cemented casing" of the well and found that the concentration of methane in the Crawleys' water had spiked to seventy-two milligrams per liter—over ten times the DEP safe standard.[32] The DEP went a step further, issuing a rare "positive determination letter" that explicitly blamed natural-gas drilling for the migration of methane into the Crawleys' and the Bodles' water wells. The Bodles, who lived next door to the Crawleys, in a double-wide trailer, also saw their water mysteriously turn brown. The dishwater stained Peggy's fine china; Doyle showed me the turbid reservoir of their humidifier.

The gas company denied responsibility for the spike in methane levels, but as part of its "good neighbor policy" it installed a ten-foot-tall pipe over the Crawleys' water well to vent the gas before the water was pumped into the house, placed methane detectors in their house, and commenced delivery of bottled water. But, after concluding its own investigation into the incident the following year, the company mailed the Crawleys a 1.5-inch-thick final report, which I later reviewed, and informed them in the cover letter that it was terminating delivery of bottled water, since its analysis determined "that methane levels and composition . . . were present in the area before [we] began our gas well development activity." Unsurprisingly, the Crawleys were contemplating filing a lawsuit with their four neighbors whose water was also impacted. But Tom wondered aloud how "an average Joe like me" could possibly prevail against "a corporation with hundreds of millions of dollars and all of their lawyers," and how, even if he was ready to forfeit his ancestral land, he could afford to move somewhere else. "We have our life's money invested in this property," he lamented. "We're stuck."

It is a great irony that the water well of the elderly couple whose property hosted the troublesome gas well was unaffected. (For their part, the retired farmers believed that the methane that turned up in their neighbors' well water was naturally occurring; they sympathized with the Crawleys, but accused the DEP of having a vendetta against

FIG. 4.2. Tom and Mary Crawley sit in front of the methane vent that the petroleum company placed over their water well. Photograph by Tristan Spinski.

the gas company.) The Crawleys and their neighbors were arguably complicit in all of this; after all, they did lease their own land. However, their decision to opt in was in part based on the reasonable calculation that leasing exposed them to minimal risk. They faced little threat of drilling or development in their backyards because their properties were too small to host infrastructure like well pads—at most, a horizontal well would be drilled a mile or more below the surface. But what Tom and Mary could not anticipate, let alone control, was the extent to which the neighbor's private land use decision (to allow gas drilling in their backyard) exposed them involuntarily to harm.

It is also worth noting that the Crawleys and their neighbors would have suffered the exact same debasement of their property and quality of life even if they had refused to lease. This was the insult added to injury: their personal liberty, their capacity for self-determination, was violated. The experience of folks like the Crawleys, the Bodles, and

Scott McClain made me question the moral footing upon which the "natural right" of private property rests. Perhaps it was only in some idealized past, when homesteaders lived in solitude on windswept expanses, that people were justified in doing whatever they pleased on their land. These days, fracking is but one of many ways that private land-use decisions create externalities (e.g., pollution) that rob others of their free will. The Jeffersonian idea that land sovereignty secures self-governance is fallacious, if not dangerous.

CHAPTER 5

The Public/Private Paradox

The private land use decisions made by the Crawleys' neighbors resulted, through the petroleum company's negligence, in externalities that degraded the commons that Tom and Mary relied on to enjoy their property—namely, the groundwater from which they drew their well water.

The idea of the commons dates back to the legal designation of "common land" in medieval England. It referred then to the pastures and other swaths of land set aside by feudal lords for "commoners" to share for the purposes of grazing livestock. The post-Enlightenment enclosure of the commons banished, for the most part, both the term and the concept (i.e., communal resources) from public discourse in much of the West, especially in the UK and the US—until, that is, the ecologist Garrett Hardin resurrected it in the late 1960s. The context is important: this was a time when Western society's space-age optimism was upended by ecological catastrophe and dire predictions of impending resource scarcity and overpopulation. Two of 1969's biggest cover stories were the massive oil spill that blackened the pristine Santa Barbara coastline and Cleveland's infamous Cuyahoga River fire (the water was so polluted with flammable toxins that it ignited). In 1962, Rachel Carson published her earth-shattering book *Silent Spring*, which exposed the deadliness of pesticides and common household products. The decade ended with Paul Ehrlich's apocalyptic book *The Population Bomb*, the first line of which read, "The battle to feed all of humanity is over. In the 1970s the world will undergo famines—hundreds of millions of people are going to starve to death."[1] Concepts like "carrying capacity" and "Spaceship Earth" gained currency as technocrats began acknowledging that there were natural limits to growth and to the amount of pollution the planet could absorb. Today, these terms feel a bit anachronistic. But Hardin's "tragedy of the commons" remains, even for those who reject the treatise's Hobbesian premise, a touchstone idea among environmental leaders like Bill McKibben trying to tackle the problem of climate change.[2]

Hardin's landmark 1968 essay "The Tragedy of the Commons" argued that environmental problems are, at their core, *collective-action problems*. A collective-action problem arises when individuals perceive greater incentives for pursuing their own self-interest (defecting) than for cooperating for the common good, even though total defection is worse for everyone. To illustrate the problem, Hardin asked readers to imagine a group of herders whose livelihood depends on their cows' ability to graze in a common pasture, to which they all have equal claim.[3] Because each herder reaps the full benefits of each extra cow they add to the pasture (because they get to keep the milk or meat for themselves), they have an incentive to graze as many cows as they can. The eighteenth-century Scottish economist Adam Smith's influential "invisible hand" thesis, arguably the credo of capitalism, proposed that those who compete this way in a free market benefit the commonwealth, even if they only intend to enrich themselves. In this example, the benefit is cheaper and more plentiful milk and meat for consumers. But Smith ignored the environmental costs. Hardin argued that the freedom to self-maximize obstructs rather than promotes the public interest, because it degrades shared resources. And total freedom has the ironic effect of nullifying choice: each herder "is locked into a system" that compels him "to increase his herd without limit" until the pasture is overgrazed and unusable.[4] Were one herder to altruistically decide *not* to increase his herd for the sake of the common good, he would still bear the environmental cost of others' selfish herd expansion.

This is the tragedy of the commons, a quintessential resource dilemma: people see no reason not to pursue their self-interest, even when doing so is contrary to the common good and degrades communal resources, because they know that their self-sacrifice will have no positive effect unless others cooperate with them. (Population growth, Hardin controversially argued, is the archetypal case: if I voluntarily abstained from having a large family because I realized the strain it puts on the planet, it would not matter so long as others kept freely "breeding"; so I have more kids.) Hardin urged us to view national parks, air, water, and the atmosphere as commons that are threatened by the same competitive logic of exploitation that, if left unchecked, will ruin nature's commonwealth.

Hardin suggested that we must abandon the system of the commons to avert ecological catastrophe. He seemed to put more faith in private property. Under a system of ownership, he alleged, "the men who own property recognize their responsibility to care for it, for if they don't they will eventually suffer."[5] (Consider this: Are you more inclined to clean a public bathroom or your own?) Statements like these made Hardin a hero to neoconservatives—as did his "lifeboat ethics" thesis, which used the problem of resource scarcity to justify cutting off aid to poor countries and closing the border to immigrants.[6] Many of his market-oriented acolytes used Hardin's arguments to justify the privatization and monetization of shared natural resources. The "Wise Use" movement of the late eighties, backed by timber companies and Ronald Reagan, argued that selling off America's public forests would not incite the excessive harvesting of trees or water, because private owners would have to personally bear all the costs if their overexploitation destroyed the land's productivity.[7] (It was a dubious argument; even less clear is how something like strip mining, which removes the entire surface layer of vegetation and soil to access subterranean coal seams, is compatible with conservation.)

Hardin has, with good reason, become a reviled figure among many progressives and environmentalists (the Southern Poverty Law Center labels him a white nationalist who supported fascist policies).[8] But critics who box him in as a champion of neoclassical-economic solutions to environmental problems are caricaturing his position. After his nemesis, the political economist Elinor Ostrom, famously documented numerous case studies from around the world where communities successfully conserved shared natural resources over generations, Hardin clarified that he meant to imply only that "ruin is inevitable" in instances of an *unmanaged* commons. While privatization was one means of creating a so-called managed commons, he concluded that socialism could work as well.[9] What's more, although Hardin believed that the "concept of private property deters us from exhausting the positive resources of the earth," his original essay warned that it potentially favors pollution. The "air and waters surrounding us cannot readily be fenced," and the "owner of a factory on the bank of a stream . . . often has difficulty seeing why it is not his natural right to muddy the waters flowing past."[10] What this problem necessitated, Hardin concluded, was state coercion, in the form of regulations or taxes. (The US's Clean Air Act of 1963 and Clean Water Act of 1972 were enacted precisely to address the issue.)

Importantly, Hardin could have been wrong about the inherent selfishness of people but still have penned a relatively accurate description of how large segments of the American (and world) population respond to real-world resource dilemmas. The critical question to ask is this: Why is it that so many of us find ourselves mired in Hardin's dystopian world, in which circumstances compel us to prioritize our self-interest at the expense of the public good? There's nothing natural or inevitable about this state of affairs; it is our legal-political system that makes it hard to escape.

To wit: during my time in Pennsylvania, I was struck by how land leasing bears out Hardin's admonition that, absent strong regulations, it is difficult "to keep private natures truly cordoned off from the rest of the world" (Hardin's far-left intellectual adversaries concurred).[11] The exemption of fracking from federal regulations like the Safe Drinking Water Act, in combination with the Pennsylvania Department of Environmental Protection's (DEP) apparent disinterest in punishing industry malfeasance, meant that there were insufficient coercive mechanisms in place to prevent or ameliorate the spillover effects of gas drilling on private land. Also, with the state preempting municipalities' ability to restrict fracking locally, communities lacked the tools to try—à la Ostrom—to collectively manage shared local resources like groundwater, roads, and air.

Rather than mitigate the tragedy of the commons, private property facilitated it. Lessors were akin to that factory owner on the bank of a stream: in exerting their autonomy over, and right to benefit from, their property by leasing, they contributed to the production of spillover effects that figuratively and sometimes literally muddied the waters downstream. The cumulative impact of countless individual choices was a degradation of common-pool resources like air, water, roads, and less tangible rural "goods" such as dark skies and quiet. This doesn't mean lessors were the bad guys or that they were particularly greedy. Rather, they were forced to make difficult and sometimes tragic decisions aimed at making the best of a situation in which they usually had incomplete or inaccurate information from the industry, and in which their government—which many distrusted anyway—offered little guidance or protection. In different circumstances, they may have acted differently.

Like Hardin's herders, many residents were aware of at least some of the externalities that they would be forced to endure from fracking in the area and took them into account when deciding whether or not to lease. Mary Crawley recalled thinking that, since her property was so small, she and Tom could not buffer themselves from the land use decisions of the large farms around them (an observation that turned out to be tragically prescient). "If you didn't sign it [the lease,] . . . you were still gonna be affected." Tom added, "You're not gonna stop it." Asked how that reality affected their decision-making, Tom said he concluded that they would, in effect, be carried along by others' decision. "I'm just nine acres amongst everybody else . . . so you folks [the farmers] make the decision and we can go from there." Tom remembered thinking that, even if he and Mary had private reservations about leasing, it would have been foolhardy to hold out once it became clear that the large landowners around them all planned to lease. "They're gonna be drawing gas out all around me. I may as well be in on what little bit of money there may be there [for] myself."

It was widely believed that petroleum companies often locked up all the large landholdings in a particular region first. For those owning dozens of acres or more, a lease was almost irresistible, because it offered potentially life-changing sums of money. Small landowners like Holly Bendorf and Chriss McDonald, middle-aged chemistry professors whose house sat on just two acres, recalled that when the landman showed up at their door he bore maps indicating that most of the surrounding area was already leased. The message, Holly said, was clear: "It didn't matter whether we signed or not. The drilling was going to happen." Chriss noted that the landman was "not pushy at all"; he seemed indifferent as to whether they leased. "In my mind," Holly added, the landman's nonchalance only "confirmed the idea" that "it's already a done deal." They also affirmed their belief in an oft-cited urban legend that petroleum companies would illegally steal the gas from under their property if they refused to lease, despite the fact that the direction and length of all wellbores (which is public information) must be preapproved by the DEP. (Some states, such as Texas, *do* have a "forced pooling" law, which compels landowners to lease if enough neighbors have.)[12] "How's anybody gonna check" where the wellbore actually goes, Holly wondered. "I don't think they can control what direction those fissures run. You can't say, 'We're only gonna make fissures to the left.'" "It's a polite fiction," Chriss added curtly.

Holly and Chriss both expressed doubts that natural gas can be extracted in a way that is socially responsible and that doesn't cause irreparable damage to the environment. And the comfortably middle-class couple was well aware that the leasing bonus, and any future royalties they might obtain, for just two acres would have little impact on their financial portfolio. Chriss called it dirty money. In the end, they signed anyway. In exchange for a non-surface-disturbance lease, they received $7,000 ($3,500/acre). The decision to lease, despite leaving them "resigned and conflicted," made sense. On the one hand, they understood that holding out would have no discernible positive effect so long as everyone else defected. "It doesn't matter what I do," Holly shrugged. On the other hand, they were already sharing the costs—both economic and ecological—of others' decision to lease while getting none of the benefits. For instance, they paid $1,000 for an exhaustive baseline water test soon after fracking commenced in Trout Run so that they could blame any subsequent impairment of their water well on gas drilling on neighboring properties. And they felt that the quiet and solitude that drew them to the wooded lot on Turkey Trot Path—a dead-end dirt road that branched off from another dead-end dirt road that you arrived at via one of the most idyllic stretches of country road I have ever encountered (Rose Valley Road)—had been taken from them. They talked of helicopters buzzing overhead "like every fifteen minutes," making it "feel like M*A*S*H" (the Korean War comedy-drama television series); the endless caravans of water trucks and the "busted-up roads" they left behind; and the clear-cutting of nearby stands of trees to make way for well pads and pipelines. The din of drilling, flaring, diesel engines, generators, helicopters, and dynamite explosions all combined to create a "low-level ambient noise, all the time." Chriss mourned the loss of the "pristine aural environment," calling it a scarce resource you can't put a price on. Similarly, flare stacks produced fire plumes so intense that they lit up the entire valley floor with an atmo-spheric orange-and-gold halo, blotting out the night sky. "I don't feel guilty about the [leasing] money," Holly added defiantly. Because of "all this has cost" them (i.e., the cumulative impact of their neighbors' leases), "we might as well get paid for our aggravation."

Perhaps nobody mourned the deterioration of the community's bu-colic character more than Cindy Bower, who lived less than two miles from Holly and Chriss. When I caught up with her in the waning days of the summer of 2017, Cindy led me, Ralph, and a photographer—Tristan Spinski—up the mountainside behind her house to inspect the disruption caused by Seneca Resources' latest development: a clearance for a pipeline right-of-way and a bright-orange drilling rig that hulked over her property like a hilltop castle. Before the appearance of the rig, Cindy had indulged in the fantasy that perhaps the worst was over. The low price of natural gas had dramatically slowed fracking operations in the area beginning in the late fall of 2013; in 2016, there were only three gas wells drilled in the entire county, compared to 207 wells in 2012.[13] What's more, the long-shot lawsuit that Cindy helped the Pennsylvania Environmental Defense Foundation (PEDF) bring against the state for profiting from gas leases on public land was tentatively decided in the plaintiff's favor in June 2017.[14] It was a landmark case that she hoped would mark a turning point in the battle to preserve local forests for future generations.

Although the leaves had not yet begun to fall as we gathered in Cindy's yard to begin our ascent up the mountain, winter, for her, had already come. Fracking was back with a vengeance. Seneca had cut a "horrific gash into the side" of the mountain next to her estate to construct an access road for the drilling rig at the peak. "Ancestral hunting grounds destroyed," she lamented, and "we have been listening to the screech and grind of heavy equipment all summer." As a precaution, they had their water tested—for the sixth time (it was fine). A second drilling rig sat by the road a half mile from her house, and Trout Run was about "to get hammered" by a new well pad to be built on the other side of Rose Valley Lake, in a residential area. Cindy described the "noise and disruption in every way during the entire development process" of the nearby well pads as "appalling, if not mentally and emotionally debilitating." This story, she resignedly pointed out, "could go on for a long, long time." Sadly, time was something that she worried her husband Jim might not have. In June 2016, the hotel magnate was diagnosed with stage 3 non-Hodgkin lymphoma, which required three-week cycles of in-patient chemotherapy. When at home, he was mostly restricted to an electric scooter and a walker. "It wasn't what either of us had in mind for this time in our lives," she lamented. Between caring for Jim and her ninety-two-year-old mother (who lived next door), Cindy had "essentially dropped out of other activities" and was no longer volunteering for the PEDF.

After helping her husband baby-step his way into the house, Cindy seemed eager to attack the mountain. Decked out in running shoes, a fleece vest, and pegged jeans held up by a belt she bought in Costa Rica made from recycled plastic bags and aluminum can tabs, the silver-haired and rosy-cheeked matriarch set a vigorous pace. By the time the rest of us even realized she had departed from our gathering place (a secluded, grassy hillock by the pond, where her father was buried), Cindy had already disappeared into the woods. I labored just to keep her in view as we followed the faint dirt trail, and Ralph found himself leaning against a tree and gasping to regain his breath. At a picturesque fern-covered clearing, I persuaded Cindy to stop and wait for Ralph and Tristan. She told me she used to make this walk daily, but had not done so since coming upon piles of felled trees several months earlier, as Seneca began clearing the way for the access road and a pipeline.

Our path connected up with an old dirt logging road, which wended its way around the back of the mountain before depositing us near the ridgeline. After a final scramble up a steep stretch of scree, we popped out of the dense forest into a scene right out of *The Lorax*: a barren expanse of rocky dirt pockmarked by stumps and uprooted trees that were too puny to be carted off as lumber. It looked like a colossus had ridden a larger-than-life lawnmower along the mountain rim for half a mile or so, all the way up to the drilling rig. Pink ribbons marked trees still to be felled. Cindy stood on a stump, holding back tears and looking broken. 'I haven't been up here since they cleared it all,' she whimpered. 'This used to be one of my favorite places, but I haven't been able to bring myself here since . . .' Her voice trailed off as she swept her arm across the sad scene. We looked down upon a verdant valley, silently watching workers in the distance lay a pipeline through a crop field. The excavated dirt was so red that the right-of-way looked like a massive bleeding cut. The pipeline would go right up the mountain to where we stood before following the ridgeline to the well pad.

Ralph and I dipped into the woods to give Cindy time to compose herself. A bald eagle briefly alighted on a branch directly above us, but by the time I got my camera out it was soaring over Rose Valley Lake. Having recovered her resolve, Cindy called to us, 'Let's see how close we can get to that rig.' Aware that we were trespassing, we slinked our way along the edge of the lumpy, 150-foot-wide clearing and slipped into the woods whenever we passed signs of human activity like a parked bulldozer or a security guard shack. Once we got within a thousand or so feet of the towering rig, we could hear the steady hum of its engine. We crept through the woods until we were within spitting distance. Cindy stood erect behind a tree while the rest of us took cover behind a dirt mound. Workers, who shouted over the din of the rig to convey

FIG. 5.1. A pipeline right-of-way and drilling rig atop the mountain behind
Cindy Bower's house. Photograph by Tristan Spinski.

instructions, swarmed around the base of Seneca Rig #339 as it methodically hammered forty-foot segments of steel pipe into the well known
as Rhone Gamble 96H. It would take over two hundred of those pipes
to kiss the Marcellus (a depth of 1.6 miles), and just about as many more
threaded together horizontally to unlock the gas from the shale layer.

FIG. 5.2. Cindy Bower hides behind a tree to spy on a gas well being drilled by
Seneca Resources. Photograph by Tristan Spinski.

Cindy shuddered and turned away from the orange rig and ant colony of workers decked out in fluorescent vests and fire-retardant pants.
'It looks like an alien landscape, like aliens are at work.' As we skulked
back down the ridgeline, I thanked Cindy for bringing us up here.
I knew it was not easy for her to see all this, especially given the stress
of caring for her husband. 'You're right,' she responded, 'it's heartbreaking. If you guys weren't here, I'd be bawling.' As we set off down the
mountain, Cindy's gait betrayed her anxiety that we had kept her away
from home for too long. Less than five minutes into the hour-long de-
scent, she was gone. Jim needed her. Ralph, Tristan, and I ambled along
a gurgling creek as dusk darkened the forest, eventually popping out at
the far end of the Bowers' pond. A mowed path greeted us, inviting a
leisurely stroll along the shore. Tristan remarked how beautiful and
tranquil the scene was compared to the industrial site we had just left.

He sympathized with Cindy's mournful state, so much so that he was incredulous to learn that she was implicated in all this. She was earning royalties from the very gas wells whose presence she abhorred.

* * *

I had such a hard time reconciling Cindy's environmentalism with her decision to lease her land that I asked her to sit down and explain it to me. We talked at a sturdy oak table surrounded by picture windows overlooking the property's crown jewel—Halls Pond—while enjoying the warmth emanating from a wood-burning stove by the kitchen. The sun shone over the mountain, part of which the Bowers owned, slicing through the mist clinging to the valley floor and creating the effect of a soft-light filter. Geese honked; ducks splash-landed in the placid pond. As she began elaborating her rationale for leasing, Cindy chose her words carefully and was by turns indignant and repentant.

"We leased because we didn't feel that—we felt that it was the right thing to do," Cindy stammered. "Right in what way?" I prodded. "The only compensation for everything that's happening to us is money. If they could have guaranteed me that the noise stops at the property line, any possible contamination stops at the property line, the odor stops at the property line—if they could guarantee me that, that my property would never be affected, I wouldn't have leased." At that moment, I remembered the flimsy orange netting that used to trace Cindy's property line across the street from an Atlas Drilling well pad. The year before, she told me, she fought like hell to make Atlas erect the droopy plastic knee-high fence as a means to ensure that the double-wide tires of the big rigs that constantly entered and exited the well pad did not encroach on her grass. She seemed proud then, laughing that she never saw fencing anywhere else. But the pathetic barrier came to symbolize the futility of trying to keep the spillover effects of fracking at bay: the trucks blocked her driveway and kicked up dust that coated her grass; the diesel engines rattled her windows and flooded her yard with fumes; the flaring of the gas well obliterated the stars and forced her to close the windows and sleep with ear plugs. The gas companies "don't really have any control," Cindy seethed as she cupped her hands over the steam rising from her teacup. "We were forced to live with the consequences." Like Chriss and Holly, Cindy believed that the petroleum company would steal her gas if she did not lease. "We didn't need the money," Cindy admitted. "But am I stupid? Just let them take it for free? Looking at all those things, yeah, we decided to lease."

Cindy emphasized how restrictive the non-surface-disturbance lease was. "We got everything we wanted, and the lease had to be approved by the Western Pennsylvania Conservancy," which granted their conservation easement. The estate's pastoral landscape, she assured me, will remain "untouched by the human hand." For three years, the Bowers had remained steadfast in their refusal to lease, and it had done nothing to slow the sullying of the landscape in their neck of the woods. Meanwhile, they had absorbed the collateral damage of George's, Holly and Chriss's, and other neighbors' self-interested decision to lease. Enough was enough. The state government had failed to protect them, and it wouldn't let the municipality step in. Maintaining a principled boycott that, given others' defection, was purely symbolic struck Cindy as a fool's errand. "I'm not gonna be a martyr for this," she resolved. "I'm going to lease."

The fact that even a well-to-do, civically engaged environmentalist leased her land punctuates how, without rules in place that limit externalities and regulate the consumption of finite public goods, resource dilemmas compel people to prioritize self-interest over community resilience. People act this way because they know that individual altruism will yield no positive results unless everyone else behaves unselfishly as well. Just about every landowner I met, regardless of their economic circumstances or environmental politics, applied this logic. Truck traffic, along with the smells, noise, light pollution, and occasional water contamination associated with fracking did not stop at lessors' or beneficiaries' property lines. Everyone experienced a diminished capacity to enjoy the commons—that is, peace and quiet, unbroken vistas, dark skies, unhurried country roads, the sounds of nature, and clean air and water—whether or not they leased. It seemed sensible to lease and make some money for oneself so long as everyone else is usurping the commonwealth already.

From afar, it might be easy to dismiss Cindy as a hypocrite. Indeed, Cindy called herself one on several occasions. But I realized that most of us, myself included, are in no position to claim the moral high ground. Case in point: although the state of New York banned fracking and "exported" fractivists like Yoko Ono and my NYU students to rural Pennsylvania to protest on behalf of a ban there, I learned that natural gas powers more New York homes than any other energy source; much of that gas comes from Pennsylvania.[15] In the wake of the fracking boom, homeowners across America have been swapping out their old oil-burning furnaces for methane ("dry" gas) or propane ("wet" gas) heaters, which produce less particulate matter and greenhouse gases and are significantly more cost-efficient.[16] The Bowers made the switch in 2013. "We're all guilty of this energy situation," Cindy pointed out. "Jim and I were in Africa . . . [in] the Serengeti. The Maasai live there in stick huts, round huts that could fit in this room, and eight people live [in them]. I figured out that over a hundred Maasai could live in our house. Now, who is living more responsibly on the land?" Answering her own question, Cindy noted that Americans are 4 percent of the world's population yet consume close to a fifth of the world's energy and account for more than 15 percent of global carbon dioxide emissions. "Americans have gone all over the earth and plundered and raped the land and destroyed cultures so that we could have a better lifestyle than anyone else, and now we say 'not in my backyard.' To me, that is ethically not right." Viewed in this light, leasing was a small way to atone for Cindy's—and the nation's—guilt.

Cindy agonized every day over the contradictions of being an affluent member of an affluent society and being an environmentalist. One the one hand, she wondered if it would be more ethical to "give up this place and move to town so I can walk and ride a bicycle" everywhere. "There's the hypocrite again," Cindy huffed, "because I travel and I drive and burn fuel." On the other hand, she wondered if "this place [would] be

protected if we hadn't bought it and put an easement on it in perpetuity."
She seriously doubted it, because she "know[s] of at least one developer
that was looking at it that would have put a road through all the woods
down there." Momentarily brightening, Cindy added, "So I feel that I've
done something good." Locking eyes with me, seemingly in hopes that
I would offer counsel (or at least forgiveness), Cindy implored, "What
should I do?" She sounded exasperated. "Where does this take you? It
leaves you in a quandary of mixed feelings all the time."

* * *

Many of us have a vague sense that our everyday actions impact the
commons in ways we neither desire nor intend. We may even buy carbon offsets with our plane tickets to account for such externalities. But
we can usually avoid the "quandary of mixed feelings" that goes along
with taking personal responsibility for fouling the communal nest.
Why? Because we are often disconnected in time and space from the
nonconsenting others whose livelihoods suffer from the "slow violence"
caused by our lifestyle choices (e.g., our outsized energy consumption)—
faceless people like climate refugees displaced by rising sea levels in
Bangladesh, or future generations (an infamous leaked memo allegedly
written by Lawrence Summers in 1991, when he was the World Bank's
chief economist, urged "more migration of the dirty industries to the
Least Developed Countries," which would "help ease the growing pressure" caused by not-in-my-backyard activism in rich nations).[17] Many
of us are no less complicit in the tragedy of the commons than Cindy.
It is just that few of us are forced to encounter decision-making situations like she did that *feel* like collective-action problems.

Land-leasing dynamics imply that locals always acted independently—
and selfishly. But Tocqueville would applaud the region's associational
life. Perfunctory town hall meetings with the state representative in a
hamlet of two thousand inhabitants routinely drew almost a hundred
of them. Dozens of residents in outlying municipalities, many of which
were populated by only a few hundred taxpayers, regularly crammed into
township meetings to discuss topics such as whether to add a stoplight

at a busy intersection, replace a damaged guardrail, or allow trucks to park in an empty roadside lot. (Each meeting began with the Pledge of Allegiance. Typically, though unnecessarily, residents would state their name and address before speaking. Elected township supervisors would listen, debate, and, ultimately, vote.) At a Wysox Township meeting I attended, held in a cramped outbuilding with a crusty drop ceiling lit by fluorescent bulbs, guests were asked one by one if they wanted to talk about anything. An elderly lady said that the supervisors should pay a particular loan on a quarterly basis rather than annually to reduce the interest; they briefly conferred and accepted her proposal. A young man suggested that the township give its impact fee money from gas drilling to the fire department rather than increase the millage rate to fund the all-volunteer unit; the supervisors promised to consider it. The group resolved to buy a new township truck from John, who owned a local dealership, and the supervisors voted to accept the crowd's suggestion to go with the lowest of four bids to replace a guardrail. This was civic association in action, a time to figure out "what connects us together as a town" and what we owe our neighbors.[18]

When it came to matters thought to be in the *public* interest, many locals endorsed collective action—even George, who as an elected member of the Montoursville School Board passionately fought an epic (losing) battle to prevent the historic old high school from being torn down.[19] But mineral rights, perhaps the ultimate expression of personal land sovereignty, fostered the illusion that deciding whether to develop the subsurface of one's estate was purely a *private* matter. This belief was bolstered by the fact that landowners could, and often did, lease or sell their mineral rights with the stroke of a pen at their kitchen table. Every lease to extract shale gas was a private contract executed by two nominally free agents (landowner and petroleum firm). Not only was there no obligation to check with others before leasing, there were no formal mechanisms in place to facilitate community consultation and cooperative decision-making. Leases typically did not require consent, let alone input, from a third party (e.g., one's neighbors). There were no public referenda or town hall debates about whether the community should allow land leasing, even though other issues that impacted the commonwealth *were* debated and decided in town-hall-style forums. Placing a cell tower in one's yard, or getting a liquor license for a new business, required more public input than leasing.[20] This was no accident; it was by industry, and federal and state government, design. Land leasing, then, was an overdetermined resource dilemma, given the legal and regulatory context.

Most residents endorsed this arrangement, or at least took it for granted. Yet as I watched residents like the Crawleys involuntarily absorb the sometimes-catastrophic spillover effects of neighbors' ostensibly private land use decisions, a deep irony became apparent: the legally protected freedom to exploit one's mineral rights routinely eroded the freedom of others—their right to be left alone, and their sovereignty over their estate (the violation of land sovereignty associated with leasing is most acute in split-estate cases, where the surface owner may not be able to stop development on their own land and reaps no benefits).[21]

While behavioral scientists have endlessly analyzed resource dilemmas through the anodyne concept of game theory (focusing on, e.g., defectors and free riders), few consider how they threaten civil liberty and community. It was the loss of freedom that Cindy cited as the reason for leasing: her neighbors had violated her land sovereignty; the leasing bonus was *reparation*. In Pennsylvania, a gas company is lawfully guilty of trespass if, in the process of extracting gas from a lessor's property, any resulting fractures or frac fluid extend into a neighboring subsurface estate for which the operator does not have a lease.[22] Yet many of the aboveground trespasses that Cindy and others experienced (e.g., noise and light pollution) are largely unregulated.

Much like a community of rural California ranchers studied by law professor Robert Ellickson in his aptly titled book *Order without Law*, many long-term Lycoming County residents prided themselves on resolving property disputes that arose in the community through informal norms of neighborliness rather than through appeals to legal entitlements.[23] While the residents were fiercely committed to individual sovereignty, the codependency so often required in the past to eke out an existence in one of America's poorest and most-isolated regions fostered a surprising legacy of cooperation.[24] However, the spillover effects of individuals' choice to lease their land sometimes affected their neighbors' quality of life to such a degree that it contravened the covenant of letting others live. This breach in turn weakened the community bonds that had traditionally facilitated cooperation. The financial and environmental stakes of fracking could be so high, and the customary ways of getting by that once fostered association, like collectively owned dairies, had become so scarce, that neighbors and kin now routinely filtered their interactions and relations through the law.

When Scott McClain begged Poor Shot to stop allowing gas trucks to use *his* driveway—which he said he had granted access to, as a good neighbor, through an easement, he recalled that the hunting camp highlighted its legal entitlement to the right-of-way. Both parties had sued and called the police on the other; subsequently, they only spoke through lawyers. Next-door neighbors who never knew or cared about the exact location of their property lines began researching deeds at the courthouse to ensure no one else got a dime of their rightful lease bonus. Generations-old hunting camps and family farms were incorporated as LLCs. (When the Shaner clan gathered to discuss their ancestral estate, now organized as Penn Brook Farm, LLC, someone always took minutes; a lawyer was sometimes present to ensure that decisions and profits were fair to all ten siblings.) And some residents who joined with their neighbors to collectively bargain with gas companies for better leasing terms became spiteful toward the handful of lucky lessors in their group who were picked to host the gas infrastructure that generates continuous royalties, while the rest of them absorbed spillover effects that debased their land—without receiving additional compensation.

It would be imprudent to say that fracking is destroying community. But for some residents, the collective-action problem introduced by private leasing seemed to confirm their worst suspicions about human nature: it suddenly appeared as if everybody was out for just themselves. The sociological effect was a noticeable turning-inward among residents, a heightened sense that they were going it alone rather than in the same boat. Even the Crawleys, Bodles, and their three neighbors— who collectively sued a gas company that tainted their water—stopped holding weekend barbecues and gradually grew apart after they gave in to the gas company's insistence that they accept individual, and disparate, settlements. Forced into a situation where the optimal strategy was to defect rather than cooperate with one another, their sense of interconnectedness and mutual obligation withered.

*   *   *

The live-and-let-live ethic that traditionally governed community relations in Appalachia is a staple of American political discourse.[25] It is grounded in the premise that there is a domain of private life that is distinct and separate from the public sphere. We are granted the liberty to love whom we want, worship where we want, and express ourselves how we want because these are considered private actions that don't trespass upon others' freedom. We are *not* granted the freedom to rob a bank or act out vigilante justice, because the arbitrary expropriation of others' property or right to due process erodes their freedom. Under the Rousseauian social contract, then, personal lifestyle choices ought not be subject to oversight or restriction *to the extent that they do not undermine the public interest.* But as the historian Naomi Oreskes and her colleagues note, macro environmental problems can erase the barrier between private and public domains. Seemingly "innocent and inconsequential" individual acts such as turning on a light or driving a car, which "would traditionally have been construed as private," they write, are "amplified by technology and indefinite iteration," such that they infiltrate the public sphere in the form of greenhouse gases or other pollutants.[26] And when they do, they harm the common good by contributing to global plights like species extinction and climate change.

The private *is* public. In the aggregate, our personal lifestyle choices trespass on others' sovereignty in ways not so different from how the spillover effects of George's decision to lease impacted Cindy's ability to enjoy her own property. It's just harder to trace the connections around the globe, compared to down the road. Consider one of the most private acts of all: defecating. It turns out that some of my excrement travels a thousand miles from New York City to landfills in Alabama, on "poop trains," creating a public nuisance by fouling the air of the surrounding communities it passes through (Parrish, Alabama, had to cancel Little League games when one train loaded with sludge parked nearby for more than two months).[27]

"It did not much matter," Hardin noted, "how a lonely American frontiersman disposed of his waste."[28] But the global commons cannot handle the amount of literal and metaphorical poop trains (e.g., nuclear waste, noxious fumes, greenhouse gases) that would result if all of Earth's seven-billion-plus inhabitants guzzled resources like middle-class Americans. As political scientist Robert Paarlberg observes, Americans' prolific rates of consumption and pollution are fostered by the country's unusually weak national political institutions. The US favors free-market mechanisms over governmental rules and regulations more than perhaps any other nation. Paarlberg implies that the problem of excess does not originate in the moral failings of individual Americans. It results from a lax regulatory system that permits—nay, encourages—unsustainable lifestyles.[29] Consider this: the US government effectively nudged automakers to prioritize gas-guzzling SUVs, pickups, and minivans—which today encompass 69 percent of the auto market in America—by exempting "light trucks" from the fuel-economy standards required under the Clean Air Act.[30] Rather than training our ire on the consumers who buy SUVs, we should ask why the auto industry and our own government foist them on us.

Fracking brings to light another distinctly American legal-political structure that favors excess pollution: its unusually strong protections of private property. Only in America does the fateful (for the entire planet!) decision of whether or not to frack mostly come down to individual property holders. When the landman and the lessor sit down to hash out the terms of a lease, there's no seat at that kitchen table representing the public interest. But the entire premise of land sovereignty rests on the fiction that what happens on one's estate stays on one's estate. Leasing one's land for gas drilling degrades others' ability to enjoy their property, and sometimes their well water and their health. Pesticides and excess nitrogen from farmers' use of synthetic fertilizer routinely drift into neighbors' properties and waterways, sometimes sullying entire ecosystems.[31] The federal government has spent decades, and billions of taxpayer dollars, trying to clean up "superfund sites," in which manufacturers freely buried toxic waste containing carcinogens like arsenic, lead, and mercury on their premises that subsequently sickened nearby communities.[32] And so on. Contra Locke, it should also be noted that those who "improve" their land by making it productive—whether by leasing, farming, manufacturing, and so forth—often rely on *public* goods like groundwater and roads.

There's no such thing as property whose use value is not reliant on communal resources and whose development does not impact others' land or the commons. Private property, then, is not—or should not be treated as—a natural right equivalent to civil liberties like freedom of expression.

We have already crossed the threshold where exercising our individual rights to liberty and property alienates others from those same rights. In the epoch of climate change, personal liberty increasingly becomes a zero-sum game: my gain is your loss. This is the *public/private paradox*. The individual, Hardin wrote, benefits "from his ability to deny the truth even though society as a whole, of which he is part, suffers." Paarlberg maintains that, in America, this denialism is exacerbated by the nation's unique political culture, which celebrates individual freedoms over social responsibility. This primes many of its citizens to become personally invested in defending liberalist policies.[33]

Fracking has forced heartland communities like Lycoming County to confront the public/private paradox directly, neighbor to neighbor. As Oreskes and her coauthors point out, the public/private paradox is the new normal. This means that, sooner rather than later, we all have to "figure out how to live with it."[34] The social contract, and the health of our planet, hangs in the balance.

CHAPTER 6

Indentured

"I'm gonna walk you around here," George Hagemeyer said as I tagged along with him for his morning constitutional to the well pad on what was shaping up to be a lovely day in May. "Technically, I'm not supposed to let anybody on it," he huffed. "But there's nobody down here working right now, except for the fence guys." He scowled at a few contractors wrapping cyclone fencing around a valve protruding from a newly buried pipeline. "They won't have anything to say about it," he dared. Whenever I visited George, no matter who was working on site, he encouraged me to walk right up to the lip of the pad and take pictures. He enjoyed reminding the hard hats that it was *his* land, and he was watching. After George allowed a film crew from the Children's Network to document the well pad in the spring of 2013, he said he got an anxious phone call from an Anadarko representative. "Tony's a little upset," George smirked. He said he reminded Anadarko that nowhere in his lease did it say that he and others cannot take pictures or videos of gas-drilling operations. Upon being told that "the company doesn't want it," George felt aggrieved. So when Ralph Kisberg came calling soon afterward, asking if he could bring Lehigh University students to shoot a video as the wells were being readied for fracking (the most intense stage), George enthusiastically agreed.[1] "Of course, I had to take them down [to the pad] and show them," George snickered. "Oh my god, they [Anadarko] just about had a fit!" Two months later, in June 2013, George happily hosted the League of Women Voters, after they told Ralph they wanted to see an active fracking site. "I said, well, I don't quite understand what they want, but hey, if they wanna see it, go ahead."[2] When I asked George why he let people he didn't even know document his property, he implied that it was in part to send a message to the gas companies. The message, he told me, was this: "Buddy, it's my land. I'm gonna take any pictures I want. Don't tell me I'm not allowed."

Despite George's rebellious antics, his jurisdiction over his land had waned considerably. This reality set in a little more each day, as fracking moved from one phase of operations (e.g., building an access road and the pad) to the next (e.g., fracking the wells and connecting them to a pipeline). Through it all, his hands were tied by the lease he signed in February 2006 with East Resources, even though East relinquished all claims to George's land in 2009. East first created a fifty-fifty partnership with Ultra. East and Ultra then transferred ownership to Chesapeake (two-thirds) and Statoil (one-third), both of whom subsequently sold 50 percent of their share to Anadarko. The last-three-mentioned companies later signed a "joint operating agreement" with Matsui. Chesapeake vouchsafed 2.5 percent of its share of George's lease to Larchmont Resources, which, scandalously, turned out to allegedly be a personal piggy bank for Chesapeake's own CEO at the time, Aubrey McClendon.[3]

Although George ran his three-page lease by a lawyer first, "As time went by, I found out there was a couple of things . . . that I thought—excuse the phrase, but damn, I wish I had known that ahead of time." Motioning toward the gravel road that Anadarko carved through his backyard the year before to access the well pad, George sighed, "I wish—if it was on the other side of the trees, if they would have went down the side I wanted, I'd never see it at all." He went on, "Am I happy about that? Not really. But my lawyer never told me what I was allowed to do and what I wasn't." Anadarko didn't consult with him about it, he said. When a company spokeswoman turned up in 2010 to discuss a signing bonus for a pipeline, George was tantalized by the money but said he wanted to think about it. That's when he said he learned that "it was in my lease that they had the right to put the pipeline through my property." George was reportedly told, "If you don't sign, we can do what we want anyways." I was skeptical that this was true after reading George's original lease and its subsequent bills of sale: they said nothing about the conveyance of a right-of-way. But he was adamant in his belief that the pipeline was a fait accompli.

In mid-July 2013, after George's gas wells had been drilled and fracked, I stood with him on the berm while a gaggle of workers completed installation of six large "separators" on the pad—one for each well. The purpose of these cream-colored metal boxes, each the size of a small car and topped by a twelve-foot-high missile-like vent, was to remove most of the sand, brine, and condensate (liquid hydrocarbons) that were mingled with the unearthed natural gas. Two massive, newly erected cylinders next to the separators would then remove any remaining water vapor so that the gas was "pipeline ready." Called glycol dehydrators, they looked like twin vertical submarines and were each attached to a metering shed. On the other side of the separators stood four large condensate tanks (sometimes mistaken for oil tanks), which, once connected to the separators via thick steel tubes, would store the residual liquids. It was a lot to take in. The tangle of pipes, tanks, smokestacks, and metal cylinders looked, to me, like a smaller version of facilities I passed on the New Jersey Turnpike as I drove through the industrial zones of Elizabeth and Newark, such as the Linden Generating Station, the state's second-largest power plant. Only this was in George's backyard, in the rustic foothills of the Appalachian Mountains.

George looked taken aback. I asked whether he had a sense what would go on the pad. "Nothing, nothing, nope. They showed up and started doing their work, and what you see is what I see. I had no idea." Although George had told me several months before that he was thrilled with Anadarko and considered them a partner, he spoke differently now. "I'm not saying they lie to people . . . but they don't get their point across to the ordinary guy that doesn't ever deal with this. They're not saying you also have to let these separators [be] down there. I didn't know anything about the separators. All of a sudden, we have all these buildings down there." At least, he added, they're temporary. I instantly felt queasy, realizing that George thought most of the infrastructure be-

FIG. 6.1. The separators on the well pad in George Hagemeyer's backyard.
Photograph by Tristan Spinksi.

fore us would be carted off once the wells were hooked up to the pipeline. Gas companies and landmen often emphasized, in public (e.g., at
town halls), their commitment to shrinking well pads to minimize permanent disruption. Most notoriously, presentations and brochures I
saw commonly depicted an Arcadian meadow dotted by almost indis-
tinguishable wellheads, which the industry euphemistically called
Christmas trees. The implication seemed to be that one's land would be
similarly reclaimed after drilling and fracking operations concluded.
Left unsaid was that gas wells may be fracked multiple times and produce for decades, and that the company could target deeper layers of
shale from his pad after that. The condensate tanks and separators,
which George had the impression would be gone by the end of the year,
would very likely outlast him. I felt terrible breaking the news to George
and asked if he was OK. "Do you really wanna know? I question whether

it's really worth it. Everybody says, 'Oh, once you get your first royalty check you'll say it's worth it.' I don't know."

It wasn't just the big surprises. George seemed just as incensed, if not more so, by the small, unanticipated insults to his property. Like the white wooden billboard Anadarko planted in his front lawn that read, "George Hagemeyer Pad," with "all the permit signs on it and everything." He sighed, "That stays there." George went on to bemoan the mailbox that Anadarko placed at the foot of his driveway (every well pad must have a street address), along with a bevy of new signs. "I have 'Caution Overhead Wires' signs, I have 'Slow, Children at Play' signs, I have 'No Trespassing' signs, a white Anadarko sign, another sign for the well pad, a consumptive water use sign, and now they're telling me they need another sign out here for emergency 911. That's nine signs! I'm out here in the country and it looks like I-80!" The more he thought about the signs, "the more pissed off I got." George recounted calling state senator Gene Yaw's office "and bitching him out" about it. "I says, I live in the country. I like the freedom. I like the openness. Now I've got all these freaking signs all over the freaking place? The government doesn't care! That ticks me off to no end, because now I have to put up with that for the rest of my life." It felt like a big "fuck you" from Uncle Sam.

* * *

Perhaps the ultimate irony of leasing is that landowners like George experienced unexpected affronts to their autonomy not only from others' land use decisions, but also from their own. As analysts like Stephanie Malin have observed, private contracts between petroleum companies and lessors provided structural advantages to the former that disempowered the latter. Landowners often felt impotent to negotiate the terms of their lease or control what happened after they signed; some scholars call this lack of meaningful participation "procedural injustice."[4] Indeed, many gas companies and landmen seem not to have prepared lessors for the reality that the "guests" they invited onto their properties sometimes operate as if they have the run of the place, and that leasing their land elicited heightened government intrusion into their everyday lives (it was the state, after all, that required Anadarko to post all those signs by George's driveway). George and others had unwittingly signed away, in effect, their freehold rights, becoming akin to tenants on their own property.

George met me in his driveway one July afternoon, anxious to know if the security guard had asked me to check in with her on my way in. He grimaced when I said she stopped me, wanting to know my name and the purpose of my visit. The guard was only authorized, he said, to regulate ingress to the gas company's access road (which branched off from the driveway), not the entire driveway, which also served his sister's house. "My niece came here the other day and the guard stepped out and put out the slow sign. I told her not to do that. Then my nephew came and they put the stop sign on him! Well, that ticked me off. This is *my* property; it's *my* driveway." Ever since then, George reminded anyone who came to visit that the guard "doesn't have the authority to stop anybody; they're not the cops." Things reached a head a few weeks later when the guard reportedly stepped in front of his SUV with the stop sign and told George to wait, because they were moving heavy equipment off the pad. George "hollered" so loudly to Anadarko, he said, that they left the guard shack empty for a day to cool him out. He advised Anadarko that "They'd better never stop a gray Ford Explorer again." However, when George complained to his lawyer about the incident, he was told that it was a public-safety issue and that Anadarko was within its legal rights.

Lessors found themselves bearing witness as things happened *to* their estate, often having no input or forewarning. One August evening, George said, he was watching the six o'clock news while eating his supper when a sand truck rumbled past his house down the access road. The big rig startled him, both because of the relatively late hour and because Anadarko had no need for sand on his well pad anymore. Jumping out of his chair, George recalled shouting out the window, "Idiot! You've got the wrong place!" He said he told himself, "George, shut up. It's their business. Mind your own business." But an hour later, the sand truck was still down on the pad. "What the frick is he doing," George asked aloud. He walked over to ask the security guard stationed at the foot of his driveway, who informed him that they were bringing the sand truck to George's pad to store it. (Regarding the security guard shack and portable toilet, which had sat on George's lawn for five months at that point, he lamented, "I can't believe it's been that long! I thought it'd be in and out of here.") George was flabbergasted. It had never occurred to him that Anadarko's lease allowed it to use the well pad as a parking lot; the wording, in fact, did. "It's been over three years since they started," George complained to me. "I'm tired of the traffic up and down my field and in my road." He had expected that things would quiet down, and that his days of dealing with truck traffic were over, now that his six wells had been drilled and fracked and hooked up to the pipeline. But it turned out that Anadarko was preparing to use portions of George's leased land as the staging ground for other, nearby fracking operations.

"I'm sick and tired of these people coming on my property. [They] opened my property up for every Tom, Dick, and Harry to come in here!" In George's mind, "They're trespassing." But "I don't have a say in it! It's the same way with this telephone pole" that Anadarko had just installed on the pad. "They tell me it's . . . for this radio antenna. I mean, they never said anything to me. They never called me and asked me if they were allowed to, but yet they're putting it on my property." George said he learned of the company's plan to erect the towering antenna from his sister, who happened to be at the township supervisors' meeting where the permit was approved. And it was only by reading a public notice in the *Williamsport Sun-Gazette* that he discovered that Anadarko had applied for a permit to withdraw up to three million gallons of water per day from his creek (it was approved).[5] As if these indignities weren't bad enough, the security guard warned that George could be arrested for trespassing on the well pad. A few days prior to the warning, George had poked around on the empty pad ("I'll go where I damn well please," he recalled thinking. Anadarko can "go F themselves"), but a camouflaged security camera that the company mounted on one of his trees recorded his transgression. "Arrested on my own property?! I dare them," George seethed, "This land is *mine*, and just because they've got a lease doesn't mean they can do anything they want."

But the truth was that George's contract granted near-total authority over portions of his leased land (e.g., the pad) to Anadarko, who was often not even required to inform him of its activities and their expected duration. George spent hours on the phone trying simply to find out what was happening on his own land ("Trying to get a hold of my landman is like trying to get a hold of my dead grandmother. It ain't gonna happen"). "I still have water trucks coming and going almost every day," George reported to me in a Christmas e-mail greeting, five months after work on his property wrapped up. More frustrating was that a crew of roughnecks living in a temporary "man camp" on his pad had left, only to be replaced by another. "I thought they were done Friday," he wrote, "but I came back from getting groceries on Saturday to see another crew moving in." Back in midsummer, George told me he was "so disgusted at this point" and had "no way of knowing when things would calm down." A half year later, little had changed. He still couldn't "get answers from nobody," and now a colony of strangers was squatting in a make-shift trailer park in his backyard.

The subtle ways George sometimes played the role of supplicant to Anadarko hinted at the power they wielded over him and his land. He never did, to my knowledge, venture onto the well pad again, after the "trespassing" incident. When George mentioned to a hard hat that I was writing a book, the worker suggested that he run it by the site manager. I was shocked (and annoyed) to learn that George followed this advice, recounting the questions I asked and writing down the exact spelling of my full name. "I'm sure they checked you out," he shrugged. And when the site manager paid a visit to George's outpost on the berm one afternoon as the workers prepared the dehydrators, George made a humble request that, to him, would make a big difference in his capacity to tolerate the "hideous" industrial equipment. "Well, if you just paint em' a different color where the opening [in the line of trees] is, I wouldn't notice it as much." George suggested painting the dehydrators green "to match with the trees and the grass and everything," adding, "That's what I have to look at the rest of my life." As usual, the Anadarko representative listened respectfully. He noted that cream was the standard color, but promised to see what he could do. In the end, they were painted cream. Although there may have been a good reason why, George never heard it. And I could not help but notice that Anadarko did paint its equipment green on some of its pads in state forests, at the insistence of the Pennsylvania Department of Conservation and Natural Resources (DCNR).

George's modest acts of resistance against Anadarko only underlined his impotence. He pulled up a thin yellow pipeline marker ("A deer must've run over that one already," he joked. "Broke it right off. Boy, that didn't last long"). He pushed Anadarko to mount a camera along the access road to record alleged breaches of contract, like workers leaving a pile of cyclone fencing outside the right-of-way. He strung cones together with plastic chains along the edge of his field to remind trucks not to drive on the grass. "They won't let me put a board with nails in it, and my lawyer didn't think that would be a very good idea," George laughed. "I do, and I think it would work!" Whenever he felt acutely wronged, George called his lawyer—perhaps the clearest indicator that this self-styled mountain man, who presented himself, in the words of Horace Kephart, as a "law unto himself," had been defanged by his lease.[6]

* * *

George and most of his neighbors signed five-year leases. But "five-year" is, in many ways, a misnomer. Most contracts had a "held by production clause," often buried several paragraphs under the boldface preamble, that allowed the operator to unilaterally extend the lease beyond the "primary term" under certain conditions. Most common was a rider extending the lease *in perpetuity* "so long as oil or gas is 'produced' from the leasehold" before its expiration.[7] It was whispered that Anadarko and other local operators were not above hastily drilling wells in the days or weeks before five-year contracts were set to lapse, just to trigger the "secondary term," sometimes catching lessors like George unawares.

When I met Drake and Andrea Saxton, the retirees were counting down the days until their lease expired. Their worst nightmare was that

XTO would show up on the 1,825[th] day and drive a hole in the ground, locking them into a compulsory contract extension. The lease had come to feel, they said, like serving time in prison, and they understood that the secondary term would be a life sentence.

"My grandparents bought this place in 1948," Andrea recounted, as the limping sexagenarian gingerly coaxed her new hip along a mowed creekside path behind her house. She said she lived with her grandparents, who raised her, on the forty-acre estate, located at the dead end of a mile-long gravel township road in the sparsely populated (and sparsely paved) township of Moreland, for a few years in her childhood before her grandfather—a plumber—moved the family back to Philadelphia. After stops in Long Island, South Jersey, Syracuse, and Chicago, the divorcee returned to the farmstead in 1987 to take care of her grandmother until "she passed away in a good way with her tummy full and no pain." Andrea then married Drake, a former long-haul trucker and commercial pilot who, with his thick tuft of blond hair and relatively fit build, looked younger than his sixty-five years. For the last quarter century, they'd been "trying to put the place back together." The original house was "in such bad shape we had to take it down." But the salvaged wood was given new life in a quaint cottage that the couple hand-built where the field met the woods, overlooking Little Muncy Creek.

"When I was a little kid," Andrea smiled weakly, "I came down here and got the eggs." The dense copse behind us was then a pasture. Drake pointed to the stone hearth and wood stove. "One day I came home, [and] there was a hole cut, and there was a pile of stone laying out on the porch. These big stones. Andrea's cutting out the wall! I said, 'What are you doing?' Well, this is what she was doing!" A handsome wooden ladder behind the hearth climbed to a sleeping nook brilliantly lit by skylights. "Of course," Drake said proudly, "the ladder's a throwback from her sailing days." When her kids went off to college, Andrea said, she sailed around the Gulf of Mexico for four years. "And the handrails are like a boat as well." A framed collage on the wall documented how, in the years before age and an ailing hip sapped Andrea of her strength, she and Drake had hauled stones from the creek bed, hewed beams and joists from trees they felled ("Each of those beams have a little over eight hours invested in them"), and laid plumbing not only for the cottage we were standing in but also for a nearby log cabin and a much larger main house. They also bought an old barn for $400, had it disassembled and transported from Trout Run, and reconstructed it piece by piece (Andrea color-coded every board with crayons). "We did everything in here [the barn]," Drake boasted as he pointed to the pictures. "Plumbing, lumber, floors. Here I am cementing the floor we're standing on. Even the countertops we built right here."

The foyer and living room of the main house featured soaring cathedral ceilings and an open staircase ascending to loft-like bedrooms. Framed by timber and anchored by a cast-iron wood-burning stove, the space emanated warmth and coziness. A kettle atop the stove perpetually boiled water in the colder months, beckoning visitors to linger for a cup of tea (and a serving of Andrea's homemade bread). Drake joked that they built the manor and moved out of the cottage, where they had lived for fourteen years, because Andrea needed more closets. When a friend came and stayed in one of the cottages after they had moved into the main house, she was enchanted by the estate's tranquility and the cottage's charm—especially the view of the creek from its deck and of the stars from the bedroom skylight. Upon joining the Saxtons in the main house for breakfast, the couple recalled, she insisted that they open a bed-and-breakfast. In 2006, they christened the two outbuildings the Treehouse and the Log Cottage and launched Creekview Country Cottage Bed and Breakfast. Rave reviews soon followed online (e.g., "THE place to unplug, unwind, and appreciate your world!").[8]

The B and B was still getting off the ground when the landman first came calling, in 2008. "It's embarrassing to see yourself" having been so naive, Andrea admitted, especially since she had "a little bit of background"—a degree in geology from Bucknell University—that should have helped her see the downsides of fracking. Drake recounted the landman's cliché pitch: "We're prepared to offer ya all this money, but really, when we're done, you won't even know we were there." He shook his head sheepishly. "There'll just be this little thing we call a Christmas tree. We'll put some plantings around that, and you won't even see it." Though the Saxtons didn't hire a lawyer to review their lease, they did join "a little group of a couple dozen people to try to learn from each other." The landowner coalition collectively represented about 3,400 acres. It was able to secure $900 an acre for all its members—a tidy sum for the Saxtons, who leased forty acres. "It sounded somewhat innocuous," Drake sighed, as if "nothing bad could really happen." Andrea said they took comfort in knowing that locals had already been leasing their land for fifty years; nothing ever came of it. And besides, "We were surrounded anyway," by large leased farms. "Now our gas lease is going to expire," Drake smirked, "and they'll never pay another one." Andrea allowed herself a giggle: "We're gonna have a party, because we're so excited to get rid of this thing." Drake offered a sober reminder: "The sad part is, we're completely ringed. We're gonna get it anyway, but we're not going to sign onto it."

On a gray March afternoon thirteen days shy of their lease-expiration date, I joined the Saxtons as they strolled hand in hand along a grassy trail (mowed almost daily by Drake) that wended through a grove of towering hemlocks they called "The Cathedral." The gurgling of Little Muncy Creek, where Andrea had learned to swim and where we stopped to skip stones, provided the soundtrack. The B and B, Drake mused, gave them "a new awareness of what we really have here." Visitors, he noted, come for solitude. "They wanna see the country. They wanna see rural. They want quiet." Through their eyes, Drake said, he is reminded that "this is how you're supposed to live." But a brown metal pipe sticking out of the ground, which slightly obstructed the picture-perfect view of the creek from the Saxtons' living room, was a daily reminder of how precarious their serenity was. In May 2011, seven water wells in the vicinity were found to be laced with methane. The following month, the creek that flowed through the Saxtons' backyard bubbled with natural gas. The state determined that the source was faulty cement casing associated with two nearby XTO gas wells. The state Department of Environmental Protection (DEP) assessed the Exxon subsidiary a modest fine ($95,000), and as a precaution the Saxtons had a vent placed over their water well.[9] The vent seemed to keep the concentration of methane in their drinking water within acceptable DEP standards. But it was cold comfort. In the year after the XTO incident, the couple said, their privacy was routinely invaded, as XTO employees repeatedly showed up at their door, unannounced, with "gas-sniffing" equipment, to check if methane had entered their home. Their lease, Drake said, meant that "we don't have a choice." And when "they come in, your home is theirs." They claimed that gas workers had gone through every corner of their house, sometimes while paying guests were staying there. And they reported that business was down 50 percent between 2012 and 2013, which they attributed to the local increase in drilling activity.

"It's grown for us to the point that now we both feel as though we're under siege," Drake growled. "We don't live here to have our life impinged upon by someone who's come here to make a profit. I really don't have the command of the English language to impress upon you how disturbed I am over that." His voice crescendoing in righteous indignation, Drake went on, "They don't have the right to come in here after we've spent twenty-five years building this and run us out. If they ruin the water in that well, that's what they will have done. And they will have destroyed our lives." Drake hissed, "They lied. As far as I'm concerned, they got these leases fraudulently."

Several weeks later, the Saxtons had a pig roast and raised a glass. Their lease had expired. The couple was experienced enough to know that it was not the end of their troubles—after all, no development had actually occurred on their property during the five-year contract. Nonetheless, it felt as if a great weight had been lifted off their shoulders. They had clawed back some of their autonomy. A wrong was righted.

* * *

The contract as imagined in liberal theory, legal scholar Margaret Radin writes, is a "bargained-for exchange transaction between two parties." The hallmark of a freely agreed-upon contract is *negotiation*. It is "supposed to involve consent by each party to give up something of his or her own to obtain something he or she values more"; if one's rights are violated in the process, "there must be the opportunity to seek a remedy" in court.[10] This presumption undergirds contract law. However,

Radin finds that the negotiable-term contract is increasingly being su-
perseded by "take it or leave it" *boilerplate* agreements—most infamously, the software-user agreements most of us accept without reading
and the liability waivers we must sign to enroll in many organized physical activities. On a daily basis, Radin observes, many of us sign away
basic liberties, such as the right to privacy and the legal entitlement to
bring one's grievances before a jury of one's peers.

Why do so many of us agree to boilerplate contracts in the modern
era, and why do so few of us read them? The most insidious reason,
Radin says, is because we need the product or service and "have no access to a supplier that does not impose onerous clauses." Other consid-
erations are the belief that the company has power over us, such that we
are stuck with what it imposes on us, and that we wouldn't understand—
let alone be able to alter—the terms of the contract anyway.[11]

The terms of gas leases were certainly not as immutable as, say, the
Twitter user agreement. A few lessors secured multiple concessions
from gas companies, some of which imposed significant restrictions on
the lessee (most notably, the Bowers' non-surface-disturbance clause).
However, most lessors recalled landmen strongly implying that the
terms—with the exception, perhaps, of the amount of compensation—
were nonnegotiable. "They deliberately make it sound," Andrea remarked, "as if, if you don't sign up now, we're moving on." Drake added,
"You're not gonna get this offer next week." Indeed, the nonchalant
pitch so often proffered by landmen—this is the lease that all your
neighbors signed, and we can simply drill around you if you won't accept these terms—fed into lessors' belief that most if not all of the lease
was boilerplate. The industry line was that leases are "standard." This is
especially ironic since, as analysts have noted, there are no requirements
for uniformity in leases. But the structure of private negotiation meant
many lessors didn't know that.[12]

Even some lessors who hired counsel reported being told by their lawyer
that they had received the "standard lease," and so it was a simple decision to take it or leave it. And, like boilerplate user agreements, taking
it often meant unknowingly relinquishing autonomy because of hidden
or obscure clauses that George called "a bunch of lawyer mumbo-jumbo"

(George confided he "never read the entire thing," because his lawyer implied the terms of his lease were fixed.) Sure, George admitted, he didn't understand some parts of his lease. But he didn't feel like he could go back to his lawyer to clarify every little thing, because there were only so many billable hours—at $200 a pop—that he could afford when he hadn't even "gotten any money out of that hole yet."

Many people, Radin notes, are surprised to learn that boilerplate is treated by law as binding. This was certainly true of George. As we watched contractors erect the radio antenna that George didn't know Andarko was allowed to install in his yard, he groaned, "Granted, they're leasing the property. But now wait a minute! Shouldn't you have somewhere in the agreement something saying that you can't do anything you damn well please on my property without having my permission?" George could not comprehend why he and the gas company couldn't just sit down and talk through his concerns. He was sure they could readily come up with solutions that both parties could live with. "It's just the little things," he insisted. Unfortunately, George was quickly learning how doing business with a $38 billion corporation was much more of a one-way street than the working relationships he had forged with his plumber or his auto mechanic. "I don't care what the contract says, that you can put this here, you can put it there, or whatever," George grumbled as he glared at the access road through his field. "Work with the property owner. Why sit there and piss 'em off or make everybody mad at you, when it's their property?" As he spoke, sour industrial fumes wafted from somewhere on the well pad into his field. "Oh my! I don't care for that at all," George yelled. "Rest of my life. The contract's signed, nothing you can do about it. Oh well." I asked what George would do if he could go back in time. He said he would have found out first "what all is involved." He would have put in his contract that the gas company couldn't leave "all of that junk sitting around" (the separators, tanks, etc.) on the pad. He would have forced Anadarko to place the access road on the other side of the line of trees. There would be a clause reading, "My place is not for storage." There would be no antenna, no security guard shack. It sounded sensible. It was fantasy.

There were few things lessors like George valued more than their freehold rights. Had they known the extent to which their lease's fine print alienated them from authority over their own property (through, e.g., the automatic extension of the five-year term if a well was spudded), or the degree to which the contract's terms were negotiable, I suspect, more of them would have had major reservations about signing a so-called standard lease. This was Drake's logic in accusing the petroleum companies of having obtained contracts fraudulently. The insinuation was that his lease "delete[d] rights that are granted through democratic processes" without his full consent.[13] This type of procedural injustice runs contrary to the guiding principle of contract law, which is premised on negotiation between nominally free and equal parties who *knowingly* surrender certain entitlements in return for something more valuable.[14] But, as sociologist James Coleman observed decades ago, the rise of corporate actors—which are legally recognized as persons—has institutionalized inequality in legal and economic transactions. The corporate actor, Coleman wrote, "nearly always controls most of the conditions" of the contract, holds much of the information that a citizen would need to make an informed decision, and has access to vastly different resources that it can use to structure relations to its advantage. The resulting asymmetry of relations—in which "a natural person, as the weak party to the relation, has little control over the actions of the strong party, the corporate actor"—finds expression in boilerplate user agreements and standard gas leases.[15]

The hardest thing I ever had to do in the time I lived in Billtown was explain to George that he could have potentially received the same amount of royalties without allowing Anadarko to step foot on his property. While ideas about the sanctity of home led a few landowners to reject leasing, some who leased professed the same priority—to preserve their estate. George viewed the bonuses and royalties as a means of ensuring that his property would be a prized inheritance, rather than a millstone, for his descendants. "I already have my will set up," George told me the first time I met him. At that time, he viewed the disruption in his backyard as a godsend. "You know, I never could have imagined it would work out like this," he remarked. "Those holes in the ground," he believed, would allow him to "take care of this land" beyond the grave. "The property has to stay in the family" in order for his heirs to inherit the "gas money," which he thought would ensure the integrity of his dad's land for generations to come. "I love my home too much" to *not* lease, he told me then. As the royalties began flowing in, George was grateful. But he was also confused, because he heard that his next-door neighbor, whose property did not host the gas wells, was receiving more money than him. To me, it was clear why that was the case. I showed George his "pooling agreement" (which I got at the courthouse), which showed that he had 73 acres folded into a rectangular "unit" consisting of 637 acres. The units' wellheads were on his property, but the wells branched underneath the surface of his (leased) neighbors' properties. Twelve and a half percent (the state minimum) of the proceeds from the gas that came out of the ground in the unit would be divided among the landowners based on the amount of acres they had in the unit. Because his neighbor had a hundred acres in the unit, I explained to George, they were entitled to more royalties. George's (mis)under-standing was that 'the big money comes from having the pad.' As we looked at the pooling agreement in the yard, with Halliburton trucks rumbling right behind us, George began boiling over. 'That doesn't make any sense!' Pointing toward his neighbor's hundred-acre property, he yelled, 'They're gonna make more money than me, and I'm the one that's going through all this?! I'm the one who got my trees cut down! I'm the one who got the road put through my field!'

It was clear that George was under the misconception that the best—and perhaps the only—way to secure large royalty checks was to actu-ally host the natural-gas infrastructure on his property. He was paid a bonus up front for the surface disturbance associated with the pad and access road on his land, but it was so paltry ($14,000) that he could not believe that was all he was entitled to for his troubles. 'I should have said, go put your damn wells somewhere else!' The best way to describe how I felt sharing this information with George was shitty. It was dawn-ing on him for the first time that he may not have had to compromise his beloved land to profit from natural gas. Perhaps, if he had signed a non-surface-disturbance agreement, Anadarko could have placed the well pad on his neighbor's property instead and still put his property in the unit. 'That don't seem right,' George muttered dejectedly. 'Why did I go through all this trouble if they're gonna get more money?' He grew even more disgusted when I pointed out to him the clause that Anadarko could alter or dissolve the unit at any time, meaning it could redraw the unit boundaries to include less of George's land. In fact, according to courthouse documents I found, it had already enlarged the unit once, possibly impacting his share of royalties.

It took George a few months to confirm what I told him that summer. "I had one 'H' of a time trying to get in touch with someone" from Anadarko, George wrote to Ralph and me via e-mail in October 2013. "They feel that I got compensated for the road and pad and trees. What a joke!" In a follow-up e-mail, George was so worked up that he considered calling his township supervisors to "ask them to stop handing out any more [gas well] permits to the gas people because of the mess that was just told to me." It was apparent that George had never seen, let alone consented, to his "pooling agreement," because he started complaining to his state representatives about Anadarko "taking gas from under me to pay my neighbors." His lease did not spell out that he would be pooled into a unit (even though pooling is the default), abetting George's illusion that the gas beneath his property was "his," when it was in effect collectively owned by everyone in the unit.

I felt sad for George but suspected there would be no hard feelings once he received his first royalty check, which arrived after the new year and totaled almost $35,000. I invited him and Ralph to speak to my class in April 2014, the idea being that Ralph would represent environmentalists who were skeptical about fracking and George would represent lessors who benefited from and endorsed it. George had told me he was having a ball since the money began rolling in, and he surprised Ralph by picking him up in Williamsport for the ride to Manhattan in a stretch limousine. For the first half of class, things played out as I expected. Ralph troubled the popular idea that fracking is a tool in the fight against climate change, emphasizing the massive problem of greenhouse gas emissions resulting from "fugitive methane" leaks. The leaks would only increase, he argued, as the cement casing in gas wells aged in the coming

FIG. 6.2. Ralph Kisberg (left) and George Hagemeyer (center) next to the limousine George rented for them to come from Williamsport to New York City to speak to my class. Photograph by Colin Jerolmack.

decades and began to crack. In contrast, George railed against the media's emphasis on the horror stories associated with fracking. He then talked at length about how much fun he was having with the gas money: after purchasing a new kayak and a passenger van to transport it, he said he was considering getting a toboggan to sled down his pipeline right-of-way. My students' eyes grew wide when he told them how much he received in his first royalty check. But once students began asking George about his own experiences, he focused on the negatives. A truck recently spilled transmission fluid on his driveway, he complained. And all the traffic was bringing the noise and filth of New York City ("You can keep it!" George said of Manhattan's concrete and congestion) to his backyard, ruining his experience of the country. One student seemed to catch George off guard, asking as we looked at pictures of the pad in his backyard if he ever felt like he no longer recognized his family farm, given all the disruption. His eyes became solemn and watery, and all

George could muster was, "Yes, I do." Another student gently prodded him: "Do you regret leasing?" George silently nodded as his eyes drifted upward, as if looking beyond the lecture hall. "What would my daddy say if he saw the way they used this land?

"They want you to think you don't have any rights," George went on, "because they want to do everything their way." It was then that I realized it was always about natural rights for folks like George.[16] The value they placed on land sovereignty justified their decision to lease. In turn, the feeling of having involuntarily forfeited his right to liberty and property soured George on the industry. Yeoman no more, he was now indentured.

* * *

There's another, perhaps more insidious way that oil and gas companies stifled some lessors' autonomy and concealed information that would have helped potential lessors make a more informed decision about fracking: nondisclosure agreements (NDAs). In many cases where such companies offer any kind of settlement to impacted landowners, they require them to sign an NDA.[17] I became acutely aware of this issue when I was in the final stages of editing this book. I had come to know a couple whose bucolic dream home, which they built from scratch, became close to worthless after a gas well drilled nearly a mile away from them flooded their water well with methane and turned the water brown. The couple had no problem talking to me on the record even though they were in the midst of a heated lawsuit, because they had already made their story public by reaching out to media outlets and speaking at anti-fracking events. Everything changed, however, when the couple received a settlement (one that, in my opinion, was quite paltry given all they had endured, and continue to endure).

I received a curt text message from the husband in the summer of 2020 that told me, "You cannot reference us in your book," because they had signed a nondisclosure agreement. I called him back and offered to use pseudonyms and remove any identifiers, adding that they had told their story to me long before they signed the NDA and that it was already out there in the world through newspaper articles. But, his voice trembling, the husband told me they were too scared. 'They have us by the balls, he said.' (My encapsulation of the couple's story, which I shared with them, was to appear in chapter 4.)

The ubiquity of NDAs makes it difficult to assess how many cases of water contamination from shale gas exist. And, for lessors who already felt like they had had their property rights run roughshod over by powerful corporate actors, the NDA stifled the one weapon they had to push back against the industry: freedom of speech. It was with great reluctance that the couple relinquished this right: the husband had planned to write a scathing memoir about their experience called "Fractured Fairytale." But after a decade wasted battling the industry while drinking bottled water, eating off paper plates, washing their hands with towelettes, and having to go into town to take a shower, they were 'tired and beaten.' So they gave in, they said, despite the injustice of it all.

CHAPTER 7

Unmoored

It was a serene fall morning in Trout Run. The sun peeked over the mountains, illuminating the tricolor foliage and burning off the fog that hovered over the Bowers' pond. Things had been remarkably quiet around here the past few weeks. No helicopters. No drilling. No trucks. Cindy was delighted that she could fling open the windows and hear the chirping of birds and the quacking of ducks. Like the old days. After putting on the kettle, Cindy pressed her forehead to the glass in her sunroom to drink in the scene. That's when she noticed something unusual: the stillness was ruptured by staccato tapping—like a woodpecker, though higher-pitched. It took a moment to realize that the grating sound was coming from inside her home. Glancing sideways, she noticed that her spherical stained-glass suncatchers, which dangled from strings in front of the picture windows, were rattling against the glass. "They have never done this before in the fourteen years that we have had a house here," Cindy told me. She took the worst offender down, and worried that she'd soon have to remove the others. The clinking was barely audible, but to Cindy it was "unsettling and unnerving." Something is "definitely shaking the earth," she concluded, "and it is new." Though she could only speculate on the source ("Is it mini earthquakes? The sucking of the gas out of the shale?"), Cindy was certain it had something to do with the extraction of shale gas thousands of feet below.

When the Bowers constructed their estate—replete with timber-framed chalets, a boathouse, footbridges across the stream, and hiking trails, they envisioned it as a rural sanctuary. The conservation easement

FIG. 7.1. The well pad across the street from Cindy Bower's property, at night, with potholes caused by industry trucks in the foreground and flaring in the background. Photograph by Colin Jerolmack.

they placed on the land would preserve its sylvan charm forever. That gave Cindy peace of mind. But then fracking came to Trout Run, and everything came to feel up in the air. The sleepy rural outpost increasingly resembled an industrial park, and the contrasts could be jarring. Just around the bend from pastures, unspoiled forests, and a lake popular with anglers, there could be dynamite explosions drowning out birdsong and diesel fumes mingling with the mist coming off the mountains. Security guard shacks and portable toilets dotted the country lane known as Sugar Camp, which was routinely jammed with big rigs squeezing past each other on hairpin turns. The trucks left behind bone-jarring potholes and kicked up so much dust that the apples growing in a neighbor's orchard were coated in a brown film. Cindy never knew how long the disruptions—or lulls in activity—would endure, leaving her in a constant state of uncertainty.

Sometimes, the most disconcerting encroachments on individual autonomy were the least tangible. For Cindy (and others), the acute sensory disturbances associated with fracking were much more than an annoyance. The incessant industrial hum, the clattering of windows, the putrid odors, and the artificial light had, over time, burrowed into her psyche, manifesting as a chronic state of anxiety and disarray. The loss of rural tranquility felt to her like a security blanket had been yanked away. Cindy found herself unable to sleep because of worry and unmotivated to go on walks. She and Jim also began spending more time at their upstate New York cottage (until Jim was diagnosed with cancer) and considered abandoning their cherished home, even though their property was intact.

While fracking promised a modicum of economic security, the price for some residents was not only their land sovereignty but also their *psychological* sovereignty. When I asked landowners to describe their mental state, a common refrain was, "under siege." For many, their land had long been a fountainhead of comfort and stability—an anchor, and a refuge. What made even seemingly minor disturbances like the clanking of Cindy's suncatchers so unnerving was that they were uncanny signs that landowners could no longer be sure they stood on solid ground. To be on solid ground is to feel at ease, confident, and safe. The power of the metaphor lies in the fact that standing on terra firma feels more secure than being in air, at sea, or in motion. But fracking at times upended the rhythms of country life and literally shook the earth, leaving some people feeling profoundly dislocated. Their surrounds were no longer a haven; they were a source of unpredictability and even danger. The effect was a pervasive mental state of disquietude, vulnerability, and fear I call *ambient insecurity*.

* * *

Four months after I moved out of Williamsport, in January 2014, I came back to the area to check in on the Saxtons. Drake had recently bought a new plane, and he and Andrea had just returned from a trip to Florida. As I settled into their couch, Drake dramatically slammed a plastic bottle of water down on the table. 'Our water has been impacted, and we are no longer drinking it,' he proclaimed. Sometimes, when he was traveling, Drake explained, he'd buy bottled water and then refill the bottle from his tap when he returned home. He said he filled one up and left it in his Kia SUV for a few days. When he got in the vehicle, he recalled, he was just about to back up when he glanced at the bottle in the cup holder. The water in the bottle he showed me looked pretty clear, but at the bottom was a half-inch layer of cream-colored sediment. 'I never had this before,' Drake insisted. 'For twenty years I've been filling these bottles up, and now all of a sudden we've got this.'

Turbidity has long been a common phenomenon in drinking water in Pennsylvania, a state in which over three million rural residents rely on private water wells (which are completely unregulated by the state).[1] It is often the case that cloudy water results from the presence of undissolved alkaline minerals, which are harmless. Drake knew this. But because he had never seen sediment in his drinking water before, he could not shake the worry that nearby gas drilling had somehow violated the integrity of his well. If sediment could now enter it, his thinking went, so too could chemical-laced frac fluid or methane. There was more. When Drake and Andrea first walked through the door upon returning from Florida, they reported that the radon detector in the basement was "screaming." An estimated 40 percent of Pennsylvania homes have levels of this naturally occurring radioactive gas that are above what the EPA considers to be safe.[2] The Saxtons, however, claimed that they never had a problem with radon until the first gas well was drilled nearby. After they installed an expensive venting system in their basement, the levels dropped, they said. But now they were back up to over twice the EPA's recommended safe level. We could hear the radon detector's high-pitched alarm as Drake and I spoke. Unlike turbidity, radon was not a *potential* threat. It is a known carcinogen. For Drake, it was too much of a coincidence that his water turned cloudy and the radon levels spiked after the latest round of drilling.

Andrea, still moving slowly from her hip replacement the year before, lumbered over from the kitchen to seek solace under her husband's arm. 'We're gonna be poisoned out of here,' she fretted. 'This could all be lost forever.' This wasn't supposed to happen. The Saxtons had built the so-called Log Cottage to house a caretaker, so that, when the time came that they were no longer self-reliant, they could still live out their remaining days on the property. Now they were forced to have a conversation they never imagined—about where they might move. A houseboat? Lewisburg, Pennsylvania? The Carolinas? When I asked what these three disparate scenarios had in common, the couple responded in unison, "They're not over shale." But the thought of starting all over again, especially at their advanced age, was agonizing. A quarter century of their labor was inscribed in every beam, cornice, and tile. To leave it all behind would be like cutting the couple down at the roots.

Whether or not they really would be poisoned out of their home, the Saxtons' belief that they would be impacted their relationship to their land. Over the ensuing years, the couple developed a fatalistic narrative, occasionally referring to their ancestral home in the past tense and talking about *when*—not *if*—they would move. The bed-and-breakfast faltered, not helped by the fact that the Saxtons felt it necessary to warn guests not to drink the tap water. Drake and Andrea eventually decided to close Creekview Country Cottage. Although Drake told me in 2018 that they closed the B and B not because of the gas industry but because they wanted more time to travel, it seemed apparent to me that the two were connected. During the time I lived in the area, fracking had taken over their lives. On some days, Drake reported, he would spend hours chasing down gas trucks that illegally used township roads not equipped for heavy vehicles. He took it upon himself to investigate foul odors and mysterious roadside spills. He plotted a class-action lawsuit against the petroleum industry, transforming his home office into a war room stacked with news articles, legal briefs, and DEP inspection reports. He and Andrea talked about being stressed, exhausted, and in need of escape. I don't think it's a coincidence that it was during this time that they bought a new plane and a mini camping trailer and began embarking on extended trips. It seemed like they wanted to spend as little time at home as possible. The estate, long their country refuge, had become a place from which they sought to escape.

Many impacted landowners like the Saxtons lived in a perpetual state of limbo, waiting helplessly to see if the spillover effects of fracking would either subside or force them to abandon their homesteads.

Although Drake and Andrea were still residing in Creekview when 2019 rolled around, it had been five years since they stopped drinking or cooking with their well water. This state of permanent emergency, Andrea lamented, meant that nobody—including her grown daughters or their children—would want to live here. Looking visibly pained, Andrea imagined her grandmother turning in her grave at the thought of the family farm disappearing.

Landowners around here traditionally viewed themselves as stewards of the land for future generations—often their children or grandchildren. Now some fretted that the chain would be broken on their watch. The uncertainty could breed mental paralysis, leaving them unable to make decisions about their estate. By the time I met the Crawleys, they had been drinking bottled water at their own expense for over two years. Much of Tom's free time was consumed by fruitless phone calls and meetings aimed at resolving the issue by forcing the gas company to either install a water filtration system or buy out his home. Drinking from plastic jugs of water and eating off paper plates with plasticware was not something Tom and Mary envisioned doing for the rest of their lives. But they had no idea if and when their water issue would be resolved. On the one hand, so long as the issue remained unsettled, they could not sell their house. On the other hand, their uncertainty about whether they would be able to remain in their home meant that they were not willing to invest in several longed-for home improvements (most notably, an addition off the back of their house and a carport). "We're in a holding pattern," Tom complained. "It's a lot of waiting, waiting, waiting."

Jim and Jenni Slotterback, RDA members who owned a quaint house on a one-acre lot tucked into a hollow near Trout Run, were in the same boat. They had been about to gut renovate the kitchen and bathroom and install solar panels when fracking came to town. Even though they had already laid conduit pipe for the wires that would connect to the solar array, they put everything on hold. The holding pattern ate at Jenni. "I like to have a home that we're putting our time and our effort into making it sustainable," she sighed. "Our gardens and our rain barrels and all that. Our own little oasis." But it made little sense to sink their money into building a private Eden "just to lose our water" and have to move.

Anne Nordell could relate. Since 1983, she and her husband, Eric, have owned and operated Beech Grove Farm, located on eighty-nine idyllic hilly acres near the hamlet of Cogan House. The Nordells, I discovered from my older brother (who runs an organic farm in Maine), are folk heroes to many small-scale organic farmers, due to their pioneering closed-loop sustainability methods—and their Luddite philosophy. A sprightly sexagenarian with wire-rim glasses, perpetually dark fingernails, and a mop of tangled gray hair, Anne was a fixture at the Williamsport Growers Market, which is where I met her. (Anne worked the stand with two part-time helpers; Eric, who was much more subdued, preferred to stay on the farm and hide behind his Amish-inspired beard.) She was openly anti-fracking; she even let Ralph leave flyers for a *Gasland Part II* screening at her farmstand.

One steamy July evening, I made my way to Beech Grove Farm from Williamsport. After navigating a gravel portion of Buckhorn Road that forced me to drive no more than twenty miles per hour to avoid skidding out, a stretch of newly paved asphalt suddenly appeared in front of me, along with a security guard holding a stop sign. Although Buckhorn is a public right-of-way, I had to tell the guard where I was going and wait to be waved through. A gas company working in the area had paved the road, and it posted guards at either end to control the flow of cars during the hours when gas trucks were operating. I soon popped out of the thickly forested game lands and found myself overlooking a stunning vista of the valley floor, dotted with farm houses amid the green swirls of crop rows. Soon after descending onto Cogan House Road, I was met with an incongruous roadside message board warning of "heavy truck traffic" in an area with more cows than people. Fair warning. I soon had little choice but to pull into the lot of a small roadside church and wait out the tractor trailer convoys, one of which numbered more than a dozen. Water trucks. Sand trucks. "Residual waste" trucks. Trucks towing massive rectangular "frac tanks." A slothful flatbed carrying modular trailers, chauffeured by pickup trucks with flashing lights and "wide load" signs. Signs of gas activity were everywhere, including

FIG. 7.2. Fracking behind a cemetery in the hamlet of Cogan House.
Photograph by Colin Jerolmack.

right behind the church, where a large coiled tubing rig was poking through the concrete plugs of a newly drilled gas well to allow the gas to flow to the surface.

The farm was one of the prettiest I'd ever seen. A gravel two-track driveway split by a verdant grassy median led to a quaint whitewashed farmhouse and an unpainted barn that housed horses. The seven acres that the Nordells actively cultivated were perched high atop a grassy hill out back. I spied Anne coming out of a greenhouse, looking every bit the archetypal farmer, with her muck boots, dirtied and torn button shirt, blackened nails, and unkempt ponytail. We hopped into her crud-covered pickup to make it up the hill before sunset. The perfectly manicured rows of organic lettuce and broccoli looked out over rolling farmland in one direction and forested foothills in the other. The late-day sun threw pink across the sky as it tried to poke through the clouds left over from an afternoon shower. "Man, this is beautiful," I remarked. Then the fog began to lift, revealing an access road, well pad, and pipe-

FIG. 7.3. Anne Nordell surveying her field at Beech Grove Farm.
Photograph by Colin Jerolmack.

line right-of-way cut through a portion of state game lands. Anne sucked her teeth, "They've cleared five acres of forest just for the freaking road." A drilling rig atop a distant hill glowed like a festooned Christmas tree. "That's the one [well pad] that's most depressing," Anne sighed. Convoys of water trucks, seemingly going well over the posted speed limit, screamed down Route 184. The revving of their diesel engines bounced off the valley floor, puncturing the pastoral tranquility. The other day, Anne said, she counted over 125 big rigs in just a few hours. "We never appreciated how silent it was until it wasn't anymore," she grumbled. "And that's gone forever." Because of the noise, she said, she woke up angry every day. "Psychologically, it's just grating." Anne added, "There's days where I just say, we need to get the hell outta here."

"This is our dilemma. Do you stay? Cut your losses and get out? We're of the age where we're too old to start over." Anne acknowledged they could probably survive "doing a little homestead thing" somewhere else. But they could never duplicate the cornerstone of their thriving vegetable business: the soil. The Nordells' famed silky loam was weed-free without the use of pesticides. And it was so fertile that cultivating just 3.5 acres of it each year yielded enough crops to keep the farm going. The secret to the soil's health was labor and experimentation. Decades of each. As Anne explained, she and Eric had developed a complex system of crop rotation that virtually eliminates weeds, waste, and the need for irrigation.[3] Their storied "reduced tillage" method meant relying on draft horses pulling small manual tools that barely scraped the surface. It also meant taking half their arable land out of production every year and turning it over to cover crop.

More than the mountains, the rolling fields, and the community, Anne said, their attachment to this place lay in the soil. "We've been here, building this soil all these years. We've developed this system." The soil was their wellspring. They'd always been able to trust in knowing that if they took care of it, it would take care of them. More than their home, their horses, and their customers, Anne felt an obligation to the earth beneath her feet. "I can't walk away from the soil."

These days, Anne worried that the soil that sustained her livelihood and nourished her community was in peril. She told a *New York Times* reporter that they would shut down the farm at "the first indication that we have any type of contamination." Anne added, "I eat the food that I grow, and I will not sell anything that's unsafe."[4] But what gnawed at her was the question of how she would know. As she stooped to sift the coffee-grounds-like loam through her fingers, Anne fretted that it could be carrying invisible toxins. "We're totally surrounded by leased land," and so groundwater contamination always lurked as a catastrophic—if unlikely—possibility. There was also the possibility—less remote—that a truck crash or on-site well pad accident nearby might cause chemical-laced flowback water to spill into local tributaries that fed the farm (it had already happened multiple times in the county[5]). And what about the air? With hundreds of big-rig trucks trundling daily along Route 184, which bordered Beech Grove Farm, was she crazy for worrying that the benzene, formaldehyde, arsenic, and other toxins spewed from their tailpipes might settle in her fields and penetrate the earth? Anne was in the midst of trying (and failing) to convince Penn State's

Marcellus Center for Outreach and Research (MCOR) to set up air monitors on her farm to answer that question. (She once lamented to me that Penn State Extension, which oversaw MCOR, had been 're- duced to a clearinghouse for natural gas propaganda' and 'doesn't really work on behalf of farmers anymore.') Indeed, some members of the RDA expressed worry that the crops they purchased at the Growers Market from Anne and other local farmers might be compromised by fracking.

* * *

"The central problem of our age," famed biologist Rachel Carson de- clared in the 1962 book *Silent Spring*, is the "contamination of man's total environment" with "substances that accumulate in the tissues of plants and animals and even penetrate the germ cells to shatter or alter the very material of heredity upon which the shape of the future depends."[6] Car- son wrote these doomsday words in a halcyon era. Many postwar Amer- icans bought into Dupont's motto of "better living through chemistry," embracing pesticides, plastics, abrasive cleaners, and synthetic beauty aids. Yet Carson showed that most of these household products— which were never tested before going to market—contained toxins that could amass silently in the body for years before manifesting as disease.

Silent Spring dropped like a bombshell, igniting the environmental movement and helping inspire the creation of the Environmental Pro- tection Agency. Americans were concerned enough about the threat of nuclear war with the Soviet Union in the 1960s that many built backyard fallout shelters. Yet all the while, they had been unwittingly surrounding themselves with carcinogens in the name of convenience. Carson made that connection explicit, comparing pesticides and household chemi- cals to nuclear fallout. The message was clear: the world around us— including the intimate spaces where we live, work, and play—was in- creasingly being infiltrated by microscopic hazards. Indeed, the past half century has witnessed a steady stream of federal manufacturing and import bans on chemicals once commonly found in our food, home goods, and carpets and walls (DDT, PCBs, CFCs, and asbestos come to mind). Yet the number of threats posed to us by the environment still seems to multiply over time. One need only spend a day in California to come to the paranoid conclusion that nowhere is safe. Thanks to a law requiring businesses to publicly disclose if they use or produce any chemicals that have been shown to be potentially carcinogenic, people are bombarded with cancer warnings as they park in a garage, purchase liquor, stay at a hotel, lounge at a coffee shop, or visit an amusement park. ("The metal dust and diesel fumes given off by your favorite amusement park rides could give you cancer, and the state of California needs you to know," a *Popular Science* article sneers. "Also, the food you eat there might be fried, which could give you more cancer, and you might drink a beer there which also could give you cancer. The whole park is basically a death trap.")[7]

Hyperbole aside, it is often said that we live in a "risk society," in which environmental hazards are not mere by-products of the modern economy but some of its main outputs.[8] Yet many of these "manufactured risks" are unevenly distributed. Because industry and heavily trafficked roads cluster in economically vulnerable urban regions, poorer and minority city residents are at greater risk of premature death from exposure to particulate matter, ground-level ozone, and other pollutants.[9] Notwithstanding notable exceptions like Louisiana's so-called Cancer Alley (an eighty-five-mile stretch along the Mississippi River where dozens of petrochemical companies belch formaldehyde, benzene, and other carcinogens into the air and water surrounding suburbs and small towns), exurban and rural residents tend to enjoy cleaner air and water than their urban counterparts.

Almost everyone I came to know in Lycoming County cited the area's natural amenities, and its distance from what they saw as congested and polluted metropolitan regions like Pittsburgh and Philadelphia (aka "Filthadelphia"), as a major reason why they remained in or moved to the area. The advent of fracking, however, meant the imposition of an industrial infrastructure onto rural communities like Hughesville. Nationwide, over seventeen million Americans now live within one mile of an active oil or gas well.[10] Although no research to date has definitively proven a causal relationship between fracking and disease, "all phases of gas production involve complex mixtures of chemicals," including some with "significant toxicity."[11] Several studies have preliminarily linked shale gas extraction to low birth weight, respiratory ailments, skin rashes and headaches, and the death of pets and livestock.[12] Toxicology tests on residents in some "frack zones" have revealed elevated levels of heavy metals, arsenic, and carcinogens like benzene and tetrachloroethylene—to name just a few of the hundreds of toxins used in shale gas extraction that could potentially find their way into the surrounding water and air through faulty cement casing of gas wells, truck spills, flaring, and exhaust from compressor stations and on-site generators, dehydrators, and separators.[13] New York governor Andrew Cuomo (D) cited such studies to justify a statewide ban on fracking in 2014, saying more research is needed to prove it is safe. (Pennsylvania's then governor Tom Corbett (R), whose election campaign reportedly received about $1 million from the gas industry, removed a provision from Act 13, a 2012 overhaul of Pennsylvania's oil and gas laws, that would have funded a health registry—crucial to conducting robust health studies—for people living near gas wells.)[14] I met few people who claimed to be sickened by fracking. But that does not necessarily mean more such people don't exist. Gas companies have been known to buy claimants' silence through out-of-court settlements that include a "gag order."[15]

Even if fracking does increase morbidity, it could be years or even decades before its effects become apparent. The philosopher and antifracking activist Adam Briggle has likened the rapid proliferation of shale gas wells despite this uncertainty to "a drug that skipped over all the clinical trial stages . . . to go directly to mass commercialization."[16] In the end, it might prove impossible to tease apart the distinct health impacts of fracking from other contributing factors—whether environmental or genetic. Some people, like George, seemed unperturbed by the threat of toxic exposure. In July 2018, for instance, he mentioned to me in passing over e-mail that a foul industrial odor wafting from his well pad was so pungent that he had to close all his windows. This was not the first time; I too had smelled it in his yard before. Although he mocked a gas worker's explanation that it was just diesel fuel, he never investigated further or filed a complaint. Others, however, lived in a near-constant state of paranoia.

"The other day," Holly Bendorf told me, "I drank a glass of water that tasted funny. Now, it could just be because I didn't wash all the soap out of it. But you just get nervous and wonder if you are contaminated." Jim Finkler, who lived down the road from the Crawleys, couldn't help but wonder if his chronically swollen lymph nodes were somehow connected to fracking. When he and his wife Noreen were considering whether or not to purchase their property, in the 1980s, Jim—an avid angler—said that the presence of a creek in the backyard with abundant trout sealed the deal. But ever since 57,000 gallons of flowback water from an XTO wastewater storage tank spilled into the Sugar Run tributary in 2010, "I haven't seen a trout in this creek." Jim scoffed at the Pennsylvania DEP's conclusion that there was "no lasting environmental impact"; the state attorney general filed criminal charges against the Exxon subsidiary.[17] Like the Crawleys, the Finklers were also suffering from the effects of the nearby gas well's faulty cement casing, which infused their well water with methane. Strangely, their well water began leaving pink stains in their dishwasher, blender, and sink. Although Jim's ear, nose, and throat specialist was reportedly skeptical of any connection between his swollen lymph nodes and fracking, Jim told me he always made sure to remind the doctor that they had issues with their well water. His family refused to drink from the tap or cook with it. But they still used it for showers, owing to a lack of practical alternatives. That made Jim anxious.

The potential psychosocial effects of fracking are understood even less than the potential health effects. However, a review of the nascent research on this topic (most of which is based on surveys) suggests that "persons living in fracking communities" may endure "worry, anxiety, and depression about lifestyle, health, safety, and . . . changes to the physical landscape."[18] Simona Perry, who lived with and studied landowners in Bradford County, Pennsylvania, claims that the mental impact of fracking on many local residents was more severe than what we typically associate with stress. She describes a collective sense of "loss or fear of loss" so pervasive that it "consume[d] and alter[ed]" their everyday lives. Even many residents who supported fracking, she writes, worried that it "had forever altered the connections they had with their family histories, childhood memories, their lands, [and] their neighbors and communities."[19] According to Perry, the most apt descriptor for this experience is *trauma*. Although trauma is usually associated with specific horrific incidents, Kai Erikson long ago argued that "chronic disasters" (e.g., living in poverty) can be as traumatizing as episodic disasters like an earthquake. A chronic disaster, he writes, "is one that gathers force slowly and insidiously, creeping around one's defenses rather than smashing through them." It can produce "a numbness of spirit, a susceptibility to anxiety and rage and depression, a sense of helplessness . . . [and] a heightened apprehension about the physical and social environment."[20] Erikson contends that communities forced to endure uncontrollable insults to their environment and ongoing threats to their health may display these traumatic symptoms.

I'm not especially interested in whether the stressors associated with fracking can trigger reactions that satisfy the medical definition of trauma. It is clear, however, that some people I met in Lycoming County wrestled with feelings of loss, helplessness, and anxiety related to changes in their physical environment. Yet more than any of these somewhat narrow and clinical terms, the notion of *ambient insecurity* helps make sense of the range of distressing and disorienting experiences that folks like Cindy and Holly associated with fracking. Energy firms' capacity to reconfigure, or even erase, seemingly permanent features of the landscape shook some residents to the core: each time Cindy and I passed the well pad across the street from her property, she shuddered and shook her head, barely able to comprehend the God-like capacity of the energy firm to level the side of the mountain seemingly overnight. The extent to which residents' peace of mind and sense of community were supported by the serene rhythms of country life and the perceived safety of the natural environment only became apparent now that it seemed as if that foundation were crumbling.

Perhaps the most disquieting manifestation of ambient insecurity was the phenomenon of flaring, which occurred when petroleum companies burned off the gas of a newly drilled well before it was connected to a pipeline, so that the pressure would not build up. I will not soon forget the first time I encountered it. It was dusk, and I had just left Holly and Chriss's house. As I drove past an old cemetery, I slammed on my brakes in the middle of the road and gasped. The flame—over a mile away—raged higher than I could have imagined, looming over tree stands and fields and bathing the tombstones in an orange glow. The roar, like a hot-air balloon burner, echoed across the valley floor. I continued down Old Cemetery Road, drawn to the flare like a moth to a porch light, but began to get nervous as I approached it. It was night now, though one wouldn't even know it, because the fire cast sunset-like streaks across the sky. After pulling over on the side of the road, I had to psych myself up to leave the safety of my car. I was scared, even though there were two farmhouses closer still to the flare stack than where I had parked. I wondered what it felt like for those residents, whose homes looked like they would be engulfed in flames. From here, the flare sounded like a jet engine, only louder. Occasionally, it let off a deep, low rumble that caused me to jump into the woods on the presumption that a tractor trailer was approaching. I only took my fingers out of my ears to take pictures and video, though I was so unnerved by the awesome sight and sound that my hands shook uncontrollably. After about ten minutes, the din was getting into my head, scrambling my thoughts. I had to leave. Once in bed that night, the roar reverberated in my brain. The flare felt etched onto my retinas. It was one of the most startling things I've ever experienced.

The flare stack was only about a hundred feet from Cindy's property line. The next day, I e-mailed her to check in. She reported that, thankfully, the flaring had subsided—for now. "It is the first we have had peace in a year, at least, maybe longer," she wrote. When I met with her a few weeks later to share the videos I recorded that night, she was stunned all over again at the spectacle's intensity, even though Cindy had lived through it several times. It seemed alien, she said, and apocalyptic. She told me she felt like the flaring, which went on for days, would never end. Although the weather was finally warming up (it was late April), Cindy shuttered all her windows and plugged her ears. But the flare's sonic fury rattled the windows, which rattled her nerves. Just as disturbing was the obliteration of the stars. Flaring, in concert with construction lights, cloaked the environs in a gauzy orange—a phenomenon that Holly contemptuously called fracker borealis. For Cindy, it was literally disorienting, because the sky no longer reliably signaled the time of day. It felt unendingly like twilight, that odd and usually brief interlude between day and night. As a result, she felt in limbo. "I miss the dark," Cindy lamented, before adding fretfully, "Will it ever look like night again?"

* * *

The geographer Yi-Fu Tuan developed the evocative concept *topophilia* to describe the psychological experience of feeling strongly attached to a particular place.[21] Topophilia can entail much more than feelings of pleasure and aesthetic appreciation toward the environment. It can also be an anchor for identity and community. After all, local histories and folkways are often embedded in—and shaped by—the land. Residents' invocation of "rural values," and the way they contrasted the goodness of country life to the alleged ills of city living, signal how much their sense of personal well-being and attachment to their neighbors were bound up in the region's pastoral topography.

While the Arcadian landscape was a source of stability, security, and belonging for residents like Cindy, fracking instilled a *landscape of fear*. The notion of a landscape of fear, which refers to "a psychological topography that exists in the mind of prey" about where predators lurk, comes from ecology. The idea stems from the fact that the mere presence of predators in the environment can induce some animals who feel endangered to remain in a permanent state of hypervigilance and apprehension. The problem with this ostensibly adaptive response is that it can be debilitating—for instance, prey spend so much time watching out for predators that they devote insufficient time to foraging food or raising their young. The ambient insecurity triggered by fracking had an analogous effect on some people.[22] Everything they loved or relied on seemed threatened all at once: the air they breathed, the water they drank, favorite vistas, the tranquility of country roads, the integrity of the forests and the night sky, and their relationships with neighbors whose land use decisions impinged on their quality of life. The feeling that fracking augured, to quote author Seamus McGraw, "the end of country" left some feeling unable to plan for the future and alienated from their environs.[23] The angst this aroused could be crippling. The only obvious remedy, some concluded, was to evacuate.

CHAPTER 8

Overruled

On a brisk evening in March 2013, about thirty-five residents crammed into Fairfield Township's tiny municipal office to hear about and discuss one of the first proposed gas wells to be drilled in this rustic exurb (population: 2,700) six miles east of Billtown. As required by law, Inflection Energy, a small petroleum company headquartered in Colorado, had posted an ad in the local paper announcing its "conditional use" permit application to "construct a natural gas well pad or pads and drill a well or wells" on John and Shirley Eck's property. In accordance with the Fairfield Township Zoning Ordinance of 2007, the municipality's elected Board of Supervisors (BOS) convened a public hearing to receive written and oral comments about the proposed drilling and, in turn, decide whether or not to allow the project to move forward. Although leasing one's land required no public input, a permit to actually drill for gas did.

A large American flag hung from the white cinderblock wall. The three supervisors, all Republican white males dressed in blue jeans, casual button-up shirts, and sneakers, took their seat behind a Formica table that looked out on cramped rows of metal folding chairs. The locals occupying those Spartan seats were disproportionately male; their preferred uniform was work boots, plaid shirts, and Carhartt jackets or coveralls. To the supervisors' left, almost comically overdressed in a smart gray suit, sat Mike Wiley, the township solicitor. To their right sat a stenographer. It was apparent that the issue at hand, natural-gas wells, had attracted a greater crowd than the BOS was used to for its monthly postsuppertime meetings. Noting that almost every seat was taken,

BOS chairman Grant Hetler drew chuckles when he deadpanned, "It's great to see all you people here."

Chairman Hetler kicked off the proceedings by leading the Pledge of Allegiance. The solicitor then asked everyone wanting to speak that night to sign their name and address and be sworn in. I sat in the back row next to Ralph, who had arrived early and saved me a seat. Scanning the room, he wondered aloud if soon-to-be Hall of Fame pitcher Mike Mussina, who lived next to the proposed drilling site and already had a well pad on his own land, was in attendance (he was not). Three representatives from Inflection Energy sat immediately to my right, poring over a fat binder labeled "Eck Pad B." Ralph chatted up a young man next to us with a crew cut and piercing blue eyes, Joe Earnest, who said he was concerned, because he was raising two kids in a house just three hundred feet from the proposed development. Ralph asked if Joe had got a baseline water test so that he would know if drilling impacted his water. 'Yeah,' Joe huffed. 'I got twelve pages of shit I don't understand.'

Inflection's lawyer, a young man who sported a dark suit and damp blond curls, made his way to the front of the room with Tom Erwin, the company's chief engineer. Few would mistake the fast-talking attorney, whose bravado came across as a bit unseemly in this context, for a local. But Tom, who spoke plainly and dressed even plainer, in blue jeans and a flannel, blended right in. This was just as Inflection intended. When the small, Colorado-based company began operating its first drilling rig in the area, it entrusted Tom—with his thirty-plus years of experience working in the oil and gas industry—to take up residence in Montoursville and act as the public face of the company. His job title, senior field operations manager, was a misnomer. His métier was community outreach (and, it turned out, persuasion). It felt like I saw him everywhere: an information session about gas royalties at Penn College, a Democratic Party policy committee hearing on drilling on state land, the Little League World Series, the Bullfrog Brewery—you name it. He seemed to get along with everyone, and he often lingered after events for as long as anyone wanted to talk. He kind of reminded me of Ralph.

Occasionally sounding impatient, Inflection's lawyer asked Tom a series of generic questions (required by law) about the details of the permit request and what the community could expect as far as traffic, noise, and light pollution. Tom responded to each query earnestly and deliberately. Making eye contact with residents, Tom pointed out where the company planned to place Eck Pad A and Eck Pad B on a map and described how many acres (about seven) they would need to clear for the pads. 'They're basically going right by my house,' Joe Earnest grumbled. 'I didn't realize it was gonna be two pads.' Tom promised that the well pads would be hidden from the road, then he moved on to discussing the one-acre impoundment pond that would be built to store the millions of gallons of water used to frack the wells. One of the supervisors, betraying a slight smirk, interjected, "How many tractor trailers to fill the pond?" A number of attendees let out a knowing, nervous laugh. Tom looked down before uttering, "Roughly 1,600." The audience groaned, and two of the supervisors grimaced. Tom tried to reassure the BOS that Inflection would look into using a water pipeline in place of the tanker trucks. 'We want pipelines as much as you do because it's easier for us,' he explained, before conceding in response to the chairman's request for clarification that they were seeking permission to drill before knowing if a water pipeline was feasible.[1] Another supervisor asked if wastewater would be stored in the impoundment pond, and Tom calmly assured him that the pond would hold only fresh water. "Produced water," he explained, would be held in on-site "frac tanks." When asked how it would be disposed of, Tom acknowledged that their wastewater management plan was not finalized; it could be reused for a future fracking job or hauled to a treatment facility. 'How do you keep the brine water from contaminating the groundwater,' a supervisor asked while stroking his mustache with a forefinger. Tom patiently walked through the multiple safeguards (e.g., several layers of steel and cement casing) designed to ensure the integrity of the well. The supervisor nodded his head and stayed silent, indicating satisfaction with Tom's testimony.

The conversation returned to truck traffic. Tom estimated that there would be between 150 and 300 big rigs running up the country lane each day during the three–five-month construction phase. During the subsequent two-month "completion phase" (when the wells are fracked),

FIG. 8.1. A water impoundment pond (iced over). Photograph by Tristan Spinksi.

residents could expect to see about 225 big-rig trucks on the road daily
(mostly hauling water and sand, the main ingredients of frac fluid).
These figures rankled some residents, who began murmuring about the
dangers and inconveniences associated with such heavy truck traffic
on the township's narrow and twisty roads. 'We won't run the trucks
during school [busing] hours,' Tom offered in an effort to allay their
concerns.

It was shaping up to be a long night. After an hour and twenty minutes of questioning, Tom looked relieved to be turning the hot seat over
to Inflection's Director of Regulatory Affairs and Environmental Health
and Safety, Thomas Gillespie. A "licensed professional geologist,"
Thomas gave off a grandiose air in his dark blazer, vest replete with a
gold pocket watch chain, trimmed gray beard, and spectacles. He began
his testimony by highlighting that he has taught at numerous universi-
ties and consulted for the DEP. In response to the Inflection lawyer's

first question, Thomas confidently asserted that in his expert opinion the proposed drilling would have no adverse effects on the environment or people's health. (Although Ralph and I whispered about whether a master's in geology and a professional license gave one standing to determine that fracking did not pose a threat to public health, we stayed silent when the township solicitor asked if anyone wanted to challenge the witness's expertise.) He then proceeded to describe the process for securing the water-withdrawal and drilling permits ad nauseam, grinning as he ticked off all the environmental codes and agencies involved (e.g., filing a "water management plan" with the SRBC [Susquehanna River Basin Commission]; filing E&S [erosion and sediment] and EC [environmental control] plans with the DEP). Thomas's rapid-fire barrage of information and acronyms seemed intended not so much to educate residents about the permitting process as to convey the message that lots of regulators (perhaps too many!) had looked at Inflection's proposal and determined that it was safe.

In response to a supervisor's question about testing local water wells before gas drilling, Thomas noted that the DEP "basically makes us test wells," even though, in his interpretation of the state law governing gas drilling at the time (Act 13), they were not mandated to perform baseline water tests. But he hastily added that Inflection was glad to test all water wells within three thousand feet of a gas well, because it benefited them too. When a resident complains about water contamination from fracking, Thomas noted dryly, "If we want the DEP on our side, we have to have that baseline test." Residents' ears seemed to prick up when a supervisor asked about a resident complaint regarding her well water after Inflection drilled a nearby gas well. Joe looked worried, furrowing his brow and sighing. But Gillespie quickly parried, claiming that the DEP concurs with Inflection's conclusion that the problem was "internal to her water system."

By the time the official question and answer portion of the hearing rolled around, it was past many residents' bedtime (10:00 p.m.). Yet most dutifully remained. Harvey Katz, a retired field biologist and widower who cofounded the RDA and was a regular at BOS meetings, was one of the first to stand up. Known for his long-windedness, Harvey was asked how long he would speak for by the sniggering chairman, who then called a ten-minute break so that the stenographer could rest her hands before taking Harvey's question. An expert on wetlands, Harvey expressed concern that the excess stormwater runoff created by clearing trees for the well pads would deplete well water. Things got a bit testy after Harvey pointedly asked Inflection's geologist if he was aware of a "New Hampshire study" showing that increased runoff leads to slower recharge rates for groundwater.[2] Gillespie tried to evade the question, emphasizing his expertise as one of the consultants on the DEP's updated regulations on runoff, until Harvey cornered him by asking, "Are you familiar with the study or not?" Thomas admitted he was not, which prompted Harvey to lecture him about its findings until Chairman Hetler gently cut him off by exclaiming, "Thanks, Harv! Got it."

A gentleman asked whether it was the homeowner's responsibility to determine if something went wrong with their well water after gas drilling. Thomas conceded that it was. Although Thomas offered assurances that Inflection would "honor all concerns" for "as long as we are operating in the valley," the man shook his head in disappointment. For the remaining half hour, the conversation returned to the chief complaint—traffic. An older man blurted out that he'd like to see respect for homeowners' quality of life. Restricting trucks' use of "jake brakes" (noisy, compression-release engine brakes) at night, he said, would be a start. Though he made no promises, Tom Erwin said Inflection would tell its drivers to minimize their use of jake brakes. A supervisor voiced skepticism that heavy equipment would be able to safely navigate the S-turn at White Church Road, which led more than one resident to shout aloud that the road couldn't handle it. As evidence, a man in the back yelled that big rigs got hung up there already. What would happen, someone else asked, if an emergency vehicle needed to get through? Joe, who had been doing back-of-the-envelope calculations of how many trucks would bypass his house, stood up and bitterly interjected, "So we're talking about 18,000 to 20,000 trucks coming past *my* house?!" Tom stared at the floor to avoid Joe's glare and muttered yes. Two of the supervisors sneered, betraying their disgust at the volume of trucks and Inflection's apparent nonchalance. Tallman Hollow and Carey Hill

FIG. 8.2. Gas truck traffic and resultant road conditions on Carey Hill Road in Upper Fairfield Township. Photographs by Colin Jerolmack.

Roads, which Inflection was currently using to service a well pad, were a complete nightmare, they complained. Tom looked ashamed, admitting that they had underestimated how much the heavy trucks would cause congestion and tear up the road. He guaranteed that they would be better prepared this time. But when an astute resident followed up by asking if they had done a traffic study of White Church Road, Tom was caught flat-footed. He hesitated, then looked back at his lawyer for guidance. He eventually shook his head no, but quickly added that a traffic study could be done if need be.

The hearing was finally called to a close at 10:40. After a brief huddle, the supervisors—who looked exhausted and ready to go home—announced that Inflection needed to perform a traffic study before the BOS would consider voting on the application. The hearing would continue at next month's scheduled BOS meeting. Inflection's lawyer, geologist, and engineer looked surprised. They fully expected, it seemed, to walk out of there with an approval. After all, their permit applications in the neighboring township had been a cakewalk. The drilling rig, which probably cost over $10,000 each day to keep in the valley, was sitting idle on another well pad waiting to begin its work at the Ecks'.

* * *

The hearing seemed like archetypal self-governance in action: informed citizens and their directly elected, unpaid representatives came together in free association to deliberate about a local issue and collectively decide what course of action served the public interest. To be sure, state bureaucrats (e.g., the DEP) played a major regulatory role. But the hearing implied that it was civic voluntarism in Fairfield that ultimately controlled how fracking proceeded in the community. This is the essence of *home rule*, whereby communities are empowered to "craft ordinances and make decisions based on local needs, rather than having to follow a one-size-fits-all state code that's decided by state legislators."[3]

It didn't take long, however, for me to come to the discomfiting conclusion that municipal permit hearings pertaining to fracking were little more than Tocquevillian artifice. The reality was that the state enjoyed

almost complete jurisdiction over the placement of natural-gas infrastructure. Indeed, the subsequent "continuance" hearing for Eck Pads
A and B in Fairfield provided the community with an unwelcome civic
lesson regarding its lack of decision-making power over fracking in its
own backyard. The parking lot was so full I had to leave my car in an
illegal space. A number of the same skeptical residents, including Joe
Earnest, were back and seemingly spoiling to fight against Inflection's
planned invasion of truck traffic. The township solicitor began the hearing by noting that Inflection had performed the requested engineering
study; its findings allegedly confirmed that White Church Road offered
a sufficient turning radius for oversized vehicles, with the caveat that
"traffic control procedures are required." The solicitor then put forth a
list of conditions that had to be met for permit approval. All of the conditions, though, were trivial requests that were either already required
by law or were standard industry practice—e.g., the gas company must
create a road maintenance agreement, post warning signs on the road
for motorists, and obtain all required federal, state, and local permits;
gas trucks may not operate during school busing hours, park on public
roads, or go over the speed limit. As soon as these conditions were read
out, and only minutes into the hearing, the supervisors moved to vote.
Only after Joe interrupted the first "yea" to ask if the audience could
speak did the BOS reverse course and listen to testimony from
residents.

Joe had taken the supervisors' decision to issue a continuance last
time as evidence that the BOS was taking residents' ambivalence about
the project seriously. Because the proposed drilling site was in an area
zoned "Residential-Agricultural" (R-A), fracking was not "permitted as
a matter of course."[4] On paper, the BOS had the authority to determine
if gas drilling was allowable as a "conditional use," based on their judg-
ment of whether it was compatible with other uses in the R-A district.
Joe was confident that he and other residents had shown last time that
it was not. But it was now obvious that approval was a foregone conclusion. The continuance was simply due diligence. Now that the BOS had
the traffic study in hand, its members seemed intent on avoiding any
more public debate and quickly approving the wells—even though

Inflection's study didn't address several of the concerns raised at the last hearing. Joe was livid, arguing that there was no way trucks could make the turn on White Church without going into the other lane. Inflection's claim that they could, he said, just proved that they didn't drive on that road. Joe added, "Last time we talked about brake retarders, but I didn't hear anything about that." Inflection's lawyer insisted that the issue was beyond the BOS's control; only PennDOT (the Pennsylvania Department of Transportation) could regulate noise from jake brakes. The township's solicitor nodded, "That's why we worded the condition the way we did—'best efforts to encourage.'" As some in the audience hissed, Tom Erwin jumped in to smooth things over, promising to "talk to our guys" about not using their jake brakes unless they had to.

Harvey Katz, the retired biologist, pressed Inflection about inconsistencies he said he had discovered between the plan Inflection submitted to the BOS and the plan it submitted to the DEP. Thomas Gillespie, who seemed caught off guard by Harvey's sleuthing, stuttered a bit as he responded. They gave the BOS a simpler plan, he said, because the DEP plan had a lot of unnecessary details that the public didn't need to see. Although Harvey and a few others shook their heads in disgust, Gillespie seemed oblivious to how his statement could be understood as belittling to residents. The BOS, however, seemed unperturbed by Gillespie's confession, just as it seemed untroubled by the plan's lack of clarity about how many gas wells would ultimately be drilled, whether or not Inflection would use a water pipeline rather than tanker trucks, and how it would dispose of wastewater.

Harvey pursed his lips and sniped, "We'll leave it at that." As soon as he was seated, the BOS chairman hastily called for a vote (again). In deference to grumbles that one of the supervisors, Scott Harris, had a conflict of interest, since he lived next door to the Ecks and had also leased his land to Inflection, the chairman announced that Harris would abstain from voting and noted, "He's part of the deal." (Harris had not said a word during either of the permit hearings and spent a lot of time looking at the floor.) The two remaining supervisors moved to approve both pads. Within fifteen minutes of our arrival, everyone was heading for the exit. I asked Joe if he felt like his concerns were addressed. He smiled wanly. 'As much as they're gonna be. They're gonna approve it no matter what. It doesn't matter what we say.' Tom Erwin, who seemed uneasy about the lingering tension, intercepted Joe in the parking lot. After giving Joe his card, Tom invited him to call anytime if he had any problems with the trucks. 'We're not gonna let them keep you up and make all that noise with the jake brakes,' Tom pledged. It seemed like a good-faith commitment on Tom's part. Nonetheless, it followed a pattern that Inflection had established throughout the course of these hearings: make oral promises to be good neighbors and minimize impact, but avoid putting it in writing.

From Joe's perspective, his elected representatives had sold him out. But the truth was that the BOS had no choice but to approve this and every other fracking-related project that came before it. At the time, Pennsylvania municipalities were subject to the full force of Act 13. Signed into law in 2012, by Tom Corbett, the Republican pro-growth governor whose largest individual campaign donations came from oil and gas companies, Act 13 asserted that the regulation of oil and gas is a "statewide concern" and is therefore "within the sole authority of the state to regulate." Municipal governments were forbidden from establishing more stringent rules than the state's uniform standards. And, in what many "home rule" proponents saw as an unconstitutional assault on local sovereignty, the act mandated that municipalities allow oil and gas operations "as a permitted use in all zoning districts."[5]

Historically, zoning has been the most powerful—if not the only—tool available to small towns to mediate between private-property rights and the public good. Pennsylvania municipalities like Fairfield designated R-A zones to foster "quiet, medium-density residential environment[s] while encouraging the continuation of agricultural activities and the preservation of farmland." Industrial uses are typically discouraged, if not forbidden, in an R-A district. Should someone seek to site an industrial use in an R-A zone, the burden of proof is on the applicant to demonstrate that the proposed conditional use does not conflict with the goal of preserving the area's rural character.[6] The oil and gas industry was keenly aware, it seems, that fracking might not pass muster in many locales as a conditional use in an R-A zone, and that municipalities could wield zoning as a cudgel to severely restrict, if not ban, fracking. It found many friends in the Republican-controlled legislature, which was eager to entice energy companies to bring their jobs and investment to Pennsylvania instead of, say, West Virginia. Act 13 killed two birds with one stone: it ensured that Pennsylvania remained the only major gas-producing state not to impose a severance tax based on the amount of gas produced, and that municipalities could not impede fracking through local zoning ordinances.

The oil and gas BOS hearings I attended, like many others, amounted to little more than a tragic simulacrum of civic engagement. Energy firms were still required to seek a conditional-use permit, but municipalities had no authority to deny one on the grounds that it was inconsistent with existing uses in an R-A zone. Writing about a similar situation in Texas, philosopher Adam Briggle observes that the public-hearing process "made it look like [local governments] had the power to deny a gas well, but they really had no such power."[7] Not only was the Fairfield BOS obliged to approve the permit, it was also unable to impose conditions that went beyond state regulations. This explains the supervisors' indifference to Inflection's lack of specificity regarding its plans for transporting fresh water to the site (and wastewater from the site). Because the BOS could not mandate that Inflection pipe water to the Eck pads to mitigate truck traffic, it couldn't use Inflection's noncommittal response as a basis to deny the permit.

It makes sense that petroleum companies, many of which leased thousands of contiguous acres that spanned municipal boundaries, would consider it onerous to deal with a patchwork of distinct regulations across the towns where they operated. The architects of Act 13 said it simply required municipalities "to treat all industrial uses as equal," meaning that they could not "require different and potentially more stringent restrictions" on fracking "than those for other industrial activities."[8] But the zoning preemptions that Pennsylvania and other ostensibly home-rule, shale-rich states like Texas and Colorado enacted to enable the "reasonable development" of petroleum make fracking "a uniquely invasive industry," Briggle argues.[9] Case in point: at the same BOS meeting where supervisors could do little but gripe as Inflection described its plans to put thousands of big rigs on the road, the BOS rejected a local firm's request to make permanent a temporary gravel parking lot for twenty trucks. Even the company's plea for an extension of the temporary permit was denied. "They gotta be out of there," Chairman Hetler growled, adding that the road could not handle that amount of heavy trucks entering and exiting the lot. He spoke with authority, and the BOS's word was final. Similarly, Briggle notes that, in places like Denton, Texas, zoning rules bar uses as innocuous as a bakery from residential districts on the grounds that they are "incompatible land uses."[10] Yet caravans of diesel trucks, massive drilling rigs, raging flare stacks, dynamite explosions, pipelines, and "man camps" must by law be considered uses that are compatible with residential and agricultural zones.

Seven townships in Pennsylvania filed a lawsuit against the state alleging that Act 13 was an unconstitutional usurpation of local sovereignty (see *Robinson Township v. Commonwealth*). Only two, however, dared to assert their claim to home rule in the face of Act 13 by enacting local restrictions on oil and gas operations: Grant (population: 741) and Highland (population: 492) Townships both voted to ban so-called injection wells (disposal sites where frac wastewater is buried) after learning that the DEP had approved permits for an injection well to be sited in each community that would receive up to 45,000 barrels of toxic waste per month. For many local leaders, Grant and Highland served as a cautionary tale about the perils of saying no to fracking. PGE (Pennsylvania General Energy), which sought one of the injection wells, teamed up with a powerful industry lobbying group to file a lawsuit in federal court claiming that Grant's ordinance violated the corporation's constitutional rights. Not only did the judge nullify the town's home rule ordinance, she sanctioned the two attorneys representing Grant for $52,000. Highland's "Community Bill of Rights" met a similar fate at the hands of Seneca Resources and the same federal judge. In both cases, the Community Environmental Legal Defense Fund (CELDF) represented the townships pro bono and absorbed the penalties. But the outcomes shook other townships. Several municipal leaders privately expressed to me their fear that denying a conditional-use permit could, in theory, trigger a lawsuit that would bankrupt their town.

*   *   *

Residents who participated in or were familiar with BOS meetings sometimes had a hard time wrapping their heads around their municipality's distinct lack of jurisdiction over oil- and gas-related matters. Perhaps nowhere was this more apparent than in a series of public hearings held in the spring of 2013 at the volunteer fire hall in Old Lycoming, a suburb of Williamsport, to consider a conditional-use permit for a water withdrawal facility. The proposed site of the facility, which would siphon up to 275,000 gallons of water a day from Lycoming Creek to service gas wells located further north, was directly behind the Marcellus Operations Center, a large commercial warehouse catering to gas companies that was surrounded by a parking lot and adjacent to a strip mall.

Ralph, who as usual had his finger on the pulse of community sentiment, predicted a big turnout for the first hearing and vocal opposition to the conditional use. Because Old Lycoming was a densely populated, quasi-urban district contiguous with Billtown, no land leasing or gas drilling had taken place there (or ever would). That meant that locals had nothing to gain from supporting the permit. The fact that the nearby Stroehmann Bakeries production site and hundreds of area residences relied on shallow water wells fed by Lycoming Creek meant that they potentially had something to lose.

When I arrived fifteen minutes before the start of the hearing, I had to drive to the back of the lot next door to the fire hall to find a spot. Almost all of the 150 or so metal chairs set up inside were full by the time the meeting began. One by one, as news cameras rolled and the township solicitor and permit applicant sat staidly behind a table, over twenty impassioned residents took the microphone to denounce the proposal and send the message that Lycoming Creek was not for sale. At the outset of the hearing, one of the supervisors, Janet Hall, dramatically left the table where the supervisors sat to join the audience, announcing that she recused herself to join the "aggrieved parties." She was the first to testify during the public comment period, pleading with her colleagues to recognize that the conditional use was inappropriate, even though the area is zoned industrial, because over five hundred residents and the bakery relied exclusively on the creek for water. As locals rose to their feet to celebrate Janet's audacity to join them in solidarity against the permit, she beseeched, "Please do not destroy the sanctity of Lycoming Creek Valley by robbing it of its vital water supply!"

The "sometimes unruly public hearing," as the *Sun-Gazette* called it, was a flexing of grassroots community anger against the industry that, to me, seemed unimaginable in the rural surrounds.[11] Some residents screamed and even cried about the preciousness of their water. A few threatened that they would personally come for the developer if their well went dry. When the township solicitor interjected with a plea for a "modicum of respect," he was heckled. The crescendo came about an hour into the public testimony, when an elderly man wearing a flannel shirt and a trucker's cap stared down the supervisors as he intoned, "We all know our wells are gonna go dry." Many in the crowd yelled, "Yep!" as he continued, "When it goes dry, what's my house worth?" Like a call and response, residents shouted, "nothing!" "What we have here," the man concluded as residents hooted and hollered, "is one man's greed against everyone else's lives!"

The audience was whipped into a frenzy. The next speaker threatened that the BOS didn't "want to make this many people angry"; another added, "we're all in this together." But the township solicitor admonished residents for their lack of legal acumen and threw cold water on the idea that their testimony could affect the outcome. The Susquehanna River Basin Commission (SRBC), he reminded them, had certified that the withdrawal of 225,000 gallons per day would have no adverse impact on the Lycoming Creek watershed. On that basis, it had already approved the permit request. The solicitor noted that there was a thirty-day window during which residents could try to appeal the SRBC permit; no one had. The BOS didn't have the authority to dispute the interstate agency's assessment or revisit its decision. As a conditional use (as opposed to a zoning variance) under Act 13, the BOS *must* allow the withdrawal permit so long as "reasonable conditions" are met. To deny a permit, the solicitor intoned, residents have to demonstrate that the proposed use would have "unmitigable adverse effects" on safety and well-being. In his view, they failed. Because the SRBC determined that the creek would not be impacted, any claims about dry wells had no merit.

Given the extraordinary level of public interest in the issue, it had already been decided before the hearing began that the BOS would not render a decision that evening. In the end, the BOS dedicated a half dozen consecutive monthly meetings to the water withdrawal permit. Residents wised up. In subsequent hearings, they changed the narrative away from dry wells and toward the hazards allegedly posed by the fifty-five to sixty trucks that would come and go from the site each day if the permit were approved. Much of one hearing was dedicated to attacking the credibility of an engineer who worked for the permit applicant, in order to throw doubt on his testimony. Against all odds, residents' strategy worked. The two remaining supervisors denied the water withdrawal permit on the grounds that it "did not comport with the health, safety, and welfare needs of our citizens." They noted that the engineer's witness testimony was "seriously flawed," and that the application was troublingly vague—for instance, there was no initial lighting study, and over the course of the hearings the boundaries for the project kept shifting. Insufficient evidence was provided, they added, that dozens of big rigs could safely enter and exit the property. Finally, in an apparent nod to the traditional power of municipalities to maintain the character of communities through zoning, the BOS argued that the applicant did not give "much effort" to "address the generally residential characteristics of the neighborhood."[12] Of the twenty or so residents present— attendance had gradually waned over the previous five months—most stood and triumphantly applauded.

The victory was short lived. A half year later, a Lycoming County judge overturned the BOS's permit denial. Noting that the increase in traffic would be less than 3 percent on a busy commercial road that already hosted trucks, he said that concerns about dangers posed by trucks servicing the water withdrawal site were unfounded. Regarding what originally was residents' chief concern—dry water wells—the judge affirmed that water was not an "issue before the board" of supervisors in the first place, and thus was not an issue "before this court," because the

SRBC had sole authority over the matter.[13] Three months later, the Old Lycoming BOS met again with its tail between it legs. It reversed its previous decision and approved the permit, subject to "reasonable conditions." Even the conditions had been dictated by the judge. Local sovereignty was overruled.

* * *

From a Tocquevillian perspective, state laws that preempt local control over the placement of oil and gas infrastructure stymie self-rule. If the essence of democracy is that people have a say over matters that affect their lives, then local government "is the political home of informed consent."[14] The primary means by which municipalities have traditionally safeguarded procedural due process for residents is through municipal zoning, which a Pennsylvania judge hearing the *Robinson Township v. Commonwealth* case implied is "the purest voice of the people's desires and interests."[15] As political theorist Theda Skocpol notes, it has historically been conservatives who pine for the purported golden era of Jefferson, "when local civic voluntarism solved the country's problems apart from—actually instead of—extralocal government and politics."[16] So it is deeply ironic that it is Republican statehouses that have passed or bolstered oil and gas preemption laws as part of what the author and MSNBC reporter Zachary Roth considers a broader "war on local democracy," relegating municipalities to creatures of the state, even as they have framed (to great success) federal oversight of fracking as government overreach.[17] Community decision-making, it seems, ought only be enabled if locals' interests align with those of state political elites.[18]

Preemption enraged many residents who turned up at BOS meetings. Most endorsed, or took for granted, the fact that this was a venue where they could voice concern over proposed new land uses (e.g., a cell phone tower) and be a part of making decisions that impacted the common good. Even BOS meetings in sparsely populated townships on mundane topics—like whether to replace an aging salt truck—routinely drew a critical mass and sparked spirited deliberation. Locals treasured their capacity to decide these matters for themselves and took that responsibility seriously. At the Old Lycoming water withdrawal permit hearing, many questioned why an interstate bureaucracy located eighty-four miles away (in Harrisburg) had the authority to sanction the sale of the creek water that fed their water wells. Some, who admitted they had never heard of the SRBC, said they were insulted that it did not even bother to send a representative to the BOS hearings to talk with them.

What stood out to me in some residents' remarks at the Old Lycoming water withdrawal permit hearing was not only their liberalist appeal to local sovereignty but also their message of prioritizing the public good over individual profit. They affirmed the Lockean proviso, arguing in effect that the applicant's property rights ought to be restricted to the extent that they threatened to usurp others' ability to enjoy a limited public good—water. A reverend preached about doing what is ethically right versus what is legally permissible. A fourth-generation farmer and mother stared into the eyes of the permit applicant and exhorted him to recognize that "There comes a time in your life where you have to give back to your community." She was followed by a man who asked, "What are you using the water for? Not our benefit!" He closed with a politically poignant rhetorical question: "After all, this is *our* water, isn't it?"

For Tocqueville, home rule invigorated democracy. For the political economist Elinor Ostrom, home rule was a mechanism for short-circuiting the tragedy of the commons. Ostrom won a Nobel Prize for refuting Garrett Hardin's Hobbesian conclusion that "free" actors inevitably usurp communal resources. Her analysis of communities around the world that successfully self-managed finite shared resources led her to conclude that people who feel like community stakeholders, empowered to participate in Tocquevillian self-governance, feel honor bound to pursue strategies that safeguard the commonwealth.[19] One oft-cited example are lobster zone councils in Maine, whose members prevent overfishing by agreeing to follow community-developed norms (e.g., trap limits, time/day restrictions, and trapping boundaries) and internally monitoring and punishing violators. Before the councils, lobster catches off the coast of Maine were in sudden and steep decline. The recognition that many of the beneficiaries were not state residents, combined with the fear that authorities might ban lobster fishing outright, prompted local lobstermen to self-organize. Every lobsterman licensed to fish in a particular zone is a voting member of its council. Councils develop rules based on local needs and conditions; two-thirds of councilmembers must approve any rule change. Maine's Commissioner of Marine Resources is the ultimate arbiter of what becomes law, but this state official usually follows the lead of the local lobster councils. In this way, independent lobstermen act as "co-managers," sharing authority over lobster fishing with the state.[20]

"We needn't be selfless communards," the historian Cathy Gere argues, "to escape the trap of Hardin's 'rational' herdsmen." The lesson of successful commons governance, Gere maintains, is that even if our species is fundamentally self-interested, it is also "incorrigibly social" and "perfectly capable—under the right conditions—of rational, bottom-up stewardship of commonly owned resources."[21] If we create conditions that foster trust, accountability, and egalitarian decision-making at the local level, Ostrom believed, a kind of civic environmentalism could take root. As a result of collective deliberation that helps stakeholders see how mutual restraint benefits everyone's livelihood or well-being in the long run, community members would voluntarily construct "mutual agreements that create the additional restraint required for conservation" of communal resources.[22] Locals would come to view these restraints as legitimate, because they are constructed by the very people who use the resources and are impacted by their use (rather than being designed by extra-local bureaucrats) and because they're adapted to conditions on the ground (rather than being a one-size-fits-all rule drafted in a faraway capitol). The restraints and enforcement mechanisms that result from self-governance, Ostrom has shown, may be better at protecting common-pool resources than "restrictions imposed by outsiders with little knowledge or understanding of local conditions."[23]

The extent to which BOS meetings and the mechanism of municipal zoning conform to Ostrom's "design principles" for governing a commons sustainably and equitably is remarkable. If we take a more expansive view of the commons, so as to incorporate quality of life, tranquility, the night sky, and viewsheds, it becomes apparent that zoning ordinances are effectively communal agreements to restrict private-property rights in order to conserve a finite shared resource (whether groundwater or an area's "rural character"). BOS meetings and public hearings are venues where locals can deliberate, on a case-by-case basis, whether particular private land uses are compatible with the needs of the community. If not, they can petition the BOS to reject them. Given that many locals viewed land sovereignty as a natural right, some might chafe when the time came that they faced restrictions on the use of their own property. Yet most gladly abided the municipal civic compact implied in zoning ordinances anyway, both because their own community helped make the rules and because it protected them from potential spillover effects of others' private land uses.

Although many landowners made the decision to lease their land *privately*, their testimony at permit hearings suggests that they granted some legitimacy to the idea that drilling and fracking operations were *public* issues that required some degree of community input and consent. In the absence of state preemption, there is reason to believe that some BOS conditional-use hearings would have resulted in greater restrictions on the placement of natural-gas infrastructure—if not outright permit denials.

Many locals had a dim view of the state bureaucracy most responsible for regulating oil and gas: the DEP. Sometimes, that distrust was based on the perception that the agency was in the pocket of the very industry it was charged with overseeing—a form of government failure called regulatory capture.[24] Indeed, Tom Crawley was not the only person who had the impression that the DEP was "not doing anything" to hold the industry accountable when things went wrong. "As far as the individuals," Tom opined, the people at the DEP "want to do something. I get that feeling, but I'm getting the feeling that their hands are being tied by the people above them." He asked rhetorically, "Whose hand is out and who's putting money in their pocket?" It wasn't a bad hunch. Michael Krancer, who was appointed DEP secretary in 2011 by the industry-backed governor Tom Corbett, after Krancer's father donated handsomely to Corbett's campaign and the state Republican committee,[25] was viewed by environmental groups like the Clean Air Council as an "aggressive proponent of expanding the economic opportunities tied to natural gas extraction."[26] Speaking before the US House Subcommittee on Water Resources and Environment, he dismissed research that raised concerns about the safety of fracking as "suspect science."[27] And he resisted federal efforts to investigate the most infamous case of contamination in the state, in Dimock. A DEP employee accused his office of withholding information from water well tests near active gas wells that showed evidence of contamination; a lawsuit filed in western Pennsylvania claimed that the DEP faked air test results to hide pollution.[28] Krancer resigned from the DEP in 2013 to become a fracking lobbyist for Blank Rome LLP; he later cofounded Silent Majority Strategies, which claims in its mission statement to work "with the energy industry to . . . dispel misinformation by the opponents to sensible and environmentally responsible public policy."[29]

Cynicism toward the DEP ran deeper than concerns about possible corruption. It had to do with where the agency was located: Harrisburg, a city two hours away. Sociologist Robert Wuthnow argues that Washington, DC, is distant geographically *and* culturally from heartland residents, who perceive it as "beholden to urban interests." I heard the same thing about Harrisburg from local state legislators like Garth Everett and their constituents. A common lament was about the outsize political influence of the state's liberal urban areas in the southeast and southwest. Locals complained that Philadelphia and Pittsburgh hoarded the general fund for progressive pet policies like food stamps and public transportation. "The basis of small-town life," Wuthnow writes, "is not only that it is 'rural' but that it is small, which means what happens is close enough to witness firsthand and to experience intimately enough to understand and have some hope of influencing."[30] In other words, the degree of voluntary association and face-to-face interaction with local representatives that small-town living affords creates the expectation that democracy is something that people can experience in their daily lives. "Big government" will almost always be distrusted, not just because of locals' disdain for centralized authority but because it remains abstract. They cannot see it in their community or get to know it, or yell at it in a town hall meeting or encounter it at the general store in the way they do with their county commissioners or township supervisors. (Similarly, Ostrom and her colleagues have argued that many folks resist "externally imposed institutions" that regulate their use of a common-pool resource if local communities were not involved in drafting the regulations.)[31]

The DEP did little to dispel conservatives' fears that it embodied what Thomas Jefferson called "tyranny in government." In 2017, it slapped Grant and Highland townships with a lawsuit, claiming their municipal bans on wastewater injection wells "unlawfully interfere with state oil-and-gas policies"—despite the fact that Act 13's preemption law was declared unconstitutional in 2013.[32] The DEP's argument—that there is "no constitutional right to local self-government" regarding fracking—mirrored that of the petroleum companies that had already sued the two towns for daring to assert local sovereignty. On the very same day that the DEP initiated the lawsuit, it approved new permits for injection wells in both communities.[33] In effect, the state agency ostensibly charged with safeguarding the environment on behalf of Pennsylvania residents forced two towns to live with a land use that they considered unsafe and incompatible with a rural district. "This is not a pollution problem," a community organizer in Grant contended. "It is a democracy problem."[34]

According to one of the state Supreme Court Judges who struck down Act 13's preemption law (*Robinson Township v. Commonwealth*), local control has historically been "fundamental to due process concerns of protecting a resident and his property from being harmed by other residents and their property."[35] Most of the citizens who turned up at BOS hearings in Fairfield, Old Lycoming, and elsewhere weren't opposed to fracking per se. What left locals aggrieved was learning that they had no say whatsoever over a land use that would impact them. To them, zoning preemption was state-sanctioned procedural injustice. In the name of development, the state had repudiated the tenet of self-determination.

CHAPTER 9

Town and Country

There is a threat at my doorstep that causes me to fluctuate between cowering in fear, basking in denial and screaming in outrage. I don't know how to do battle with so great an enemy. What great irony, as for 30 years, I have been a messenger of good health and well-being.

These days, I am spending hours planning how I might gather my family, pull up stakes and find a new homeland. We are no longer safe here. The gas drillers have arrived and staked their claim to hundreds of thousands of acres of Penns Woods.

For decades, the only access road to this remote, beautiful and wildlife-rich area was Butternut Grove—a narrow, "no outlet" road that goes past my driveway and used to dead end at a hiking trail at the top of the mountain. Most days, not a single car drove by during my 2-mile walk along this road. I could ride my horse up the mountain, to the place where the one-lane road became Dad-Dad Chapman trail on state forestland. That trail is now gone, gated off, and posted with trespass warnings carrying severe penalties. Chain-saws and hundreds of gravel-carrying dump trucks have changed the narrow trail into a wide gravel road through the forest and onto a well pad. Many trees were sacrificed to build that road, a vernal pool destroyed, the once loved trail on land that is called "common wealth" is now off limits to me and all who used to hike, hunt, ski and trail ride there.

The lives of all Butternut Grove residents have forever changed at the hands of the corporation claiming the right to send its trucks up the road, to foul the air with diesel fumes, to generate noise, to disturb the ecosystem on the mountain, to haul truckloads of toxic fracking chemicals up and millions of gallons of toxic water back down. This same company also has a permit to pump over one million gallons per day from the Loyalsock—a beautiful creek that begins in Sullivan County and travels 64 miles on its way to the West Branch of the Susquehanna, providing recreation for hundreds of fishermen, kayakers, inner-tubers, swimmers and summer-cabin dwellers— offering water that dances and glimmers and supports abundant fish, amphibian, bird and wildlife.

My grandfather bought these 20 acres with their mile-long creek frontage in 1933. The memories my family has made here are priceless and my grandchildren are the 5th generation to run in the meadow, swim in the creek, ride and hike in the nearby woods. In our increasingly transient society, roots this deep are precious and rare. And yet—one of my children has already moved 400 miles away off the shale.

The industry has been carefully mapping out its strategy for years, repealing both state and federal laws that would have protected us. The gas rush is here, and the special place we once called home has become the Marcellus Sacrifice Zone.

Barbara Jarmoska

* * *

Barbara—or Barb, as she is universally known—sent me this essay by way of introduction soon after I moved to Williamsport and e-mailed a query to the Responsible Drilling Alliance (RDA). She had just succeeded Ralph Kisberg as president of the RDA, the small Williamsport-based 501(c) organization that was pretty much the only fractivist game in town. I heard a lot about Barb before I met her. As the outspoken, progressive owner of Freshlife, the only area health food store (located in Montoursville), and driver of a Prius plastered with anti-fracking bumper stickers, it seemed everyone in town knew (and had an opinion about) her. When I explained my research to curious locals at gathering places in Billtown like Alabaster Coffee, people asked if I had met the "weird lady" or "crazy environmentalist" from Freshlife. Representative Garth Everett was more diplomatic, but clearly viewed Barb as eccentric. Describing what he saw as her sky-is-falling alarmism as we sat in his strip mall office, Garth chuckled, but then seemed to catch himself. "She's very—Barb's Barb. She's always been alternative. That's just Barb."

Alternative was an apt description, even in comparison to her "granola" RDA comrades (to say nothing of Barb's hidebound neighbors). At a well-attended hearing where state lawmakers received testimony from locals regarding the potential impacts of fracking Loyalsock State Forest, several RDA members spoke in measured terms about specific, quantifiable ecological harms (e.g., native birds displaced, acres of forest lost). But Barb, who told the legislators she was speaking today as both a citizen of Pennsylvania and an inhabitant of Mother Earth, went full New Age. She chastised "reductionistic Westerners" for their propensity to accept and celebrate the "invisible energy" that powers remote controls and Wi-Fi while they simultaneously "discount or even scoff" at nature's "equally powerful forms of invisible energy." Stopping to appreciate a clear stream or "woods silent except for birdsong," Barb said, can cause within our bodies a "cascade of neural transmitters and hormones that is the stuff of joy." The "people native to this land," and Eastern cultures, appreciate the healing energy of nature, she added. Gesturing toward the legislators seated at a table, Barb dramatically claimed that a tai chi master could "drop you to your knees from twelve feet away," simply by harnessing the invisible energy field that surrounds us all. She closed by quoting the author Richard Louv, whose book *Last Child in the Woods* famously argues that children today suffer from "nature-deficit disorder," which manifests in health and behavioral problems.

Upon first meeting Barb, I wrote in my notebook that this vivacious child of the sixties struck me as a "sort of modern-day benevolent witch." Perhaps it was her belief in supernatural energies—she was known to say that the rocks and trees around her had names and could speak to her—and her commitment to holistic medicine (especially homeopathy). Or maybe it was the "deeply psychospiritual" women-only writing retreats she hosted in the woods of her secluded creekside property. Or the texts she quoted reverentially (like Bill Plotkin's *Nature and the*

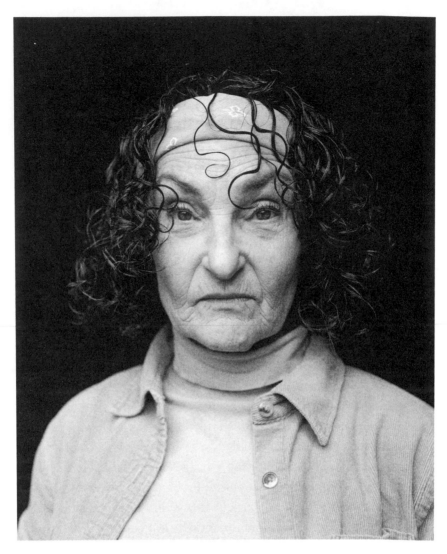

FIG. 9.1. Barb Jarmoska. Photograph by Tristan Spinksi.

Human Soul: Cultivating Wholeness and Community in a Fragmented World, which introduces "ecopsychology"). But it was also written on her face, which to me seemed wizened yet full of vitality. Her perpetually raised jet-black eyebrows, which framed hazel eyes, suggested mystery—or perhaps someone who remained in a constant state of wonder.

Though Barb's unconventional lifestyle lent itself to caricature in a place like Montoursville, in some ways she was not so different from people like George. She, too, prized self-reliance and putting family first: when her nonagenarian father was unable to care for himself, she refused to outsource his care to others (he temporarily moved in with her in 2017); she owned her own backhoe, which she used to clear debris whenever the creek flooded; she sometimes rode her horse bareback up the mountainside by her lonesome, like an arboreal cowgirl. Aside from George, I didn't encounter anyone else whose family history and sense of self were as intertwined with their land as Barb. I asked Barb in 2016 why she was still here after saying for so many years that she was so brokenhearted about fracking that she considered giving up her land. "I made myself think about what it would be like to drive out of that driveway for the very last time." Barb shook her head and waved her hand as her voice wavered. "I can't even think about it now without choking up."

At the base of Barb's driveway stood a majestic, one-of-a-kind Norway spruce tree. Eight distinct meaty trunks sprouted from the bottom and ascended about eighty feet into the air. As Barb tells it, when her grandfather bought the property, at the height of the Great Depression, that tree was so small that he hoisted Barb's mom onto his shoulders so the child could look at a bird nest tucked into the crown. An ancient sagging barn in the front yard, which according to family lore dates back to the late 1700s, served as a stable when Barb was a child. Because her father's job as a salesman required a lot of travel, Barb moved around her whole childhood, "like an army brat." The one constant was this property, which back then only had a cabin that lacked indoor plumbing. She spent every summer here. "It grounded me," Barb told me; "I grew up here." As we sat in Barb's screened-in patio overlooking a small meadow dappled with sunlight and the glistening Loyalsock Creek, Barb recalled her favorite memory from those golden years. She and her sister (who, as an adult, was tragically killed by a drunk driver) used to lie awake for hours at night on the cabin's front porch and listen to the night sounds. "It was literally a chorus of bullfrogs," Barb recounted with a faint smile. She then inhaled a large gulp of air in an attempt to mimic their calls: "Gallumph!"

When Barb's father retired, in 1975, he and Barb's mother decided to move full-time to the property. "He and my mom tore down the old cabin," Barb reminisced. "My sister and I stood in the yard and cried our eyes out." Her parents built a simple one-story ranch house that "was very typical of the seventies, with lots of little dark rooms and big, thick shag carpets and avocado[-colored] appliances." It was their retirement dream, and they enjoyed a run of thirty joyful and tranquil years there, hosting family reunions, creekside barbeques, and sleepovers with Barb's kids. When caring for the property got to be too much, Barb's parents gifted it to her (she was living in Montoursville then). "I broke their hearts the way they broke my sister and I's heart," Barb recalled with a chuckle. "It was the darkest, most closed-in little house. It was really so not me." Barb's dream was to "have a place where people can come and be outdoors and connect with nature—to open the house up to the world." She set about redesigning the space so that it embodied that spirit of openness. That meant gutting the house, tearing out every interior wall, and "literally taking a chainsaw and sawing off the roof, joist to joist." The result: an airy, two-story "sanctuary" featuring an open floor plan, cathedral ceiling, bunkbed-filled guestroom, multiple porches strewn with rockers, and firepits.

The renovations took two years (2005–7). Almost as soon as they were done, Barb began hosting a camp for inner-city kids from New York and New Jersey through the Fresh Air Fund. She was living the dream. But it wasn't long, she said, before she got a rude awakening in the form of a knock at her door. She opened it to find two friendly strangers, Jon Bogle and Ralph Kisberg. The pair was just launching the RDA and was going door to door to advise residents about the impending industrial onslaught. Barb had never heard of fracking before. "They said, this is what's coming. I said, you're kidding me." That was in 2008. In 2009, another pair of friendly strangers came knocking at the door. The husband and wife—she dressed smartly in a blouse and heels, he with an ill-fitted sport coat draped over his shoulders—told a very different story than Ralph and John had about what was to come. As Barb remembered it, they "just played best friends" and told her, "We are here to tell you the good news." Anadarko wanted to lease her property. She'd won the lottery, she recalls them insisting.

Barb wouldn't be cashing in her ticket. By then, she had joined the nascent anti-fracking movement and was working to help get the RDA incorporated as a nonprofit. But the writing was on the wall. Parades of trucks trundling up Route 87 to service gas wells further north drowned out the bullfrogs. "That contrast," Barb bemoaned, "is one of the most heartbreaking things about all this." She began sleeping with earplugs. Soon, Barb was surrounded by leased land. Butternut Grove Road was next. By 2013, when I met her, Barb had lost more than peace and quiet, or a horse trail. She lost her family. Barb's adult son, whom, she said, used to live ten minutes up the road, moved his wife and two children to upstate New York, with the express purpose of getting off the shale. The chain had been broken. The ancestral land would not be her two grandchildren's stomping grounds. Up the creek from Barb's house, the cabin she had built in the woods as her son's twelfth birthday present sat suspended upside down in a sycamore tree. It had been deposited there after a massive flood, in 2011. Barb saw little point in retrieving and repairing the cabin. Her grandchildren wouldn't be using it. So there it sat, a haunting metaphor for how fracking had upended Barb and her family's lives.

After pausing in silence at the cabin one chilly April morning as if paying respects to a memorial, Barb and I scrambled up the steep, wooded hill that pinned her property against the creek. We walked alongside a timeworn, moss-covered stone wall likely created when Appalachian settlers carved out paddocks and gardens from the dense forest over two hundred years ago. The low, wide wall took shape as they removed fieldstones. "This stone wall is really something to think about," Barb narrated. Second-growth forest reclaimed the cleared tract decades ago. But the wall endured. "I like to think of what it means that every single one of these rocks was touched by a human hand."

"We're on the land of a hunting camp now," Barb announced as we hopped over the wall. "They have leased it. They want a well on it." The grass yard immediately surrounding the cabin was filled with junk, including targets riddled with bullet holes. "They shot up their propane tank," along with a satellite dish, too, Barb huffed. It was hard for her not to judge. "It is really interesting to look at the value system," Barb said.

"Yes, I don't need the money from gas drilling," Barb admitted, noting her rental income from six properties. "But many of the people that I know [who leased] also didn't really need the money." All the members of the hunting camp have homes, Barb noted. This plot is their recreational property. If she owned a cabin in the woods, "it wouldn't look like this." Barb saw in the cluttered, shot-up yard "a disrespect for the land that is evident in so many of the places they live." Why, she asked, "wouldn't it carry over to a lack of concern [for] what the industry is doing?" She cited her next-door neighbor, who, she said, dumped thousands of tires in his backyard. He had just leased his land for a water withdrawal station, which would clog Barb's driveway with trucks.

Adjacent to the hunting cabin was the spring that once supplied the water to Barb's grandfather's cabin. It emptied into a small bog. In a few weeks, the bog would be full of spring peeper frogs. The "frog chorus," Barb smiled, "starts about five o'clock in the evening and is absolutely a symphony." Her smile quickly fading, Barb added, "It breaks my heart to think about the trucks and gas wells" that would mar the land if the hunting camp's property was developed, "and what would happen to this wetland. It could all go." Barb asked rhetorically, "I guess the question is, what's enough?" She claimed that her life "would be no different if I had an extra million dollars."

Glaring sidelong at the cabin, Barb sighed deeply as she contemplated the moral gulf that separated her and her RDA friends from the occupants of the cabin and many of her other pro-gas neighbors. "They think we're a bunch of whacked-out environmentalists who are impeding progress and their riches, and we think the only thing they care about is money."

* * *

Barb's observation encapsulates one of the most prominent tropes in contemporary American politics: environment *versus* economics. "Our best intentions regarding conservation and carbon reduction," *New Yorker* columnist David Owen writes, "inevitably run up against the realities of foreclosure and bankruptcy and unemployment."[1] It's not just the media, or politicians, who imply that we have to choose between a strong economy and a healthy environment: many well-known environmental social scientists have also characterized the environment-economy relationship as an "enduring conflict."[2] What makes this apparent (and overblown) tension so difficult to resolve is that it has become one of the major flashpoints in America's hyperpartisan political landscape.

Things weren't always this way. After the catastrophic Santa Barbara oil spill in 1969, President Richard Nixon lobbied for "preserving the beauty and the natural resources that are so important to any kind of society that we want for the future." Although he privately held that "in a flat choice between smoke and jobs, we're for jobs," Nixon presided during an era when politicians of all stripes were "falling over themselves to claim the mantle" of environmentalism. His 1970 State of the Union speech argued that "restoring nature to its natural state is a cause beyond party."[3] By year's end, Nixon had created the Environmental Protection Agency. In 1973, he signed the Endangered Species Act. Fifteen years later, as the world began to awaken to the dangers of global warming, another Republican—presidential candidate George Bush Sr.—famously promised to fight the greenhouse effect with the "White House effect." (In the end, Bush was all talk and no action.)

While the ecological crisis has worsened considerably over the past three decades, conservatives have by and large disavowed environmental protection (which is not to say that many progressives have made it a priority, at least not before the 2020 Democratic primaries). Some analysts pinpoint the 1992 Earth Summit, in Rio, as an important turning point, after which the "US conservative movement began to see global environmentalism as a threat to US national sovereignty and economic power."[4] Domestically, conservatives seized on a judge's controversial decision to halt timber sales in the Pacific Northwest to protect the habitat of the (now infamous) northern spotted owl (relying on the Endangered Species Act, the US Fish and Wildlife Service had declared the owl "threatened" in 1991). The logging industry claimed that tens of thousands of working- and middle-class jobs were lost, which helped spur conservative think tanks to begin organizing what would become a countermovement that disputed the seriousness of environmental problems and cast environmentalists as prioritizing "trees and cuddly animals" over people.[5] It worked. During Bush Sr.'s reelection campaign, the man who just four years earlier had vowed to fight global warming mocked Al Gore as the "ozone man" and threatened that, should Bill Clinton prevail in the 1992 presidential election, "we'll be up to our necks in owls, and outta work for every American."[6]

By the time Clinton moved into the West Wing, the notion of an environment-versus-economy tradeoff—and the implication that partisans have to pick sides—had crystalized in American public discourse. What was once "a modest tendency for Congressional Republicans to be less pro-environmental than their Democratic counterparts" grew into an abyss.[7] Uniting under a pro-growth, anti-regulatory umbrella, conservatives (whether Tea Partiers or moderates) now regularly frame environmentalists as "dismissive of any type of resource extraction ... and as never giving a thought to job creation or the impact environmental regulations would have on the profitability of certain industries."[8] Many mainstream Republicans also discredit the science of climate change.[9]

Conflicts over fracking seem to be just the latest manifestation of the environment-economy standoff. In one corner: liberal tree huggers who would forsake billions of dollars of economic growth and energy independence to protect the lowly sage grouse's habitat.[10] (Tom Shepstone, a Pennsylvania-based pro-gas blogger, dismissed the anti-fracking movement as "fear-mongering by those who would have the rest of us do nothing to improve our lot, while they live off money inherited or made elsewhere."[11]) In the other corner: free-market fundamentalists and robber barons ready to mortgage our children's and the planet's future for a quick buck.[12] (Shepstone's nemesis, Wendy Lee, a Marxist philosophy professor, saw fracking in dire terms: "Dead from cancer is dead. . . . Species driven to extinction don't come back. Wells that are poisoned stay poisoned."[13])

Many scholars echo conventional wisdom, arguing that it's economic desperation that drives communities to embrace potentially risky extractive industries. At first, I believed that about fracking too. But the more time I spent in Billtown, the less I thought that the disconnect between the "silent majority" of landowners who supported fracking and the small but vocal minority who opposed it could be boiled down to differences in how each side valued the environment versus the economy.[14] Rather, a major cause of the chasm that separated these two camps were perceived cultural and lifestyle differences that residents often mapped onto the rural-urban political divide. Many locals suspected that fractivists were cosmopolitan, latte-sipping liberal townies who, as representative Garth Everett remarked, "have no clue about rural values." Aside from Ralph, RDA members did little to counter this perception. They failed to craft a localistic message that validated the community's perceived values.[15] In turn, for landowners, showing support for fracking became a means of expressing community solidarity.

Local officials and landowners abdicated responsibility as well. Their distrust of government inclined them to be skeptical of environmental advocacy that purportedly served the public interest, because the means to that end—increased oversight of private land use—was at odds with their political ideology. In this way, residents were willfully complicit in maintaining the status quo even when confronted with industry malfeasance, favoring bootstrapping over resistance.

* * *

One of the biggest cultural issues that drove a wedge between the fractivists and much of the rest of the community, more important than their differences in political *ideology*, was the former group's distinct *style* of political *engagement*—namely, their tendency to engage in disruptive actions like protests.[16] In the spring of 2012, several dozen working-class and poor residents of Riverdale Mobile Home Park, a cluster of timeworn trailer homes sandwiched between Route 220 and the West Branch of the Susquehanna River, learned that they were being evicted to make way for a water withdrawal site. Most residents accepted a $2,500 payment to walk away from the park. But seven families, citing the exorbitant cost of relocating or the fact that their decrepit trailers might not survive the move, held out. As word spread of what was considered to be "the first example of outright evictions because of Mar-cellus Shale operations" in Pennsylvania, Riverdale became a cause célèbre for the nascent anti-fracking movement.[17] Among the fractivists who flocked to Riverdale to "denounc[e] villainous corporations for evicting poor families for fracking and profits" was Wendy Lee, the tat-tooed Bloomsburg University philosophy professor and outspoken fracking abolitionist.[18] For thirteen days, she and dozens of other activ-ists from as far away as Philadelphia and New York—including veterans of the Occupy Wall Street movement and members of fringe direct-action groups like Earth First!—"occupied" Riverdale to prevent the forcible removal of the remaining residents. They eventually stood down, when confronted by a private security force; the holdouts sued for settlements.

Wendy Lee called "Occupy Riverdale" a "watershed moment" in "gal-vanizing the anti-fracking movement in Pennsylvania"—on par with the infamous case of contamination in Dimock and the making of *Gasland*.[19] But Reverend Leah Schade, a self-described anti-fracking activist and ecofeminist who organized prayer services with the holdouts during Occupy Riverdale, was more circumspect. She told me that it was dif-ficult to mobilize the residents and expressed mild disappointment that, for the most part, the holdouts just wanted fair compensation. It was the residents who made the decision to stand down (rather than be ar-rested) and agree to move out. Leah recalled that the activists wanted to keep up the fight, and that they felt let down by residents' disinclina-tion to link the eviction to larger political issues of social justice and environmentalism.

A similar dynamic was on display at a town hall I attended in Hughes-ville early the following year. When representative Garth Everett opened it up for questions, Tom Crawley vented about his ongoing water prob-lem in front of the packed fire hall audience (about seventy-five people). "I've got a contaminated well as a result of [gas drilling] that you know about," he shouted from the back as Everett nodded. "You were kind enough to meet with us and we appreciate that . . . [but] I'm frustrated because I've called your office and Mr. Finkler called you twice and you never got back to us." After Everett apologized and said, "my mistake,"

Tom's neighbor Jim Finkler yelled, "Every time I draw water out of my faucet it looks like it came out of a soda bottle." The attendees politely gave Tom and his neighbors space to detail their grievances, and the state representative remained gracious even as the complainants accused Everett of abandoning them ("We were able to do what you could not or would not do," Tom hissed, informing Everett that he arranged his own meeting with the DEP. "I thought you could have helped us out more"). However, the tenor of the room quickly shifted when Wendy Lee and a companion pointing a video camera at Everett used the opportunity to level a broader critique against the industry and government.

Lee followed Doyle Bodle's complaints about the DEP's inaction by interjecting that both the agency's director and his boss—the governor—opposed the kinds of regulations needed to protect the public from an inherently toxic industry. She had already made an impassioned five-minute speech a few moments earlier, for the state to stop allowing drilling on protected forests, which drew groans and murmurs, and this time Everett's patience ran out. He sternly told her that she had spoken out of turn, and when she replied that Doyle had as well, and that she was simply trying to provide Doyle with information, Everett told her that she was not "part of the community" (she lived an hour away) and was thus "only here as a guest." Everett asked her if she wanted to stay or leave, which prompted a woman in the audience to ask aloud, "What *are* they doing here? I wish he *would* throw them out." Many in the audience nodded their approval when Everett threatened expulsion if they continued to "try people's patience." Right after this heated exchange, attendees introduced mundane questions about government workers' pensions, roads, and Obamacare. Tom Crawley and his neighbors looked disgustedly at Wendy and did not engage her. In this way, attendees ratified Everett's efforts to neutralize the fractivists and their platform.

Tom and his neighbors' complaints of industry malfeasance and government indifference were surprisingly well aligned with the thrust of Wendy's diatribe, despite their ideological differences. Everett's and the audience's different reception of the two parties was likely due in part to the fact that Tom, Jim, and Doyle were recognized as locals who were part of the representative's constituency, while Wendy wasn't. But, not to be ignored is that Wendy's grandstanding (the self-described "agitator extraordinaire" vowed to post the video online, and did[20]) and baldly political framing of the issue was an affront to community norms. After all, Ralph, who as a resident of Williamsport was not one of Everett's constituents either, was treated courteously even though he too raised pointed critiques of Everett's (lack of) response to drilling violations. The contrast was that, like Tom and his neighbors, Ralph framed both the problem and the solution as *parochial* issues (e.g., appealing personally to Everett to serve his constituents) rather than as *partisan* ones. He wasn't rude: he came to engage in civil dialogue, not to confront and shame (Ralph implored, "Garth, I'm not saying it's your fault. But now these people have bad water. What are they gonna do?").[21] In fact, Ralph and Garth had a productive e-mail exchange the day after the town hall: Ralph forwarded Garth information about a nearby compressor station that a constituent had raised concerns about the night before; Garth wrote back asking if there was a study he could cite in talking to the DEP.

Perhaps Wendy was right to think that actions like the Occupy Riverdale protest and the disruption of Everett's town hall energized the fractivist movement. They did likely attract outside attention to local issues. In the wake of Occupy Riverdale, in January 2013, a busload of fractivists from New York City who called themselves "Artists against Fracking," led by Yoko Ono, Sean Lennon, and Susan Sarandon, toured the area, stopping at gas wells where violations had occurred, unfurling protest banners, and declaring their solidarity with impacted locals. A gaggle of quote-hungry and photo-snapping journalists followed the bus. However, fractivist strategies that seemed aimed at mobilizing extra-local audiences (why else would Wendy record her standoff with Everett and post it online?) had the exact opposite effect on many locals, repelling them from anything and anyone that smelled of activism. Some viewed the fractivists' drive-by antagonistic style as paternalistic and hypocritical ("How do they heat their home? How did they power that bus?"). "These people have no interest in this area other than just creating a stink," Tom Crawley griped of Artists against Fracking. "It's just publicity for them. It doesn't do anything to help us."

Events like Occupy Riverdale and Wendy's in-your-face confrontation with Everett stuck with local residents. A year later, Tom and Mary Crawley cited both as the main reason why they were not willing to "raise a stink" about their situation to the media or environmental groups (it took me nine months to convince the Crawleys and their neighbors to talk to me). In particular, they were concerned that environmentalists from "outside the community" who heard about the case would demonize their "nice old neighbors" whose property hosted the faulty gas well, or otherwise disrupt the community. "Oh gosh," Mary worried, "no picket lines." Recalling Riverdale, she remarked, "That was awful. I drove past that I don't know how many times, and [saw] the picketers and people from out of the area that just came in and camped up there." Tom added, "We're afraid everybody will blame [our neighbors]. It's not their fault. I don't want people camping out on their property." Despite their difficulties navigating the byzantine bureaucracy of the DEP and finding a competent lawyer whom they could afford, the Crawleys and their neighbors repeatedly rebuffed the RDA's outreach efforts and offer of pro bono legal advice on the grounds that they did not want to be associated with anti-fracking elements.[22] They were adamant about not politicizing their plight.

I've come to the conclusion that many area landowners, who were predominantly conservative and proudly rural, viewed adversarial modes of political engagement of the kind commonly deployed by fractivists as inconsistent with their political and community commitments. Jessica Smartt Gullion notes something similar in her book about life in a conservative Texas suburb during the fracking boom. Even as locals became concerned about the health impacts of fracking, they were reluctant to mobilize because they viewed public forms of activism as "something that only liberals and/or Democrats do."[23] The lessors I came to know could stomach differences in political opinion. I should know; though some ribbed me for my liberal views, all welcomed me into their lives. But they could not abide divisive political strategies that, to them, bore the hallmarks of urban interlopers who either did not

FIG. 9.2. Anti-fracking activists stage a small protest in Williamsport.
Photograph by Colin Jerolmack.

understand or did not respect rural values (the Crawleys felt this way even though they were registered Democrats).

To clarify, Wendy Lee did not consider herself a member of RDA, although she did identify as a member of the umbrella group Shale Justice, with which RDA was affiliated. And all the dozen or so core RDA members I befriended lived in the area—they were not "professional protesters"[24]—and kept a lower activist profile than Lee. Rather than "occupy" a fracking site, they held a small, permitted Earth Day rally at the local DEP office. What's more, the group explicitly desired constructive relations with the community and local leaders (among their efforts to this end, they mailed out a survey to introduce themselves to the community and gauge its priorities). Nonetheless, the RDA gained little traction with neighbors beyond the city limits of Williamsport—a speck of blue in a blood-red county, where fracking was not happening. The first time I sat down with Ralph, the stout, gray-haired but youthful and perpetually agreeable cofounder of RDA, he offered a shockingly blunt assessment of his group's marginal status. He said matter-of-factly that the RDA had no credibility in rural communities; most residents considered the group a joke. I asked if any local leaders or politicians gave the RDA a seat at the table, and he simply replied with a chuckle and a head shake. (He later clarified, though, that Garth Everett "was always open to talk or e-mail with me," and that Rick Mirabito, the sole Democratic state representative in the county before he lost his seat, in 2014, "was very open to us" and "is still helpful" in his newer role as a Lycoming County Commissioner.)

Although the community's relationship to the RDA was less overtly antagonistic than its relationship to the wider anti-fracking movement, it was marked by the same degree of alienation. Despite their geographic proximity to provincial, proletarian lessors like George, RDA members—half of whom were "rusticators," most of whom lived in town, and almost all of whom were college-educated and politically liberal professionals—could hardly have been more distant socially. For the most part, they had cosmopolitan tastes and leisure pursuits that seldom led them to rub elbows with everyday rural residents of the county. That segregation meant that folks like the Crawleys couldn't discern if and how the RDA might be deserving of more trust than, say, Wendy Lee.

Just two days after the aforementioned town hall in Hughesville's Spartan fire hall, I found myself in an ornate theater on the campus of Bucknell University, watching a play called *Same River*, performed by a New York City–based ensemble. Promoted by the RDA and loosely based on real local events and people, the production focused on a working-poor couple whose marriage is torn apart by fracking. He eventually takes an industry job, but she—her name is Barb—joins the RDA and finds purpose in getting arrested for protesting the displacement of mobile-home dwellers. The play was decidedly anti-fracking, much to the liberal college town audience's delight. In one scene, a lampooned industry worker called concerns over fracking "leftist hippie barf fuck." In the end, the landscape is destroyed and water wells are poisoned. As the curtain fell, a voiceover intoned that water is sacred, the rain falls on all of us, and we are all in the same river. Afterward, the producer and cast led a "town-hall-style meeting" in which the audience could reflect on the performance. Most spectators heaped praise on the actors and dancers and called the performance moving. The director closed by ranting against the industry and encouraging everyone to get involved in the fight. The crowd broke into cheers when she added that they would be taking the message on tour across shale country.

On the ride home, I asked Ralph how he thought Hughesville residents would respond if the director brought the performance to them. Guffawing, Ralph lamented that it's amazing how people like the performers and the audience don't see that they exist in a bubble. Their liberal, anti-fracking views, he observed, are such a small minority of the population of the region. He added that they can do what they want because they're artists, but the idea that the average lease-holding farmer would attend *Same River*, let alone feel that its portrayal of fracking resonated with them, is absurd. Ralph also opined that you won't make any converts appealing to moral righteousness or ideals like environmental stewardship; 'you gotta appeal to their practical, immediate concerns.'

For the most part, Ralph's RDA comrades spent a lot of time in the bubble he described. They held their monthly meetings in the sumptuous Peter Herdic House Restaurant, a farm-to-table establishment housed in the legendary lumber baron's historic mansion on Millionaires' Row. A reservation-only "community dinner" that the RDA held there featured "an exotic vegetarian entrée using locally harvested winter squash, garbanzo beans, veggies, basmati rice and aromatic spices." One of the RDA's fundraising ventures was the creation of a limited-edition, locally sourced organic amber-style ale and a public contest to name the brew (the winner: Old Logger's Ale, named for the Old Loggers Path in Loyalsock State Forest that was threatened by gas drilling). A public lecture that the RDA hosted about the economic risk of a fracking bust took place at the Williamsport Country Club. Priuses dotted the parking lot; the audience was a who's who of the town's social elite, from the county's sole Democratic state representative, Rick Mirabito, to Matt Schauer, a young, hip developer who owned numerous luxury "artist lofts" (once housed the city's only coffee shop). These settings, and menus, were a far cry from down-home Kathy's Café in Hughesville, near the Crawleys' house, and Cohick's Trading Post, the backwoods general store where many lessors gathered (and where many SUVs and pickups with gun racks dotted the gravel parking lot). In fact, most nearby landowners I met avoided Billtown (if not microbrews) entirely. They were more likely to buy their produce at suburban chain grocers than in town at the Growers Market.[25] They, too, loved the outdoors, though primarily for hunting and angling, not hiking and picnics. I didn't meet a single fracking opponent who was a member of a hunting camp; most lessors were. The apparent urbanity and wealth of fracking opponents led some pundits to deride them as the "green gentry."[26]

* * *

Though RDA members expressed a sincere wish to connect with local residents impacted by gas drilling, few of their daily activities brought them into casual contact with landowners in the surrounding rural parts of the county. The one exception was Ralph. He lived in town in the postwar suburban-style house he grew up in. (He left its midcentury-modern decor—dark-wood panels in the den, angular sofas, and mono-chromatic color schemes—untouched.) But he spent as much time mingling with lessors in rural hamlets as he did hobnobbing downtown with activists and bohemians (whom he took in as roommates when he needed money or company).

A typical late winter day in 2013 found Ralph coaxing his antiquated Toyota Camry along snowy backroads in Trout Run. As usual, he was on the lookout for new industry activity. This time, he had some college students with him. Upon spying a drilling rig peeking out above a line of trees, he pulled over to get a closer look. A security guard reportedly attempted to shoo him, but Ralph was able to engage him in amiable banter long enough for the property owner to appear in the driveway. That was how he met George Hagemeyer, who graciously offered to give Ralph and his entourage a guided tour of the well pad. As Ralph and George recall it, they hit it off right away. Both enjoyed talking about the specifications of the rig (it was a "triple," meaning it could hold three connected thirty-foot pipes at a time). George was eager to learn what he could expect as far as gas production from the wells, and Ralph was happy to share production numbers of area wells that he found online.

As Ralph came to know George, who invited him to come back and watch the process of fracking and "completing" the gas wells in his yard, he didn't hide the fact that he had a critical view of the industry. But he related to George first and foremost as a neighbor, not as an adversary or a potential convert. Ralph's deferential and folksy demeanor meant that George—who told me, when Ralph first connected us, that he didn't want to speak to anyone who was "anti-gas"—did not even view him as an environmentalist. It wasn't that Ralph lied about his position on fracking, but rather that Ralph didn't conform to the image that George had in his mind of how a fractivist spoke and behaved. It's possible that Ralph's very presence on dead-end White Birch Lane put George at ease (with all due credit to Ralph's easy smile and calming monotone style of speaking). It just wasn't a place where George had ever encountered an environmental activist, let alone a liberal, before.

As George began experiencing problems with fracking, Ralph gave him resources rather than a sermon. When George complained that he couldn't connect with his Texas-based landman or get any details from Anadarko about how royalties would be divided among lessors in his unit, Ralph introduced him to the last remaining landman in Billtown, Russell Poole. When George grew concerned that his property rights were being violated and that the company that bought a majority stake in his lease (Chesapeake) was cheating him out of royalty payments, Ralph connected him to a lawyer who was willing to offer free advice. (George eventually joined a class-action lawsuit alleging that Chesapeake fraudulently claimed $5 billion in "deductions" from lessor checks; the firm's CEO was also indicted for rigging lease prices but died in a suspicious car crash before he could be tried.)[27] Ralph never tried to convert George, even as George grew cynical about the industry over time. George reciprocated by welcoming Ralph on his land anytime, even when he showed up to tour the well pad with several members of the vehemently anti-fracking group Delaware Riverkeeper Network.

The activists said they'd never been so close to a fracking installation; George enjoyed serving as an expert to the novices (one mistook a drilling rig for a gas well), providing lengthy explanations.

It was, in addition to Ralph's nonjudgmental disposition and ubiquitous presence, all the unglamorous behind-the-scenes research he did that was key to the rapport he developed with rural landowners. He spent hours each month at the DEP regional office and the local courthouse in Williamsport, pulling files on dozens of area wells and pipeline rights-of-way, so that he knew every detail about them (e.g., where and when they were placed; any outstanding violations; what company held the lease). He filled several notebooks with observations from countless permit hearings he attended in the area for gas wells, water withdrawal sites, pipelines, and compressor stations. His dining-room table was often given over to unfolded maps that overflowed with handwritten notes indicating the locations of every piece of natural-gas infrastructure that he knew of. (I won't soon forget Ralph's satisfaction when we found an old "orphan well" while bushwhacking through a section of leased state forest that was slated for development. We were searching for an unmarked, overgrown path Ralph knew of; he suspected the company would widen and use it as a truck access road. We eventually discovered the path, and it was indeed being graded and widened by the lessee.) His living-room end tables were stacked with dog-eared printouts of the latest academic research on frac fluid, the integrity of gas well cement casing, and methane leakage rates of gas wells.

Ralph was a font of knowledge, so much so that other environmental groups, politicians, the state's Department of Conservation and Natural Resources, and even some petroleum companies sought his expertise. But there was nothing Ralph found greater purpose in than using that knowledge to try to make life a little bit better for locals impacted by fracking. On one occasion, Ralph turned up on George's property with a retiree he was trying to help. A well pad built by Anadarko on the property next door to the retiree's was only about fifty feet from his woodshop and two hundred feet from his house (this was before the state mandated that gas wells be set back at least five hundred feet from buildings). Even though he could not stop the well pad from being

FIG. 9.3. Ralph Kisberg next to an old "orphan well" he discovered on public lands.
Photograph by Colin Jerolmack.

developed, Ralph was committed to minimizing the disruption it would
cause to the retiree. Ralph encouraged the older man to think about
how the placement of the dehydrators and separator tanks on the pad
would affect his quality of life. The man had never considered it and was
flabbergasted when he saw the massive, noisy, and malodorous equipment on George's pad. Ralph suggested that the retiree ask Anadarko to
place the dehydrators on the far side of the pad so they wouldn't crowd
his yard. When Anadarko reportedly responded that such a placement
would be problematic, because it went against their template, Ralph
volunteered to broker a meeting. He also gave the retiree copies of dia-
grams of Anadarko well pads in which the location of the separators
went against the firm's alleged template, implying that the company
could accommodate the retiree's request.

Converting rural landowners to fractivists seemed almost incidental
to Ralph's mission. But I did meet some people who bought into the

movement precisely because they were won over by Ralph. When one couple's well water was flooded with methane after a gas well was drilled on a neighboring property, they held a small press conference to make others aware of the dangers of fracking (they've since signed an NDA and asked not to be identified). Despite the fact that the couple publicly stated they weren't against drilling, they invited Ralph to speak after learning about the RDA online. Most RDA members had by that time concluded that there was no such thing as responsible drilling and debated changing its name. (Ralph was also a skeptic but supported keeping the name on practical grounds: the RDA was a known entity, and besides, "Who's gonna listen to the No Drilling Alliance?") But the middle-of-the-road stance implied in the name is what appealed to the couple. And in Ralph they found the ideal ally. One day in late January 2013, Ralph invited the husband to the DEP North-Central Regional Office in Billtown, where I helped them comb through reams of files looking for new information about violations associated with the faulty gas well. Ralph helped the man interpret the files and offered to file right-to-know requests for water and radon tests. The husband, who was initiating a lawsuit against the offending company, seemed moved by Ralph's graciousness. He said that he and his wife had felt "entirely alone" in their battle against the gas company before they befriended Ralph. He thanked Ralph profusely, adding sheepishly, "We don't expect you to fight our battles for us." Less than three months later, the couple reunited with Ralph outside the DEP office. This time, though, they came to join an Earth Day protest against fracking that the RDA had cosponsored. The couple proudly held a sign aloft that read "Shale Justice," and the wife shouted toward the DEP office, "Who are they protecting? They don't do anything! We're the casualties!" She then hugged Ralph and gushed, "Despite everything we are going through, I think of you and say, 'Ralph is looking out for us! At least Ralph cares!'" It was because Ralph invested in their personal struggle as a neighbor, rather than as a partisan with an agenda, that the couple came around to situating their plight within the anti-fracking campaign.

Ralph was adamant that fracking, though an ingenious technology, is "stupid, short-sighted, and wrong." He cherished the Arcadian beauty of Lycoming County and defiantly told me, "This is our home and we'll fight for it." But Ralph refused to fan the flames of paranoia or prey on residents' fears. After Hughesville resident Allison Rupert raised alarms about the compressor station near her home at Garth Everett's town hall, Ralph tried to put things in perspective for her. She's "scared to death," Ralph remarked. "I told her to just calm down. Let's figure out what's going on." He explained to her that even if emissions from the facility were exceeding acceptable levels, "it doesn't mean you are gonna die." Ralph reassured Allison that the compressor station's location on the top of a mountain with a lot of wind and clean air around it made it unlikely that she was at risk. "Let's just figure out what is going on and try to fix it rather than flip out and ring the alarm."

To the frustration of some of his fellow organizers, Ralph was stubbornly on the side of evidence-based activism. "Any mistake we make can get blown up and put in our face," Ralph worried. "I've got one person [on the RDA board] who's like, 'Every aquifer is gonna be poisoned.' Where do you get that?" When investigative journalists from the Pittsburgh-based *Public Herald* claimed that "hidden data" showed "widespread, systemic impact" from fracking in Pennsylvania based on thousands of citizen complaints to the DEP, the RDA was eager to rush out the story to its e-mail list.[28] But Ralph combed through all sixty-two citizen complaints from Lycoming County from 2008 to 2014, which he called excruciating, and concluded that most of the claims—for that county, at least—were most likely unrelated to fracking and showed that the DEP usually acted "quickly and responsibly." Ralph "saw the hell" that lessors like the Crawleys "went through personally in their homes" as a result of water contamination from fracking. He passionately worked to publicize their stories. But he urged the RDA to scrutinize cases before highlighting them. Some talked about cancer. "Where's the evidence," Ralph asked exasperatedly. "I'm sorry, but I don't see the evidence."[29] Ralph believed that this kind of claims-making made the RDA look like "a bunch of hysterical panicking lunatics." It was too easy for industry proponents like Tom Shepstone or Vince Matteo, the chairman of the Williamsport Chamber of Commerce, to say, "See, these people don't know what they're talking about."

Ralph seemed to be the only reliable bridge that connected anti-fracking activism to the concerns of the region's (largely conservative) landowners, politicians, and industry boosters. However, during my residence in Billtown, his peers increasingly saw his accommodationist tactics as a bridge too far. (Ralph complained to me in an e-mail that no one else except Barb "called out the gas industry, its Coalition, politicians of all levels," Penn State, the Chamber of Commerce, and the local media as much as he did. "All that gets ignored because I usually try to be decent to people.") Case in point: at the same time Ralph was engaging in a good-faith dialogue with Garth Everett over e-mail to address Allison Rupert's concerns about emissions from a compressor station (and offering his condolences for the passing of Everett's father), another RDA cofounder was having a very different e-mail exchange with the representative.[30] The individual had sent Everett an e-mail with the subject line "Still trying to educate you," in which he detailed the declining production numbers of local gas wells. When Everett wrote back, "Is there something we should do legislatively as a result of this information?," the cofounder laced into him in a response cc'ing other state representatives, Williamsport's mayor, and the chairman of the Chamber of Commerce. He accused Everett "and the rest of the legislature in Harrisburg" of having "given away the store" and "pimped out our region to the gas industry." Other RDA members were happy to see Everett called out.

Although Ralph had voluntarily stepped down as president of the RDA at the end of 2012, he remained its most influential member. As the official spokesperson of the organization and its most public figure, he was the one that other environmental groups and the media usually reached out to for comment. However, within the RDA his status became tenuous. The group had appointed Barb as its next president. Although she and Ralph were good friends, she was in many ways his temperamental opposite: in-your-face and dogmatically anti-fracking. Under Barb's stewardship, the RDA began to focus its message on a full-throated demand for a total ban on fracking in Pennsylvania. Doubting Ralph's commitment to a ban, the RDA began using other members as their spokesperson at events.

Ralph was not against a fracking ban per se. If he had his way, oil and gas drilling would cease "as quickly as the world can find a just transition to a clean, sustainable energy economy." But Ralph was pragmatic. In Pennsylvania, where he lived and focused his activism, fracking was already well under way. "It's a fait accompli," Ralph concluded, so "what's the point" of expending the group's scarce time and resources on pushing for something that was never going to happen in the Keystone State? (There was a de facto moratorium on fracking in the Delaware River Basin; Ralph and the RDA did push for the Delaware River Basin Commission (DRBC)—the governing interstate agency—to enact a permanent ban.) Thousands of residents had leased their land and were already hosting natural-gas infrastructure. Republicans, who on the whole were major backers of the industry, controlled every branch of government. And besides, it was a Democratic governor—Ed Rendell—who had auctioned off hundreds of thousands of acres of public land for drilling. Polls at the time showed that most Pennsylvanians thought fracking brought more benefits than problems.[31] Although banning fracking in Pennsylvania was a fantasy, Ralph worked hard to convince people from states, provinces, and other countries where gas drilling had not yet commenced that "you don't want this in your land."[32] He pushed a severance tax rather than a ban in his home state, because it was a realistic objective that could have a large impact (e.g., a significant tax could put the brakes on development, "give the Commonwealth a weapon of control over an out of control industry," and fund the transition to cleaner energy).

Ralph was well aware that his point of view "can't win even in my own organization," which lurched toward a more hard-line position when several of the RDA's board members joined Wendy Lee in creating the Shale Justice coalition. The RDA's official platform did not call for a ban on fracking in Pennsylvania (a stance, again, that Ralph viewed as pragmatic, not ideological). Shale Justice's mission, by contrast, was "Extreme extraction must be banned. No Compromise. No concession to 'regulations.'"[33] Senior RDA board members like Barb seemed energized—liberated, even—by Shale Justice's unrestrained messaging and activism. They cheered several young activists claiming allegiance to Shale Justice who chained themselves across a road to prevent gas trucks from accessing well pads in a state forest (one of them was Ralph's housemate at the time). They felt validated when filmmaker Josh Fox returned to town to screen *Gasland Part II* and echoed their demand to stop all industrialized fossil fuel extraction now. (Nevertheless, it was Ralph who organized Fox's visit, and about whom Fox waxed nostalgic at the microphone when recounting the screening of the original *Gasland* in Billtown.)

Things came to a head that summer. An RDA member known for his fervidity sent an e-mail to the board blasting Ralph for a radio interview in which he allegedly "took a totally pragmatic, pros and cons, middle of the road, no line-in-the-sand, position on the industrialization of PA." He went on to claim that Ralph's refusal to publicly demand an immediate moratorium on all drilling "marginalized and undermined the efforts of every RDA member who thinks a moratorium is really the only responsible course of action and is worth pursuing right now." Ralph was out of step with the RDA's current position, he suggested, and ought not act as its spokesman. Another hard-line board member followed up by chiding Ralph for not "reflect[ing] the official RDA position." RDA had, he contended, "clearly and purposively" chosen to "abandon 'responsible drilling' as an option and as an organizational moniker." He added that no one speaking on behalf of the RDA—including Ralph—was authorized to convey a message that strayed from that line, and that "diluting our message in an attempt to foster some kind of false inclusiveness is . . . counterproductive."[34]

After a few others piled on, Ralph called it quits. "This is such a waste of time. I have had enough," he wrote. He resigned as spokesperson, board member, and editor of the newsletter. "Congratulations," he wrote to his two erstwhile friends who spearheaded the digital takedown. "I have never been, or aspire to be, an alpha male, just someone who is part of something worthwhile." It was time, Ralph said, for him to "focus on something that doesn't involve so much constant negativity and anger." He signed off, "5 years of this is enough. Good luck." It turned out not to be a total divorce. A number of RDA members, including Robbie Cross and Barb, reached out to offer encouragement and urged Ralph not to leave the group entirely. But things would not be the same. It was obvious that the RDA had reached a fork in the road, and that a critical mass of its active members were intent on leading the group down a different path than Ralph was.

Only a few weeks later, Ralph was blindsided by a lengthy and scathing critique of the RDA under his stewardship that Wendy Lee, whom he considered a friend, posted on her blog.[35] Among her charges was that the RDA's historically moderate stance toward fracking meant that it had in effect colluded with the industry. In an e-mail to Wendy, Ralph made one more attempt to defend his increasingly unpopular approach to activism: "I live in a county where this is happening on a huge scale and I live among people, friends, and neighbors who believe differently and have chosen to make decisions about their private land, their homes and their businesses they are comfortable with." His inclination, for better or worse, was not to fight others' decisions and instead "fight for better outcomes for the area given what is happening." He was also inclined to "acknowledge some positive benefits" to the area from fracking. He considered it disingenuous not to. Ralph's approach, he believed, respected the community. But it was also, he hoped, a means of "bringing in people who are not opposed to shale gas" per se—which, it so happened, was most of the county's residents.

* * *

Wendy and other fractivists' embrace of unruly politics was not inherently wrongheaded. Indeed, political scientist Frances Fox Piven argues that the most powerful tool people at "the bottom end of hierarchical relations" have at their disposal to challenge the political status quo is the ability to mobilize "disruptive power." Demonstrations, walkouts, and bold demands are potent because they "disrupt a pattern of ongoing and institutionalized cooperation" that "depends on [our] continuing contributions."[36] Even if elites and the public reject the demands made by more radical elements of a movement, sociological research has shown that radicals' disruptive politics can help legitimate and strengthen the bargaining position of more moderate activists. Audiences may be moved to appease moderate activists because they fear escalating radicalism. Malcom X and other "radical" Black activists arguably had precisely this effect: the goals pursued by mainstream civil rights activists like Dr. Martin Luther King Jr. gained currency as a more palatable alternative to Black militancy.[37]

There's reason to believe that uncivil "repertoires of contention" can also further fractivists' goals.[38] The RDA hard-liner who called out Ralph over e-mail forwarded the RDA board an article about Vera Scroggins, a "gleefully confrontational" retiree and grandmother from Susquehanna County whose video-recorded skirmishes with gas company representatives and trespasses on leased land had made her a hero of the anti-fracking movement. While Scroggins' opponents accused her of "distorting the truth about fracking's impacts," they acknowledged that her activism has been effective. A spokesman for the Independent Oil and Gas Association of New York was quoted saying that if people like Scroggins "weren't doing what they're doing," New York would have dropped its moratorium (now a ban) on drilling a long time ago.[39] The RDA member's comment that accompanied this e-mailed article drew the following lesson: "Those who strive to be reasonable, polite, and non-confrontational . . . have in essence held the door open for the industry while politely asking them to play nice."

The article about Scroggins also noted that her actions led many of her friends and neighbors to shun her, because most of them "support drilling and the economic benefits it brings" and didn't buy the story that fracking will transform their community "into a polluted wasteland." Therein lies the rub. Ralph's aim was to find a community modus vivendi regarding fracking, and it seemed to him (and me) that most of the rural communities in the county supported the industry. Indeed, studies have shown that proximity to gas wells in Pennsylvania (and elsewhere) *decreases* the likelihood of political mobilization against fracking.[40] Landowners who hold gas leases or host gas development on their property are more likely to express positive attitudes about fracking.[41] In Illinois, a study revealed that the vast majority of activists pushing for a statewide ban on fracking were Democratic partisans who lived outside the targeted development region.[42] The takeaway is that many locals who have the most personal experience with fracking, and who are impacted most directly, reject fractivists' portrayal of their communities as sacrifice zones. Opposition to fracking often emanates from urban and coastal areas, most of which do not sit atop lucrative shale plays.

For the most part, fractivism is not a "Not in my backyard" movement. In the words of sociologists Fedor Dokshin and Amanda Buday, it's a "Not in *your* backyard" movement. That's how it felt to the Crawleys and their neighbors when Yoko Ono led the cadre of Manhattan-based fractivists on the "frac tour" through Pennsylvania, and when activists from New York and Philadelphia descended on the Riverdale mobile homes. It's worth noting that, with the exception of Barb, the handful of hard-liners at the center of the RDA dispute were not from the area. As Ralph highlighted in his rebuttal to Wendy, she lived and taught at Bloomsburg University, where no drilling was happening. Both of the RDA members who criticized Ralph over e-mail were rusticators who moved to the area seeking refuge from the city. (Of the six to eight board members who steered the RDA during my time in Billtown, only Ralph, Barb, and one other were raised locally.)

Wendy and the other hard-liners were, and one other more concerned with stopping fracking than making friends. Sure, the fracking ban in neighboring New York—spearheaded by liberal activists in New York City and the Finger Lakes region—alienated conservative landowners in the Southern Tier. (The ban, a *Wall Street Journal* op-ed claimed, "was more about keeping the upstate region as a pastoral retreat for city-dwellers" than "water-related environmental concerns.")[43] But they won. However, Ralph was quick to point out that the dynamic in Pennsylvania was very, very different.[44]

Consciously or not, fractivists like Wendy Lee followed a playbook similar to that of old-school Democratic operatives (who, notably, failed to deliver the state to Hillary Clinton in 2016): they made little attempt to craft a message that appealed to rural, conservative residents. Rather, the aim was to fire up enough supporters in liberal, urban enclaves to overwhelm the opposition. It was a winning strategy in New York. The same cannot be said for Pennsylvania. (It's worth noting that fractivist pressure *has* helped prevent drilling in the Delaware River Basin, which is controlled by an interstate agency, and that the industry deploys "astroturf" countermobilization strategies.[45] I met the director of "external mobilization" for the American Petroleum Institute at the *Gasland Part II* screening.)

Sociologist Fedor Dokshin has shown that, in New York State, it was only after fracking became politicized in national debates that locals' views of the industry began splitting along partisan lines. "Political identities or ideological commitments" came to matter more than perceived costs or benefits in determining whether one supported shale gas drilling.[46] Dokshin observes that partisans who line up on either side of this controversial issue "draw motivation from what the fight symbolizes: a status competition between two antagonistic social groups." The matter of gas drilling itself becomes "secondary to the deeply felt antagonism between the two camps."[47] Thanks in part to attention-grabbing hard-liners from outside the area like Wendy Lee, many rural Lycoming County residents believed that the few vocal opponents of fracking were liberal interlopers from the city more interested in community disruption than dialogue. It was also their perception that their likeminded neighbors supported, and benefited from, fracking. As has been noted in other research on extraction, community members may support industry "even if it offers them little direct economic benefit because they view it as beneficial to friends and neighbors."[48] Expressing support for fracking and dismissing fractivism became a way of standing with one's community. The impulse to show solidarity with one's neighbors in the face of opposition from perceived community outsiders could be so powerful that it could lead even those who benefited little and absorbed significant spillover effects, like the Crawleys, to maintain public support of gas drilling.

Over time, landowners like George and the Crawleys became disillusioned with the industry. They were no longer true believers. As their grievances mounted, they seemed primed to become accidental activists against fracking in their backyard. At the very least, they grew more receptive to ideas like greater oversight of gas drilling and granting more protections to lessors. But hard-line fractivists' disruptive tactics and partisan framing of the issue offended them and marginalized them from the movement. They also found fractivists to be patronizing, claiming to act on their behalf while disregarding their worldview. To some, the push for a fracking ban was a Trojan horse that would strip away home rule and property rights, even though fractivists sold it as a way to protect vulnerable rural communities.[49] (Tom Shepstone calls the conflict over fracking a war over "who controls the land," with fractivists in favor of a government-run "super land agency" that dictates from the capitol how farmers and other rural landowners use their property.)[50] In this way, fractivists played a part in turning the fracking debate into an "us versus them" battle that reinforced the rural-urban divide. In turn, local residents knew where they stood—on the side of the community, and its rural values. It became impossible for these two camps to engage in civil discourse about the issues and find common ground. Fracking had become simply another vehicle of identity politics.

For their part, most rural landowners refused to acknowledge areas of agreement and overlap with fractivists. It was almost comical to spend hours at the kitchen table listening to folks like Scott McClain and George complain bitterly that the industry is trampling on their property rights and marring the countryside and then dismiss fracking opponents as out of touch. Even as they adopted a critical stance toward the industry, lessors like Scott and George continued to insist they were not against drilling. To me, this was further evidence of how deeply one's position on fracking was connected to one's community and political identity. It was almost impossible for these residents to see themselves as fracking opponents because of all the baggage they attached to that position (e.g., being an environmentalist, aligned with outsiders, in favor of Big Government intervening in local land use decisions). Some also relied on caricatures to justify to me their decision not to engage with the RDA. I regularly heard people call the group crazy and radical, even though the positions that it had spent years carefully staking out online and in public forums were largely in line with many residents' concerns: banning the storage of wastewater in impoundment ponds that often leaked, restricting truck traffic to ease road congestion, eliminating flaring, increasing penalties for gas well violations, and—their signature (and quite popular) campaign—keeping fracking out of Loyalsock State Forest's Rock Run. What's more, the RDA's board included several politically moderate accidental activists (not just Ralph) who did not otherwise wear their politics on their sleeves. In short, most RDA members were low-key, reasonable people who prioritized practical local issues—and civility.

Lessors largely shunned responsibility for finding workable solutions to problems they experienced (or created) from fracking. With the one avenue they were familiar with to address community land use concerns—zoning hearings—blocked, most were disinterested in finding other forms of collective engagement. Their inclination to distrust government agencies like the DEP, and their knee-jerk rejection of bureaucratic regulations, fostered passivity in the face of industry malfeasance.

Interestingly, research shows that partisan identity shapes not only one's views toward regulation, but also how one assesses risk. Adam Mayer and Tara O'Connor Shelly found that conservative landowners in Colorado viewed fracking as significantly less dangerous than did liberal landowners. Part of conservatives' rejection of industry oversight resulted not from "policy preferences per se" but from their "lower risk perceptions" and greater trust in the industry.[51] (During the COVID-19 pandemic, surveys found that only conservatives felt safe at the movies.)[52]

While those exposed to contamination, like the Crawleys and the Bodles, were angry at gas companies for harming their water, they often joined other lessors in emphasizing personal responsibility. "No one held a gun to my head" to lease, Doyle Bodle reiterated even as he showed me the brown, bubbly water that came from his spigot. Their support of individual choice entailed embracing the role of acting as their own actuary rather than relying on the government or some other expert. They insisted that they knew there were some risks involved and made a personal decision to lease despite those risks. Doyle's wife, Peggy, in rationalizing the couple's decision to lease despite having some concerns and knowing that they never stood to get rich since they had so few acres to lease, compared fracking to everyday risks that people accept in exchange for convenience. "Everything at one point in time, they put stuff on it like formaldehyde when we were growing up. Stuff was put on the plants and we ate that." She added, "You could get lung cancer and never have smoked a cigarette in your life." Doyle interjected, "I agree with her. With all the chemicals that we're putting on the crops today . . . you can' t tell me they know that's 100 percent safe." Drawing a parallel to fracking, he added, "It doesn't matter where you live, you're gonna have water problems" of some kind. Now that things had gone wrong, the Bodles wanted recompense. But they viewed the gas company's apparent negligence as a breach of contract between two private parties, to be settled in civil court. Even as they struggled to hold the gas company accountable, they were hesitant to conclude from their experience that fracking posed a significant threat to the community and that the answer was more government regulations of the industry.[53] They also remained steadfast that it was not their place to say or do anything that might compromise their neighbors' land sovereignty. Justified under the "live and let live" principle, their inaction, I have come to see, is a form of *civic dissociation* that effectively emboldened the gas industry and facilitated the erosion of the commons.

CHAPTER 10

Our Land

As I made my way to Rock Run for the first time, on a frosty, snowy February morning, I wondered if it could live up to the hype. Several outdoor magazines had anointed the "ruggedly, unremittingly drop-dead beautiful" tributary of Lycoming Creek, which plunges down a densely wooded and narrow glacier-carved gorge, the "prettiest stream in Pennsylvania."[1] *Backpacker* magazine declared that its three natural pools, each chiseled out of rock from the torrents created by the so-called Lower, Middle, and Upper Falls, are "some of the best swimming holes in the entire United States."[2] Its crystal-clear waters, pure enough to earn a rare "exceptional value" designation from the DEP, are an ideal habitat for trout (who like cold, clear, and clean water); Rock Run is a legendary fishing hole. The twenty-seven-mile Old Loggers Path, which meanders alongside Rock Run and is chockablock with cascades and mountaintop vistas, is "one of the state's most popular long-distance hiking trails."[3] These wooded environs are formally recognized by the Audubon Society as a critical avian habitat.

I had planned to wait until spring to make my first foray into Loyal-sock State Forest. But then I heard that the RDA was sponsoring a mid-winter hike to Rock Run's Upper Falls, and I decided to join them. (The group took out a color ad in the local newspaper to promote the hike.) As my creaky two-wheel-drive sedan spun out in the gravel parking lot and the howling winds buffeted the windshield, I momentarily regret-ted my decision. Rock Run would still be there in sunny May. Why did I leave behind my gas fireplace? If others shared my trepidation, they didn't show it. As the snow continued to fall, the eighteen hikers—mostly older RDA members, but also a few younger locals who saw the *Sun-Gazette* ad (including a couple with a toddler strapped into her mother's backpack)—chatted excitedly as the group made its way up a closed gravel access road.

Soon, we were swallowed up by trees. It was a winter wonderland. Evergreen and hemlock branches bowed under the weight of the pristine snow. Rivulets that trickled down the rocky mountainside in warmer months were frozen in time. The snow quieted the traffic of nearby Route 14. All that could be heard was the soft crunch of boots and, eventually, the babbling of Rock Run. The creek water was perfectly transparent, allowing a clear view of the rock bed. As it careened around a stony bend, the brook created a shelf of icicles several feet long that practically glowed azure. It was stunning scenery. But it paled in comparison to what lay a half mile upstream. The headwaters of Rock Run could be seen tumbling down the mountain in the far distance. Before us, the currents banked off a two-story-high striated rock wall and briefly swirled in a pool before being sucked with force down a stone flume—the Upper Falls—and emptying into a placid pool. The group, including folks who had been there dozens of times, stood in silent awe. Smiling wide, Barb captured the collective mood: "What a spot on the planet!"

Then came the buzzkill. The reason why the RDA organized this hike, Jim Slotterback reminded us, is that the Rock Run area was one of several "special places" on ostensibly protected public land that had been targeted for gas drilling. The Anadarko Petroleum Corporation and another firm had quietly purchased the privately held mineral rights to 25,000 acres surrounding Rock Run. Internal memos written by the state's Department of Conservation and Natural Resources (DCNR), which managed the surface, revealed that Anadarko planned to build as many as twenty-six well pads in the so-called Clarence Moore tract (eponymously named for the erstwhile principal holder of the subsurface), in addition to compressor stations, water impoundments, pipelines, and new roads. The Old Loggers Path and a portion of Rock Run's watershed, which provided wetland habitat for several threatened or

FIG. 10.1. Rock Run, Loyalsock State Forest, in winter. Photograph by Colin Jerolmack.

endangered plant and animal species, like the green pitcher plant, were in the crosshairs. Saving Rock Run would become the nexus of the RDA's community organizing efforts, perhaps even its hill to die on. Peering up through gently falling snow, RDA member Robbie Cross shuddered as he imagined the alpine ridgeline pocked by drilling rigs. "What we are losing is more valuable than the gas," he mourned. "This is the people's land."

About a third of Pennsylvania's 2.2 million acres of public forest is potentially exposed to natural-gas development. The state has little say in and draws no rents from roughly 287,000 of those acres, because they, like Rock Run, are split-estate parcels; the state only owns the surface.[4] But the revenue the state generates from exploiting the mineral rights it *does* own is substantial. Between 2008 and 2010, governor Ed Rendell (D) brought in $413 million from auctions of new oil and gas leases for over 138,000 acres of state forest and game land. (An additional 195,000 acres that had been leased over the prior half century for shallow vertical gas wells was automatically made available for horizontal drilling and fracking.) In 2013, the year in which I lived eight months in Billtown, annual royalties and other gas-related payments from leased public land reportedly totaled $148 million. Only a small fraction of the money brought in each year was set aside for DCNR conservation efforts. The lion's share—95 percent, according to a lawsuit filed by the Pennsylvania Environmental Defense Foundation (PEDF)—was used to balance the state's budget (general fund). As of 2017, there were 623 royalty-generating gas wells on public land. Pennsylvania residents could expect 850 or so more, even if a fragile moratorium on leasing additional acreage in state forests and game lands holds, because the DCNR estimates that only 30–35 percent of permitted wells have been drilled.[5]

Those who support fracking the Commonwealth of Pennsylvania point out, rightly, that DCNR-managed lands are "working forests." Natural-gas extraction, according to the DCNR, "has been a use of the state forest system since 1947"; selective timber harvesting has an even longer history.[6] But the ecological disruption caused by logging and shallow vertical gas wells is a fraction of the disruption caused by fracking. In places like Tiadaghton State Forest (18 miles northwest of Billtown), where a third of its acreage is leased, it had become impossible to drive, walk, hunt, camp, or fish without experiencing the fallout from gas drilling in the form of new and widened roads, closed or rerouted sections of trails, fenced-off vistas, massive impoundments and well pads where stands of trees once thrived, and armadas of tractor trailers. And, to me, seemingly everywhere were security guards who controlled—and routinely denied—access to public roads.

Fracking has turned segments of the Tiadaghton's once remote and untamed terrain into a mining town. It threatens to do the same to the region surrounding Rock Run and to many other public wilderness areas. It is not only the "wild character" (in the DCNR's words) of these areas that has been eroded by oil and gas development. Fracking has induced the de facto privatization of actual commons. And, perhaps most troubling to many of the recreationists I met, the literal enclosure of the commons via fencing, gates, and security guards eroded the special sense of absolute personal freedom that full immersion in wilderness had long provided to them.

* * *

The Tiadaghton is one of eight state forests designated as the "Pennsylvania Wilds," which were promoted, during the time I lived in the area, as "some of the most spectacular, untouched and undisturbed wild lands east of the Mississippi."[7] Though its craggy, sylvan trails have long offered visitors a feeling of near-total seclusion, the Tiadaghton is easily accessible. The ample girth of Pine Creek Valley, whose channel carves through the heart of the park, allows for a two-lane highway peppered with trailheads and a popular rail trail that ambles from the "Pennsylvania Grand Canyon" down to Jersey Shore (PA). The quaint creekside village of Waterville, which hosts a general store, gas station, tavern, and lodge, is a convenient base camp for organizing hiking, camping, fly-fishing, hunting, biking, and snowmobiling excursions in the area. Many of the Tiadaghton's stunning vistas are accessible via car, thanks to a network of drivable trails.

The same factor—ease of access—that made the Tiadaghton area an epicenter of outdoor recreation later made it an epicenter of fracking.

Representative Garth Everett and state senator Gene Yaw held up the Tiadaghton as proof that fracking can be done in a way that is minimally disruptive. Indeed, Garth was eager to connect me to the Tiadaghton District Forester, Jeffrey Prowant, because he believed Jeffrey could show me how "sites that have been developed" are now "almost reclaimed" to their natural state. When I reached out to Jeffrey, he was happy to spend two entire days driving me around parts of the forest that had been touched by industry. But when it came to the notion that fracking could be squared with conservation, he was far less sanguine than Garth.

It didn't take long for me to realize that Jeffrey was caught between a rock and a hard place. As he gripped the steering wheel with one hand and a Diet Coke with the other, the ruddy-faced sexagenarian told me that he took a job with the DCNR because he was "always an outdoors person" and wanted to help protect them for his daughter's generation. (She was a student at George Washington University at the time; he proudly wore a tan "GW" hat atop his cropped gray hair.) But once the governor leased the Tiadaghton for drilling, it fell on Jeffrey to more or less manage fracking here. On the one hand, he was charged with policing petroleum companies for compliance with their lease terms. On the other hand, it was his duty to ensure that the companies were granted reasonable access to their mineral rights. The latter role sometimes necessitated making the hard decision to close or reroute popular drivable and off-road trails. Of late, Jeffrey said he was "taking a beating" from recreational users. He didn't sign up for this. His weary pale blue eyes, and his daily countdown to retirement (T-minus four years, ten months, and fourteen days at the time I first met him) betrayed a disillusionment with what his job had become in the fracking era. (That is not to say that Jeffrey opposed fracking per se; he was part of a hunting camp that leased its land.)

As Jeffrey eased his forest-green, government-issued SUV onto the Tiadaghton access road called Dam Run, the bustle of Route 287 instantly gave way to a thick canopy of trees and a babbling brook. But in short order we were greeted by an incongruous roadside security guard shack and a porta-potty. Mounds of gravel surrounded us, material for

FIG. 10.2. Jeffrey Prowant, the Tiadaghton District Forester. Photograph by Tristan Spinksi.

new roads that sprouted from both sides of Dam Run to provide access to Anadarko well pads that had been gouged out of the lush greenery. A caravan of water trucks with flashing warning lights forced us to pull over to the side of the recently paved and widened road. Helicopters buzzed low overhead, delivering equipment to mountaintop gas workers. Upon reaching a bend in the road where a 125-foot-wide grassy pipeline right-of-way coming down the mountainside intersected with a four-acre gravel well pad and a twelve-acre water impoundment pond surrounded by wire fencing, Jeffrey pulled over. "Prior to this, there was no—this was all forest. It was just unbroken forest." Pointing to a gravel road clogged with trucks carrying water and sand, he recalled, "There was no road. There was no pipeline." The area now felt so much like an industrial park that it was an old whitewashed hunting camp that seemed out of place. The copse that long concealed it had been replaced by gas wells, de facto parking lots, and cyclone fences. The former two-track dirt road that kinked around the lodge, once a quiet and scenic drivable trail, had become a highway for big rigs.

After a security guard had Jeffrey sign in, she lifted a gate that controlled access to a (public) gravel road. No sooner had we begun to inch up the mountain than we had to pull off to the side of the road to allow trucks to pass. We then came upon the largest impoundment pond I had ever seen. Encased in grassy berms topped by wire fencing, the rubber-lined pool occupied about fifteen acres and held fifteen to eighteen million gallons of water. "This was all forest before," Jeffrey shrugged. Continuing up the wide road undergirded by two feet of crushed stone, Jeffrey recalled that until recently the road was "basically a goat path." We drove right up to a well pad that was in the middle of being fracked. The lot teemed with dozens of white pickups and big rigs, which continuously came and went to feed the well's voracious appetite for water and sand. Roughnecks skittered about among the porta-potties and the trailers that served as temporary offices and their housing. Caterers prepared meals, and maids cleaned up the sleeping quarters. In the middle of it all was a giant crane that held aloft the wellhead. A tangle of tensile pipes stemming from ten or so pump trucks converged on the wellhead, which received the cocktail of water, sand, and frac fluid and shot it down the mile-deep wellbore at extremely high pressure. This stimulated the manmade fissures in the shale to release the gas. It was quite an operation.

From that point on, it was industry in every direction. Miles and miles of roads, which were either brand-new or converted from narrow drivable trails, branched off on all sides. Most were fronted by a security guard shack and led to massive clearings that hosted either an impoundment or a well pad. In some cases, the large trees that were chopped down to make room for industry still sat in roadside stacks. Many of the roads were accompanied by 125-foot-wide swaths of barren ground peppered with plastic yellow posts, indicating pipelines that had been laid to transport gas from the well pads. Trucks squeezed by each other. Men in hard hats roamed around the "man camps." Drilling rigs poked through the tree canopy. Warehouse-like compressor stations of corrugated metal dotted the ridges like company outposts. The air was

FIG. 10.3. An impoundment pond and fracking in Tiadaghton State Forest.
Photographs by Colin Jerolmack.

permeated with gray dust. It was impossible to escape the incessant drone of diesel engines.

"I get concerned about the disturbance to the forest," Jeffrey said. As stated in a DCNR report, "While the bureau works with companies to locate pads to avoid negative ecological effects, the selection of the general area for the pads" is made by the company "based on the presence of gas."[8] Jeffrey opined, "The companies could do more to reduce the disturbance and the impact on the forest." He pointed to two separate pipeline rights-of-way that, he said, were owned by two different companies and asked why they couldn't simply share one pipeline. It would have saved dozens of acres of core forest. Jeffrey was also frustrated that gas companies refused to reduce the size of their well pads. After all, once gas wells have been fracked and connected to a pipeline, the pads no longer need to be big enough for a tractor trailer to make a U-turn. In Jeffrey's view, even if the lessee had to come back in ten years to re-frack a well, if they rehabilitated the pad in the interim then the forest would have gained "ten years of value for wildlife or some other [ecological] aspect."

When I mentioned that Garth had promised that Jeffrey would show me a remediated site, he looked puzzled and curtly replied, "We don't have any." He wasn't optimistic there would be one soon, either. The wells, he surmised, could produce for a half century. And besides, DCNR leases, like most, "are in perpetuity" for all depths. If and when Marcellus shale gas is exhausted, the lessee retained the right to drill deeper into other shale formations (most of which were not yet economically viable). So long as the gas wells are producing, the lessee retains surface access rights.[9]

Between 2008 and 2018, shale gas extraction in the Tiadaghton resulted in over twelve miles of new road construction and forty-four miles of road modification (i.e., widening), fifty-two miles of gas pipeline rights-of-way, and 318 acres cleared for fifty-one well pads, three compressor stations, and twelve water impoundments. This equals the loss of over 3,800 acres of core forest (forested areas surrounded by more forest)—a reduction of as much as 6 percent within the leased portion of the Tiadaghton—and an increase of 586 acres of "nonforest" (e.g., tree stands turned into gravel lots).[10] This degree of forest fragmentation worried Jeffrey, and worried ecologists, because it created over 1,800 acres of "edge forests" that could attract invasive species, degrade the ecosystem services provided by core forests, increase riparian erosion and stream sedimentation, and drive out endangered plants and animals that only thrive in core forest.[11] This disruption is strikingly apparent in satellite imagery of the Tiadaghton: in every direction, the green is blemished by the brown tendrils of widened access roads and the tidy gray squares that mark well pads and impoundments.[12]

"One of [our] most significant roles," the DCNR wrote in a 2018 report on shale gas activity, "is to act, in the public trust, as stewards of the commonwealth's . . . state forest system." The DCNR says it will accomplish this mission in part by working to retain forests' so-called wild character—by which it means "scenic beauty, feeling of solitude, sense of remoteness, and the undeveloped and aesthetic nature of the state forest system."[13] Yet it was hard to reconcile that mission with the gas development that the DCNR had no choice but to administer in the Tiadaghton. Mountaintop vistas of the meandering Pine Creek Valley, where one could gaze upon miles of mountainous green folds and see bald eagles soaring on updrafts, were now blighted by drilling rigs that hulked over the ridgeline and by the tan scars of pipeline clearances and well pads. One DCNR forester lamented to me in an e-mail, "The song of the whippoorwill is now replaced by the sound of rig activity, the starry sky isn't visible due to the light given off by a well pad, the nighttime silence has been replaced by the racket of machinery and traffic." And so on. Reflecting this reality, the promotional website for the Pennsylvania Wilds has dropped the phrase "untouched and undisturbed" from its description.[14] There was no doubt, DCNR acknowledged, that the wild character of the forest was "impacted" (to put it a bit euphemistically) by fracking. Its own surveys showed that many recreationists were distressed by the displacement of nature by industry.[15]

The most common activity that respondents said was negatively impacted was hiking. As one who spent dozens of hours wandering and doing volunteer trail maintenance in the Tiadaghton, I'm not surprised.

While walking a portion of the Mid State Trail, which traverses the entire length of Pennsylvania and was the state's 2019 "Trail of the Year," I suddenly emerged from the dense, darkened forest into a disorienting, and even slightly dangerous, scene: with my eyes still adjusting to the bright daylight let in by the newly widened Schoolhouse Road and a pipeline, I had to look out for gas trucks rumbling in both directions as I crossed to pick up the trail on the other side. Huge stacks of trees recently felled to make way for a well pad made the task more taxing, as they blocked the trail. The wasteland of stumps that would become COP Tract 322 Pad C had still been intact forest when I came through the area just the week before. I scurried back to the serenity of the forest, but not a mile later I confronted another pipeline and the newly widened Hackett Road, which was trafficked by growling Caterpillar excavators and dozers. An orange drill rig loomed over a barren lot like a monument to industry. The lone sight for sore eyes was a rustic, narrow drivable dirt trail with total canopy cover that split off the access road, a reminder of what Hackett Road used to look like.

Scenic driving, the DCNR notes, is the sole purpose of many people's visit. Indeed, one factor that made the Tidaghton so inviting for daytrippers was that one could easily reach many of the forest's 190 panoramic vistas by car or a short walk while still experiencing a sense of seclusion. Yet the DCNR recognizes that, even in instances where it was able to preserve a vista's viewshed, nearby infrastructure encountered on one's approach to the vista can sully the experience. The DCNR cited one of the Tiadaghton's most well-known vistas, Ramsey Point, as "an example of an affected vista because of the infrastructure that was placed nearby."[16] After visiting the vista with Scott and Betty McClain and their friend Emily (a college student), I would say that "affected" is a bit of an understatement. We had just left behind the industrial mayhem of Dam Run Road. As Scott slowly steered us along Ramsey Road, we spotted a juvenile black bear standing amid fallen leaves right next to the road. This was the kind of wild encounter that drew us here. Yet we were immediately distracted by a well pad sitting further up the road. An acrid odor wafted from the dehydrators, whose pipes were wrapped with black trash bags held in place by duct tape. The equipment emitted a

FIG. 10.1 Trees felled to make room for a well pad along the Mid State Trail.
Photograph by Colin Jerolmack.

loud clanking sound that reminded me of zippers hitting the side of a dryer. About two hundred yards past the pad, we encountered a closed gate. A bold-print red, black, and white sign read, "DANGER. RESTRICTED AREA. NO ENTRY. AUTHORIZED PERSONNEL ONLY." Most law-abiding people would presumably turn around at this point; every indication was that the vista was closed. Ever the rebel, Scott didn't "give a shit" what the sign said and got out of the SUV. The only reason Betty and I had the confidence to join him was that Jeffrey Prowant had assured me that gas companies cannot forbid access to public roads and well pads unless gas workers or vehicles are operating. Emily stayed behind. She said she didn't want to risk getting in trouble for trespassing.

It felt like trespassing. After skirting the yellow-and-black gate, we walked by a fenced-in impoundment. We kept going until we came upon a wall of tall dehydrator stacks. We had reached the well pad. It was intimidating to step on the four- to five-acre lot, as it required ignoring

the brown billboard with multiple signs telling you not to. One, bright
red and shaped like a stop sign, shouted, "STOP. AUTHORIZED
PERSONNEL ONLY." Others warned, "You are entering a PGE location"
and "NO ENTRY." Kicking stones as we crossed the gravel pad, Scott and
I counted eleven Christmas trees (gas well caps) in the middle. On the
far side of this tangle of pipes, smokestacks, storage tanks, and sterile
void of crushed stone was the hidden vista. It was a nice one, with Pine
Creek gently curling around lush, rugged foothills. But the trip here was
menacing. The unmarked vista felt like an afterthought, not a culmina-
tion. Nor was it accessible. Now that one had to park at the gate and
walk through all the gas infrastructure, Cindy Bower lamented, her husband could no longer visit Ramsey Point with her.[17] Emily, who had
been coming up here her whole life, was physically able to walk to the
vista but no longer felt that she was entitled to go there.

* * *

Since at least the time Americans began to read Rousseau, the environmental historian William Cronon argues, they have been enamored of
the idea that the "best antidote to the ills of an overly refined and civi-
lized modern world was a return to simpler, more primitive living."[18]
This was, of course, the premise of the philosopher Henry David Thoreau's seminal book *Walden* (1854), which documented his two-year
"experiment" staying in a primitive cabin in Boston's wooded outskirts
and living mostly off the land. Living simply and close to the land, Thoreau wrote, rejuvenated the spirit and reawakened the senses. It was real
living.[19] His time at Walden Pond led him to equate immersion in nature with liberty. "All good things," he famously penned, "are wild and
free."[20] Once, when Thoreau left his sylvan haven to run errands in Con-
cord, he was arrested and put in jail for back-owed poll taxes. It is said
that this experience deepened his belief that organized government was
the enemy of personal freedom and inspired his libertarian manifesto
"Civil Disobedience."[21]

Some chroniclers argue that Americans' valorization of independence and self-sufficiency was forged by pioneers "settling" the Western

Frontier.[22] Whether or not there is any substance to this myth, the connection between wilderness and liberty has persisted for more than a century after the closure of the frontier. Even if we bracket (or, like Cronon, criticize) this moralization of nature, there is a degree of literal truth to the idea that wilderness begets personal sovereignty. There are certainly laws that one must obey in public forests like the Tiadaghton. But what is striking—at least to people like me who didn't grow up traipsing through large wild areas—is how much autonomy, and how little guidance, one is given. Trails are merely suggestions. You can walk, camp, swim, fish, and even defecate almost anywhere. You can make a fire where you like or eat wild plants. You can free-climb cliffs. You can carry an open container of alcohol (if over twenty-one). You can scream at the top of your lungs. No railings prevent you from straying too close to a ravine; no signs warn you to avoid rapids or a nearby rattlesnake den. It's up to you to supervise your own safety and comply with the DCNR code of conduct (e.g., no feeding wildlife, no littering). Most of the time, there is no technology or park ranger to monitor—or save— you. The heterodox author and activist Edward Abbey, who spent the summers of his early adulthood serving as a park ranger in some of the country's most remote national parks, recognized that this kind of autonomy was a precious resource in an increasingly urbanized, populous, and surveilled (not to mention litigious) society. "We cannot have freedom without wilderness," he opined. "We cannot have freedom without leagues of open space" where people "can live at least part of their lives under no control but their own desires and abilities, free from any and all direct administration by their fellow man."[23] For his part, the Black naturalist J. Drew Lanham writes that wilderness is the one place where he can find his "whole self, not discounted by law"; only in nature is there "no suspicion or fear generated by my brown skin."[24]

When the DCNR and park visitors reference the loss of the Tiadaghton's wild character, it is the loss of solitude, and the freedom to roam, that they have in mind as much as biodiversity loss. In a number of places, fracking has constrained visitors' movements or obstructed access altogether. In the Tiadaghton, gas drilling necessitated the long-term closure of two public-access roads, including one that led to a popular vista. On a shorter-term basis, seventeen roads totaling over fifty-seven miles were closed to facilitate shale gas development.[25] What's more, while Jeffrey Prowant was adamant that, "unless there's active drilling or some kind of active construction," gas companies could not impede public access even on well pads themselves, gas companies illegally policed people who encroached on their operations. Jeffrey was himself stopped as he stood in the woods next to a well pad while I took pictures. A security guard wearing a green vest and carrying a clipboard left her post by the pad and approached. "Excuse me!" she shouted urgently. "This is XTO property! You must leave, and you can't take pictures!" When Jeffrey replied that it was *public* property and that she could not stop anyone from walking in the woods or taking pictures, she demanded identification. It got a little tense. "You don't have the authority to ask me for identification," Jeffrey huffed. She seemed flabbergasted. "I don't have the authority?!" Jeffrey continued, "This is public land. I don't have to show you my ID." It was only upon realizing that Jeffrey was the District Forester that the guard sheepishly desisted. She reported that her boss told her to write down the license plate number of any car that drove past, and to disallow passengers from getting out of their car.

On my next visit to the forest, I found my car blocked by a chain stretched across Huntley Road. I was trying to pick up a hiking trail that I thought crossed there, and I explained to the guard that I had been back there recently with Jeffrey Prowant. Jeffrey had given me permission to show his business card to anyone who questioned my right to access public rights-of-way. "Are you telling me it's restricted access," I asked the graying, middle-aged guard, who said his name was Dom. He seemed unsure but said he thought so. Anyone who came up this way, he observed, simply turned around when they saw the chain across the road. "There's not much back there except a well pad," he added, seemingly hoping I would just go away. He wrote down Jeffrey's name and title, then wrote down my name and license plate and asked me who I was with. I politely told him I was a state resident and didn't see how that question had any bearing on my right to access the road. He didn't know what to do. I promised I wouldn't be long and encouraged him to call Jeffrey, who would vouch for me and my right of access. He relented.

I drove to within a hundred feet of the pad, which had a monstrous "walking" drilling rig on it. A hard hat made a beeline for me as I took out my camera and sternly asked, "Can I help you?" I said no, I was simply taking in the vista and checking out the activity on the pad. He didn't seem satisfied and demanded that I spell out my full name and tell him whom I was with. Though I was a safe distance from the pad on a public right-of-way, I felt intimidated. The foreman got on his radio; I decided not to hang around long enough to see whom he was calling. When I drove back down to the guard shack, Dom was on edge. They must have called him. "You taking pictures back there?" he asked, his voice trembling. I said I took a few, but just of the view of the valley. "Oh man," Dom responded, "they *really* don't like people taking pictures. I probably shouldn't have let you do it," he told me. "I won't be able to let you back there again." I felt bad for putting Dom in a tough spot and apologized, adding that I believed I had a right to be back there. He pointed to a sign implying I did not: "Authorized personnel only." (When I relayed this to Jeffrey, he said he'd make sure they got the message that the road was still public.)

Portions of the Tiadaghton have in effect become enclosed. "If a gas corporation clear-cuts trees and replaces them with several feet of limestone on a well pad, is it still state forest land?" an irate DCNR forester lamented to me in an after-hours conversation on the deck of his creekside cabin. "The land," he added, "has been successfully privatized." An entire security apparatus has emerged to regulate access to land that is legally part of the commons, a place where generations of people have enjoyed as a birthright the ability to wander the woods free from civilization's encumbrances and scrutiny. Hunters, anglers, picnickers, campers, cyclists, and snowmobilers—anyone who visits "their" forest for recreation—can expect to find public-access roads inexplicably (and sometimes illegally) closed, to be recorded by surveillance cameras in places that are so remote they lack cell phone reception, to have to show identification and explain their presence to guards who determine whether or not they are allowed to proceed on a public right-of-way, to encounter fenced-off areas and signs that warn them (sometimes incorrectly) that they are trespassing, and to be chased off areas (again, illegally) adjacent to gas installations. Indeed, I experienced all these things in the Tiadaghton, in addition to being tailgated for miles by private security cars and white petroleum company trucks whose drivers sometimes threatened to confiscate my camera. Visitors like me were made to feel like criminals for exercising our ostensible right to roam the commons (I shudder to consider the additional harassment that Black visitors may have experienced). And disgruntled foresters like the one I clandestinely met with for drinks reported having a hard time showing up to work these days, because the wilderness they loved "is being fucking destroyed."

* * *

The day after seeing all the industrial disruption in the Tiadaghton with Jeffrey Prowant, I joined several RDA members for a hike along part of the Old Loggers Path near Rock Run. A dozen or so folks convened in a gravel lot that was otherwise empty on a snowy March morning. The first part of our walk was a pleasant stroll along a gravel access road. We eventually crossed the Old Loggers Path, which, as the name suggests, was once a logging road. We picked up the trail and soon vanished into the dense second-growth forest as we slowly made our way up Sullivan Mountain. As the hike became steeper, or obliged us to traverse a shallow tributary or scramble over a downed tree, conversations were replaced by huffing and the occasional grunt. Otherwise, it was so quiet that you could hear the snow hitting the trees. My mind was alert to signs of life in the leafless winter woodlands: the staccato echo of a woodpecker's beak drilling into a far-off tree; the rustle of leaves and flash of a white tail before a deer camouflaged amid the trees bolted like a shot. Most of the time, though, it felt like we had the forest completely to ourselves. To shave some time off the ascent, we occasionally bushwhacked and met back up with the trail after a switchback. At the pinnacle was Sharp Top Vista. Whiteout conditions blocked our view of the valley, but few seemed to mind.

I couldn't help but contrast this visit to the Loyalsock with my trip to the Tiadaghton the day before. We could walk in the middle of the access road, which was narrow enough to be enveloped by the canopy, because we didn't have to make way for caravans of big rigs. The transition between Old Loggers Path and the access road was seamless: there were no denuded pipeline clearances, hulking drilling rigs, barren well pads, guard shacks, or belching diesel engines like I encountered when the Mid State Trail crossed roads in the Tiadaghton. We were free to roam as we pleased in silence through unbroken forest, removed from any signs of industry or civilization. But maybe not for long. As the RDA learned through right-to-know requests, the DCNR predicted that Old Loggers Path "will be taking the brunt of development" if and when Anadarko decided to exercise its mineral rights in the Clarence Moore tract. The gravel road that crossed the trail could become a minihighway. A compressor station and eleven well pads could be placed a mere hundred feet or so from the bosky path. Pipeline clearances would scar the woods. Sharp Top would look out on drill rigs. Security guards might interrogate visitors about their whereabouts and restrict access.

It was DCNR's position that it could not stop fracking in and around the Old Loggers Path and Rock Run. When the Commonwealth purchased the 25,621 acres from the Central Pennsylvania Lumber Company, in 1933, it didn't acquire the mineral rights. Eventually, Anadarko and the investment company International Development Corporation each purchased one-half of the subsurface; the IDC then leased its portion of the subsurface to Southwestern Energy. Because subsurface rights take precedence over surface ownership rights, the DCNR claimed that the best it could do was try to convince Anadarko to voluntarily work with it on a "surface use agreement" that would minimize land disturbance. Adding insult to injury, the state would not reap any bonus payments or royalties from development in the Clarence Moore tract, since the property was a split estate.

It was RDA members who were the first users of the park to become aware of the possibility that shale gas extraction might occur in the Clarence Moore tract. As Jim Slotterback and Ralph Kisberg recalled, some RDA members came upon survey stakes marked "APC" while they were poking around on a plateau just above the headwaters of Rock Run in 2011. After a little digging at the courthouse, the RDA discovered

Anadarko Petroleum Corporation's holding and learned that it had just contracted a firm to do seismic testing, which would allow it to locate the most optimal locations to drill for natural gas. Through a right-to-know law request, the group learned that the DCNR had been negotiating behind closed doors with Anadarko on a plan to allow drilling centered on the Old Loggers Path circuit, which included wetlands that formed part of the headwaters of Rock Run.

The RDA's discovery of what it called a secret plan to frack in and around one of the most popular and ecologically sensitive portions of the Loyalsock was explosive. It led to several front-page articles, and numerous outraged letters to the editor, in the *Williamsport Sun-Gazette*. But the RDA's digging led to an even bigger bombshell: the deed to the Clarence Moore tract implied that the DCNR may actually have, in the words of RDA board member and attorney Mark Szybist, "exclusive surface control over 18,870 acres of the Clarence Moore lands." If true, then the DCNR had the power to deny Anadarko access to almost 75 percent of the total area. It all boiled down to a "reservation clause" in the deed. When the lumber company sold the land to the Commonwealth, in 1933, it used the provision to keep to itself "the rights of ingress, egress and regress upon and over said tracts of land" to access coal, oil, and gas. Yet the clause clearly states that these rights expired after fifty years. According to Szybist, lawyers for the Commonwealth presumed that it acquired ownership of the subsurface in 1983.[26] But Clarence Moore sued to retain the mineral rights. In 1989, the Commonwealth Court sided with Moore on the question of ownership. Even so, it ruled that the subsurface owner's customary right to enter upon the surface to access its minerals was, in this case, annulled in 1983.[27]

In 2012–13, the RDA spearheaded a two-pronged offensive. On the legal front, Szybist and other environmental lawyers worked to pressure local lawmakers and the DCNR to interpret the Commonwealth Court's 1989 decision as meaning that Anadarko (and Southwestern) could not develop its mineral interests unless the state voluntarily decided to grant it a right-of-way. (Conservatives like Garth Everett remained unmoved. "These guys own the gas rights," he told me. "The law . . . says if you own mineral rights that you have the reasonable ability to develop them.") The DNCR was operating in bad faith, the RDA asserted, acting as if its hands were tied when in fact it could deny access to much of the forest. Ralph and Szybist devised what became an influential alternative development plan: the state should leverage its "total surface control" over the 18,870 acres to force Anadarko and Southwestern to agree to stringent environmental standards on development in the other 7,000 acres. In exchange, the petroleum companies would be allowed to drill horizontally under the 18,870 acres (However, they couldn't so much as scratch the surface).

On the community front, the RDA made Rock Run the centerpiece of a new public outreach initiative. Capitalizing on the news generated by its discovery of Anadarko's development plans in the Loyalsock, the RDA held a public event in the hamlet of Ralston (18.5 miles north of Williamsport) in September 2012, to unveil its "Keep It Wild" campaign. The immediate goal of Keep It Wild was, as then president Ralph said, to stop any development near Rock Run. But the larger mission was to raise alarms about the scale of disruption wrought by drilling in state forests that "belong to all of us." In front of an audience of seventy-five or so people (which, considering the distance of Ralston from any sizable town, was notable), Ralph laid out the RDA's game plan. "We've gotta do both. We've gotta push the system as far as we can push it. And we've gotta stand up and say no." Ralph recognized that "It can't just be us." They would have to "get thousands of people around the state and around the nation to say this is a special resource. We gotta hound our politicians, media. It's a lot of work." Even if they couldn't convince the DCNR to deny access to Andarko, if Anadarko met "a lot of opposition up here," it might come to the realization that it doesn't have the social license to drill here and walk away.[28]

Keep It Wild was surprisingly effective, both as a literal rallying cry and as a grassroots movement. The RDA partnered with multiple conservation organizations—both local fishing and hunting groups and a few major national players like the Sierra Club—to create the Save the Loyalsock Coalition, which helped the message reach a broad constituency. (The group later changed its name to Save Pennsylvania's Forests Coalition, to reflect a broadened mission.) After refusing to discuss the matter at all for two years, in April 2013 the DCNR offered to hold a private meeting with fifty "key stakeholders"—including Ralph and a representative from the local chapter of the Sierra Club, along with township supervisors and state legislators—to discuss where things stood regarding development in Loyalsock State Forest. A number of the people in attendance, and of the people camped outside in the parking lot who weren't allowed in (including the media), used the opportunity to denounce the DCNR's secrecy surrounding Rock Run and to demand public hearings.[29] Even the conservative-leaning, pro-gas editorial board of the *Williamsport Sun-Gazette* ran an op-ed arguing that the closed-door stakeholder meeting should be public.

The fireworks really started at a House Democratic Policy Committee public hearing I attended at Lycoming College on May 1. Organized by Rick Mirabito (the county's sole Democratic state legislator) at the urging of the RDA, the meeting catapulted Rock Run into a statewide issue. For over two hours, five lawmakers from around the state listened to testimony from angry constituents—all of whom spoke against allowing drilling in Rock Run. As well, Anadarko agreed to speak publicly for the first time about its plans. It sent its government relations advisor, Mary Wolf. Chipper, poised, and professional, the short-haired middle-aged woman kicked off the proceedings by brandishing her deep local roots: Mayor (R) of Williamsport from 2004 to 2008 and former political science instructor at Lycoming College. She proceeded to make clear that Anadarko would not back off its development plans. "Yes," she said firmly, "we are in discussions with the DCNR to access the minerals *we own* in Loyalsock State Forest." Wolf then admonished the representatives to remember that Anadarko is also a community stakeholder and "your constituent." Looking out at the skeptical audience of a hundred or so people, Wolf claimed, "We hear you, we get it." Ironically, she then announced that she could not stay to hear residents' testimony. She had to "leave out that side door," to go to a meeting in Scranton that brought together the chambers of commerce from multiple Pennsylvania towns to discuss all the benefits that natural gas was bringing to the region. (While I can't prove that Wolf didn't have some official business that day, the Scranton meeting—which I attended—didn't start until the following afternoon.)

Before Wolf could exit, state representative Greg Vitali (from the Philadelphia suburbs), the ranking Democrat of the House Environmental Resources and Energy Committee, laced into her. "Here's why I drove three hours today," he began. After hiking through the Loyalsock, he said, he understood why Anadarko's plans were secret: "Because you are gonna tear that forest apart." Virtually drowned out by applause, Vitali described the flagging he saw, which indicated where Anadarko planned to clear the forest for gas lines and well pads, and the spectacular lookout point at Sharp Top that could be impacted. As Wolf stood stone-faced, Vitali added that he's not just a representative—he's also a lawyer. "I read the Clarence Moore case, and it is pretty clear there is no right to access." He closed by suggesting ideas first floated by Ralph and Szybist: Anadarko could access the subsurface from adjacent tracts while leaving the surface intact, or it could agree with the DCNR to swap the Clarence Moore lands for less ecologically sensitive acreage nearby. Representative Eddie Day Pashinski (Wilkes-Barre) piled on, "Why do we have to drill in one of the gems of God's creation?"

Szybist then laid out the legal case for denying Anadarko the right to drill and chastised the DCNR for refusing to hold a hearing or even attend this one. A parade of witnesses, many but not all with connections to state and national environmental groups, followed. Many recounted specific memories of swimming, hiking, or fishing in and around Rock Run and called the forest magic. More than one accused Governor Corbett of using priceless state forests as a cash cow to fill in state budget gaps. Another warned that the Tiadaghton showed what was in store for Rock Run: an industrial park in perpetuity. A representative for the Audubon Society highlighted how the Loyalsock was one of only two forests in Pennsylvania where yellow-bellied flycatchers nest. The fragmentation of the woods that would result from drilling, he argued, would lead to their eviction and a silent spring. For his part, Ralph called Rock Run a rare chance to push back against the industry's takeover of the state's wild lands. He was both pragmatic and poetic. Utilizing maps and his industry knowledge, Ralph made the case that Anadarko could reach most of its assets by drilling horizontally from adjacent privately owned tracts where it had leased mineral rights. He then told a story about the famous botanist John Bartram's trip up the Susquehanna River in 1743. The "chest-high deep water," Bartram journaled, "was so clear [he] could see a pin on the rocks on the bottom." Though much of this heritage was lost "with deforestation and development," Ralph went on, "Rock Run remains that way." You can still "see a pin at the bottom in the waters in many pools." Looking into the eyes of the legislators, Ralph pleaded, "Do this for future generations." As the meeting wound down, Representative Mirabito urged everyone to plead their case to editorial boards, the DCNR, and their elected leaders. "Make yourself a pain in the ass!"

The RDA heeded Mirabito's advice. Over the next month, it organized a letter-writing and phone call campaign that flooded the DCNR with citizen complaints about drilling in Rock Run. In response, Secretary Richard Allan sat down with the *Sun-Gazette* editorial board and, for the first time, indicated that the DCNR may be able to restrict drilling. He added that the whole issue could be headed for court.[30] Perhaps more remarkable, Allan finally relented to civic pressure to hold a public comment session at Lycoming College. The June 3 meeting took on greater urgency when the RDA reportedly found new Anadarko stakes along the road to Sharp Top vista. Time was running out. When the big day arrived, the college parking lot was mobbed even though school was out. Hundreds streamed in. The line to speak stretched to the very back of the cavernous lecture hall.

The proceedings kicked off with the besuited Secretary Allan stating sternly that agency members were here simply to provide the facts in the wake of a lot of misinformation. The DCNR Marcellus Program Manager, Arianne Proctor, then proceeded to unveil Anadarko's development plans for the very first time (the agency's hand was forced, because Mark Szybist had already obtained the plans through a right-to-know request and published them on the FracTracker Alliance website). Proctor generated some applause when she guaranteed that "you'll never see development" in Rock Run Valley or "trucks up Rock Run Road." She was adamant that no development could take place until ecological surveys could assess the impact on wetlands and rare or endangered animals like the timber rattlesnake. But the next slide took the air out of the room: the proposed five hundred acres of disturbance included twenty-six well pads, over thirty miles of new or widened roads, thirty-four miles of pipeline clearance, four compressor stations, satellite towers, and five impoundments—all clustered in and around Old Loggers Path. Many of the five hundred or so attendees gasped when Proctor nonchalantly added that this degree of ecological disturbance would reduce the amount of land designated by the DCNR as "semi-primitive, non-motorized" by a whopping 45 percent. In exchange for this ecological displacement, Anadarko offered a "surface consideration payment" of $15 million. Proctor's last slide of "Next Steps" included plans to "review stakeholder recommendations for mitigation projects" and "negotiate a SDMA" (Surface Development Management Agreement) with Anadarko. Notably absent was any indication that the DCNR might consider denying development.

For hours, speaker after speaker accused the DCNR of failing to uphold its mission. Some were activists, including a few grungy Earth First! members who threatened to use direct action to stop development. But many who spoke passionately about defending Rock Run were everyday residents. The line to testify kept getting longer, and multiple people used their two minutes to belittle Allan as a political appointee who had no experience with conservation (he was formerly a sheet metal magnate). Others spoke of their rights being infringed by the leasing of "our" state forests and invoked the environmental clause of the state constitution. Some simply begged the DCNR to reconsider. Barb captured the room with a tongue-in-cheek proposal for the agency to "get a divorce from Anadarko." Kevin Heatley, an ecologist and RDA board member, added to the brief moment of levity when he testified that he once "made love to a beautiful woman" on a moss-covered rock in Rock Run, and "I'll be damned if I'm gonna let some gas worker eat his McDonald's on that rock while ruining Rock Run!" A mother tenderly recalled the time she took her two young children on their first hike through the Loyalsock. An elderly man who said his rural abode had been torn apart by drilling in the Tiadaghton brought some to tears with his plea, "Please, please help to preserve this *one* sanctuary among all the others that have already been destroyed." More than a few folks warned that fracking near Rock Run was crossing a line in the sand and would be met with fierce resistance. Eventually, a security guard approached the harried-looking Arianne Proctor and told her they had to stop; the event had already gone on for an hour more than they had reserved the room. As people filed out, chants of "Keep it wild" could be heard up and down the line.

If judged on the extent to which the DCNR conveyed new information or received new recommendations that could inform its efforts to mitigate the impact of drilling in the Loyalsock, the gathering accomplished little. But if judged on the extent to which the event illustrated the breadth of opposition to drilling in Rock Run and galvanized the movement to stop it, it was a rousing success. Less than a week after the hearing, Governor Corbett asked Secretary Allan to resign. Although the ostensible reason was a racially charged e-mail he sent to his wife on a state computer, environmentalists and the media speculated that it was related to the "increased public scrutiny" over drilling in the Clarence Moore lands and citizens' complaints over Allan's handling of the issue.[31] At a DCNR advisory-council meeting I attended in the state capital the following month, a member of the board called the hearing a wake-up call. The agency's Bureau of Forestry chief called "the intense public interest" in Rock Run "unique."[32] Energized, Ralph and Szybist sat with other advocates in PennFuture's Harrisburg office and hatched a plan that they hoped would, at the least, tie up drilling for years. The pent-up frustration that exploded at Lycoming College demonstrated, they argued, that the DCNR ignored due process regarding fracking the Loyalsock. The agency owed it to Commonwealth citizens, they maintained, to hold six formal, recorded public hearings across the state and to open a ninety-day public comment period so that more voices could be heard.

The RDA's case was bolstered when an open-records request revealed that the DCNR did not record citizens' comments at the June hearing. Activating the network that the RDA and PennFuture had built through the Save the Loyalsock Coalition, by August they gathered an astounding 12,000 or more signatures demanding public hearings.[33] The suburban Philadelphia representative Greg Vitali, who was instrumental in bringing outside attention to the issue, held a press conference in Harrisburg, in the ornate Capitol Rotunda, to echo the call of the petition. Flanked by a dozen impassive environmental advocates (Ralph helped hold a large banner that read "KEEP ROCK RUN WILD"), Vitali delivered a strong rebuke of the Corbett administration's handling of Rock Run and argued that Anadarko's plan "would destroy the wild character of Loyalsock State Forest." It's a statewide issue, he said, because Rock Run attracted visitors from all over the Commonwealth.

Anadarko indefinitely postponed its development plans after the sustained year-long public backlash. Although it's impossible to prove cause and effect, many observers agreed with Garth Everett's assessment that the court of public opinion likely explained why Anadarko was slow-walking its submission of a surface use application to the DCNR. After all, the firm had gone to all the trouble of doing seismic testing, mapping out an entire network of well pads and pipelines, and planting stakes in the ground to mark where it planned to put gas infrastructure. (Southwestern Energy, the other mineral rights holder here, remained an enigma; it never spoke with the DCNR and so it was unclear if it had any plans at all to develop its 50 percent stake in the tract.) In July of the following year (2014), the DCNR announced that it would hold a fifteen-day public comment period if and when a "final development proposal" with Anadarko was put in place.[34] Tapping into activists' outrage at the DCNR's perfunctory nod to accountability and democracy, Billtown representative Rick Mirabito held another well-attended public hearing at Lycoming College, this time to introduce and receive comments on his proposed "transparency and participation bill." The bill would "allow citizen landowners of PA public lands to have a voice regarding industrialization of these lands," by requiring public notice and input before the DCNR authorized gas development.[35] Days later, Representative Vitali announced a resolution that he drafted with input from the RDA and others that called on Governor Corbett and the DCNR to prevent drilling in the Clarence Moore lands.[36]

The winds shifted in advocates' favor with Tom Wolf's (D) gubernatorial victory over the incumbent that November. As a candidate, Wolf said he was opposed to drilling in state parks. Likely due in part to

Szybist's and Ralph's personal relationships with several people close to his campaign or poised to join his cabinet, Wolf even declared that he "will support the commonwealth's right to block drilling on those tracts of the Clarence Moore lands in which the courts have ruled that the state has exclusive surface control."[37] Upon being sworn in, Wolf immediately reinstated a moratorium on new gas leasing in state forests that Corbett had suspended. Although his options for doing more (e.g., restricting drilling on public lands already leased) were circumscribed by law and the majority-Republican legislature, he did swap out DCNR and DEP secretaries who many viewed as favorable to the industry for nominees with a track record of environmental stewardship. (Wolf's new DCNR appointee Cindy Dunn was the president of PennFuture, the organization that helped lead the Rock Run campaign.) Additionally, a general industry slowdown fomented by the glut of produced gas, which saw drilling rigs decamp to the Southwest and new hotels struggle to sustain profitable occupancy rates, helped support advocates' argument that now was not the time to frack the Loyalsock.[38]

In December 2016, Anadarko pulled out of the region entirely and sold its assets to Alta Resources.[39] Alta has said nothing to date about what it plans to do in the Clarence Moore lands. But drilling no longer seems imminent. Advocates' success in delaying drilling there for the past decade is one of fractivism's greatest victories in Pennsylvania. It was certainly the RDA's shining moment.

Like Anadarko, the public moved on from the Rock Run controversy. But Ralph kept at it, employing the same retail politics that marginalized him in the RDA. As it turned out, Ralph had been clandestinely developing an amicable relationship with a very senior official from Southwestern Energy, which held the other half of the Clarence Moore subsurface. Ralph fed the man a steady diet of information about the ecological value of the area, and presented alternative scenarios for accessing the gas without breaching the surface. When the official came up from Texas, Ralph met him for dinner and gave him an eight-hour tour of the Rock Run area. It seemed to be working. While the DCNR was complaining in 2014 that it had heard nothing from Southwestern, the official was telling Ralph that "we don't have to be everywhere" and

FIG. 10.5. Ralph Kisberg pauses to appreciate Rock Run. Photograph by Tristan Spinksi.

implying he would convince his employer to forgo developing the area. The official also reported "making headway" with trying to convince Anadarko to stall or scale back its development plans for the Clarence Moore lands. When Anadarko cashed out, Ralph reported, his connection said Southwestern was "solid on not developing Rock Run." When I called the man to verify Ralph's account, he said Ralph deserved more credit. Ralph was, by and large, the impetus for Southwestern's decision to avoid any surface disturbance in the Rock Run area, the man claimed. He added via e-mail, "If we had more people like Ralph out there trying to find collaborative solutions to energy development problems, the world would be a much better place!" So, while his more radical counterparts scoffed at his industry outreach, Ralph wrote a letter to the president of Alta in 2017 welcoming him to Lycoming County and expressing his optimism that Alta would be a "better neighbor" than Anadarko. True to form, Ralph also wrote eloquently about "the fragile beauty and spiritual significance of those 25,000 acres." Alta seemed to have gotten the message, whether from Ralph or from the public outcry about Rock Run. A DCNR representative reportedly told Ralph in a whispered hallway conversation in late 2018 that Alta had no desire to be the bad guy and was already using new, extended-reach technology to drill under the Clarence Moore lands from adjacent private lots—the plan advocated by Ralph, Szybist, and others.

* * *

Although Rock Run is spared (for now) and a moratorium on *additional* leasing of Commonwealth lands remains in place, vast new swaths of wild country are bulldozed each year as gas companies develop the tracts they leased or purchased in the past. Just across Route 14 from Rock Run, Bodine Mountain has borne witness to an industrial onslaught that rivals the Tiadaghton. That future laid in store for yet another portion of the Mid State Trail nearby, on State Game Land 75. Sportsmen were dismayed to hear that this "favorite place for wilderness rambling" and hunting was slated to be developed by Pennsylvania General Energy (PGE).[40] What's more, no sooner had Loyalsock Creek been declared Pennsylvania's "River of the Year" in 2017 than PGE announced plans for gas and water pipelines on a mix of public and private land that would stretch across Loyalsock Valley from rim to rim, right under the creek. It has become the fight of Barb's life; the planned pipeline clearance—and possibly a water withdrawal site—would abut her property. And on it goes.

In general terms, when it came to public land many locals thought more like *conservationists* than *preservationists*. While the RDA viewed protected forests as "special places" that should remain untouched, others in the community had long been comfortable with the idea of working forests that balanced recreation with the harvesting of natural resources. But public support for the RDA's efforts to save Rock Run indicates that many feared that fracking tipped the scales too far in the direction of exploitation. (The area had been the site of timber harvesting for many decades without controversy.) The public's demand for the

DCNR to prevent drilling near Rock Run—even though Anadarko had legally purchased the mineral rights—suggests that there were limits to locals' endorsement of the free market and fear of government intervention. When confronted with the choice between enclosure of the literal commons or environmental regulation, many locals revealed a preference for the latter. Akin to the broad enthusiasm for local zoning, which in effect affirmed the Lockean proviso that an owner's or lessee's property rights ought not extend to the point where they usurp others' rights to enjoy a limited public good, seemingly liberalist residents were compelled by the RDA's message that the community ought to have a say in the fate of their beloved forest and swimming holes. It wasn't about being against fracking per se. It was about being in favor of consent and self-rule. It was a rejection of the idea that energy companies could infringe on one's right to roam our land.

Many countries in Europe (e.g., Switzerland, Scotland, Austria) have legally enshrined the general public's "right to roam" the countryside, including privately owned lands and water bodies. The United States hasn't embraced a right to roam on private property. Yet there is perhaps no other country in the world that has set aside more public land for roaming. The Bureau of Land Management (BLM) and the US Forest Service oversee more than 430 million acres of protected grasslands, forests, deserts, and watersheds on our behalf—a vast recreational playground (and, of course, a refuge for threatened plant and animal species) that stretches across twelve Western states. (This is in addition to the millions of acres of *state-administered* public land.) However, over the course of the twentieth century the federal government also created a raft of laws that strengthened its capacity to profit from subsurface leases on public lands and committed agencies like the BLM to promoting the mining of coal, oil, and gas on them.[41] About twenty-six million acres of these lands are currently leased;[42] a blog post on the BLM website touts that its "oil and gas program is a boon for the US economy."[43] The fact that the federal government relies on hundreds of millions of dollars in bonuses and royalties from fracking on public land means that support for the fossil fuel industry is, sociologists Stacia Ryder and Peter Hall argue, "embedded in our nation's system of governance."[44] This leads critics like the author Christopher Ketcham to conclude that federal environmental agencies like the EPA and the BLM have been "captured" by the very industries they are supposed to be regulating.[45]

The pattern repeats itself at the state level. Pennsylvania's constitution decrees that its "public natural resources are the common property of all the people, including generations yet to come," and that "the Commonwealth shall conserve and maintain them for the benefit of all the people." Yet, as a judge decreed in a lawsuit decided in favor of the Pennsylvania Environmental Defense Foundation, politicians had illegally acted as the proprietor of what the DCNR considers a "truly priceless public asset," by funneling the spoils of drilling on state land to the capitol. The state's actions amounted to a taking of the people's land.

The industrialization and de facto privatization of large swaths of the Tiadaghton is a harbinger. If replicated nationally, it could result in significant environmental degradation and enclosure of portions of America's most ecologically significant—and majestic—commons. This is already happening. President Obama oversaw the auctioning off of millions of additional acres of federal public land for oil and gas development. In his four years in office, President Trump tripled the pace of new leasing while rolling back air- and water-quality regulations and decreasing the amount of time that the public has to review and comment on new leases. By reversing Obama-era protections for wildlife, Trump was able to open up for drilling portions of Wyoming and of Alaska's Arctic National Wildlife Refuge that were previously considered off-limits, because they provide habitats for threatened species (e.g., the sage grouse). Utah's new Bears Ears National Monument was reduced by more than two-thirds to circumvent environmental regulations that had stymied development in the area.[46] Parcels in the state's Hovenweep National Monument were reportedly auctioned for as little as $3/acre.[47] As Ketcham notes, a veil of smog and the stench of "toxic evaporation pits" cloak once-wild valleys in Wyoming.[48] Pipelines are worming their way under the Appalachian Trail. More and more of our natural heritage is being cordoned off and commodified, public in name only. (President Biden has vowed to restore and strengthen Obama-era protections and to disallow new drilling permits on public land.)

We can't pin *all* the blame for the privatization of the commons on regulatory capture. Enclosure is a collective act, to which we are all party. It is not just that too few Americans notice, let alone push back against, the auctioning off of public land. It is that too few of us demand that fossil fuels be left in the ground. Forever. To the extent that most of us continue to uncritically organize our lives around carbon-intensive energy sources, we are coconspirators.

CONCLUSION

Bust and Beyond

Since I moved out of Billtown, in the fall of 2013, the gas boom has gone bust. An industry "slowdown," as shale boosters delicately called it, was already apparent when I was packing my bags for New York City. Hotel tax revenue was reportedly down 13 percent that year, after doubling the previous three years. Anecdotally, by the end of 2013 there were noticeably fewer white pickups in the Holiday Inn Express & Suites lot, or filling up their gas tanks at Sheetz, than when I first visited Billtown in 2012. That November, the Keystone Research Center raised concerns "about the stability and permanence of even the small number of jobs that have been created" by gas drilling in the area.[1] Those concerns turned out to be prescient. Less than two weeks after Ted Cruz stopped at NuWeld during the 2016 Republican presidential primaries to tout the role of natural gas in creating a manufacturing renaissance in America, the welding and metalwork company abruptly shuttered. (The next day, Cruz abruptly ended his campaign.) Founded in 1996, the Williamsport-based company had been so busy that managers boasted of "turning down work." But now it couldn't pay the bills.[2]

NuWeld was hardly the only local business to succumb to the industry slowdown. Dan Klingerman, the builder of Marcellus Energy Park, emphatically denied to me that the industry was in retreat but quietly closed his own company, Infinity Oilfield Services. Hotels hastily built for itinerant workers from the Southwest were now half vacant. New bars and Texas barbeque eateries struggled to pay the rent. Halliburton's Muncy facility was down to about forty employees, from a peak of over six hundred. There were only 19 drilling rigs in the entire state by January of 2019, down from 114 rigs statewide in the same month of 2012. By 2019, there were fewer rigs in Pennsylvania than *before* the Marcellus gas boom began.[3] And Billtown's decades-long population decline, temporarily paused during the boom years (2010–12), recommenced. It bled over 1,350 residents—about 4 percent of the total population—between 2014 and 2020. Scott McClain, who told me in 2018 that his life was left in ruin by the gas truck caravans that eventually fractured the foundation of his home, joined those émigrés, to try to "start over in life elsewhere," in Fort Indiantown Gap, Pennsylvania (Betty, who divorced him, moved back to Billtown). The landman Russell Poole also moved on to greener pastures; gas firms weren't looking for leases.

What happened? As a Bloomberg report put it, "The numbers never added up." Fracking has always been an expensive proposition. With new wells facing average production declines of 60 percent in the first year, petroleum companies were compelled to offset the decline rates by frantically drilling more and more wells. The entire model was premised on high oil and gas prices. But nationwide, the glut of gas (and oil, though to a lesser extent) precipitated by the fracking boom depressed prices to the lowest levels since the 1990s. Fracking had become "America's money pit."[4] Once reality dashed their shortsighted exuberance, many companies decided to suspend most oil and gas drilling. Worldwide, as many as seventy-five thousand workers in the oil and gas industry were laid off between 2015 and 2016.[5] Dozens of smaller drilling companies sought bankruptcy protection. The stock prices of larger petroleum firms like Chesapeake Energy crashed. Companies like Anadarko pulled out of the Marcellus entirely. A wave of consolidations swept across the sector. Years later, the slump showed little signs of abating: in December 2019, Chevron announced it would write down between ten and eleven billion dollars in assets, "mostly shale gas holdings in Appalachia."[6] Some analysts called it the worst downturn of the energy sector in decades.[7] And that was *before* the COVID-19 pandemic brought the industry to a virtual standstill, in 2020, as global demand for oil and gas crashed. The price of a barrel of crude oil memorably fell below zero dollars. Royal Dutch Shell reported a net loss of over $18 billion for the second quarter of 2020 (compared to a net profit of $3 billion over the same period in 2019, which was already a down year) and slashed its shareholder dividend for the first time since World War II.[8] Once-mighty Chesapeake, which led the Marcellus gas boom, filed for bankruptcy in 2020.

Though lessors may have missed the writing on the wall of the New York Stock Exchange, they certainly noticed when their monthly royalty checks dropped commas. George complained to me in May 2016 that, less than two years after getting his first check, for $34,880, his most recent payment was $708. George claimed that his monthly health insurance premiums ate up much of that check.

The bust gives the lie to the industry's promise of a partnership with communities that would produce recession-proof economic growth for decades. The story, sadly, is nothing new. Researchers find that shale communities have replicated the boom-bust cycle that typifies extractive industries: there is little evidence that shale gas development brought lasting improvement to local economies; most income and employment gains were modest and temporary.[9] More than feeling angry, many locals seemed resigned to the reality that they were experiencing the lumber bust and deindustrialization all over again. But fracking was supposed to be different, because shale gas was supposed to be more than a commodity. Conservatives have often portrayed shale gas as a patriotic weapon that will finally enable the US to achieve the elusive goal of energy independence. The Department of Energy, under Secretary Rick Perry, went so far as to call natural gas "molecules of U.S. freedom."[10] Petroleum companies, however, are not servants of the state. Their primary concern, like any company's, is the bottom line. They're eager to raise the price of shale gas by liquefying and exporting as much of it as they can to other countries, rather than making sure that it is consumed in America. What's more, as recently as 2017, the US *imported* almost as much natural gas as it exported.[11]

Until recently, mainstream Democrats, and even some environmental organizations (e.g., the Environmental Defense Fund), proffered a very different—but no less moralized—narrative around shale gas that may ring just as hollow as the promise of energy independence. Because methane combustion emits about half as many pounds of carbon dioxide per million Btu of energy as does coal, shale gas has been touted as a tool in the fight against climate change and a "bridge fuel" on the pathway to renewable energy.[12] Cheap and abundant supplies of natural gas have incentivized energy providers to switch from coal- to gas-fired power plants (notwithstanding Trump's retaliation against the "war on coal"). Between 2007—just before the shale gas boom began—and 2012, the United States experienced an almost 13 percent reduction in carbon dioxide emissions. Some studies estimate that 35–50 percent of the reduction in power sector emissions "may be due to shale gas price effects" (much of the rest may be due to production declines linked to the Great Recession).[13]

However, methane itself is a greenhouse gas whose global warming potential is more than eighty times that of carbon dioxide over a twenty-year period. Even a relatively small rate of methane leakage (i.e., 3 percent) from the production and distribution of shale gas could "off-set or even reverse the entire apparent greenhouse gas benefit of fuel switching from coal to natural gas."[14] Some experts say that leakage rates are approaching that threshold.[15] And they've trended upward. Trump rolled back Obama-era regulations "that would have required oil and gas producers to more aggressively detect and fix gas leaks, and to rein in flaring or venting" of methane. In North Dakota and Texas, where the focus is on a more lucrative fossil fuel, shale gas encountered in the process of fracking for oil is an unwanted byproduct. It's actually cheaper to get rid of the gas than to pay the fees to pipe it off and sell it, so petroleum companies simply vent the hazardous greenhouse gas directly into the atmosphere or burn it off (which releases carbon dioxide). An investigation by the *New York Times* found that, in 2018, US petroleum operators vented or flared 40 percent more methane than they had in 2013. The amount of gas wasted in the Texas oilfields alone was more than Arizona consumes in a year.[16]

Many of the key questions about the net environmental impact of fracking are still unknown. We need more data. I have come to the conclusion that many fractivists exaggerate the likelihood of water contamination. But that's cold comfort to the seven families near Billtown I befriended that became a statistic and can no longer drink their own well water. It does appear that shale gas extraction is less ecologically destructive than coal extraction. But the leasing of public land for gas drilling has fragmented forests and diminished wetlands in wild areas that never experienced coal mining. And it poses a new threat to the welfare of countless animals, including endangered species: at both the state and federal levels, the industry has lobbied hard for easing rules that require operators to assess—and mitigate—the risk that development of a site may pose to endangered animals.[17] I am convinced that shale gas has played a role in reducing America's carbon footprint by supplanting coal. But we have a very long way to go in reducing greenhouse gas emissions to levels that climatologists consider a "safe operating space for humanity" (i.e., levels that would produce less than 1.5 degrees Celsius of additional warming).[18] Burning more methane won't get us there.

Although methane combustion may be less harmful than coal, the uptick in flaring and venting suggests that most petroleum operators are not committed to minimizing its environmental impact. They'll pollute as much as the law allows. They'll waste energy to increase shareholder value. After observing gas industry meetings and trade shows, I can attest that companies like Shell and Chevron are not imagining shale gas as a stopgap. They envision fleets of natural gas-powered cars, which would require the construction of thousands of new fueling stations across the country. They are building billion-dollar "cracker plants" to convert ethane, a fracking byproduct, into plastic. They are championing the completion of dozens of liquefied-natural-gas facilities that will enable them to corner the global market on gas exports. All this extra sunk cost in methane (and oil) infrastructure portends a time-consuming, greenhouse-gas-laden dead end that could delay a large-scale transition to renewable energy (e.g., sun, wind) for decades rather than serve as a bridge to sustainability.

It seems increasingly apparent that, to prevent catastrophic global warming, society must decarbonize rapidly. To do this, much of our extant reserves of fossil fuels, including methane, must stay in the ground. It's a daunting task that requires major shifts in American (and global) energy policy. But there's reason for optimism. Almost every source of green energy can now compete on cost with fossil fuels.[19] A recent University of California, Berkeley, policy study found that America could produce 90 percent of its electricity from carbon-free sources by 2035 without increasing wholesale power costs. There would still be a role for natural gas in that scenario, but it would be a minor one (70 percent less use than in 2019).[20] What's more, bipartisan support for fracking has eroded considerably in the wake of widespread, grassroots climate activism spearheaded by young people (compare a 2013 *Forbes* headline, "Obama Gets It: Fracking is Awesome," to a 2020 *New York Times* article that said energy executives were warming to then-Democratic presidential candidate Joe Biden simply because he was not calling for a total ban on fracking, as many other Democrats now are).[21] We are witnessing a felicitous coming together of investors and environmentalists, united for different reasons against fossil fuel extraction. In 2020, two of America's largest natural-gas pipeline projects—the Constitution and the Atlantic Coast—were scrapped in the face of projected diminishing returns, and popular protests. And Biden won the presidency promising to go all in on renewables.

In response to mounting concerns about both local environmental hazards and climate change, some Western European governments have placed a ban (e.g., France) or a moratorium (e.g., the UK) on fracking (and coal mining) in their respective countries. And, tied to their commitments to the Paris Agreement on climate change, many countries have mandated the growth of renewables and a reduction of greenhouse gas emissions. In the US, however, the flow of energy has largely been dictated by the market, not environmental exigencies or lofty ideals like patriotism. (This is the case notwithstanding the actions of some progressive states like New York, whose governor banned fracking, or California, which went to war with the Trump administration over its right to enact regulations on tailpipe emissions that exceed federal standards. These large, coastal states exploit the latitude granted by federalism to try to steer energy markets in a greener direction.) Fracking epitomizes America's classical liberal ethos from top to bottom. Although there is a robust national debate about the promises and pitfalls of fracking, there was never a *collective referendum* about whether exploiting shale gas and oil is in the public interest (e.g., a direct citizen vote at the federal or state level, or a congressional roll call vote or hearings). Rather, the fracking boom was the aggregate effect of millions of solitary landowners, many of whom live above shale formations in the heartland, making a *personal choice* to lease their land in exchange for payments.

Although the emphasis on freedom appeals to our Lockean instincts and resonates with our culture of individualism, this aspect of American exceptionalism leads individuals, corporations, and politicians to shirk their responsibility to cooperate with others to protect the commons (some lab studies show that accentuating the notion of choice appeals to Americans' desire for autonomy so much that it can actually *decrease* their level of support for policies that support the greater good[22]). George justified his decision to lease his land, without consulting anyone, on the grounds of land sovereignty. Yet his choice created spillover effects that impacted his neighbors—and the planet. On the national level, this logic justifies delaying the pursuit of sustainability until it is profitable—which is too late. In pulling out of the Paris Agreement, President Trump called it a threat to national sovereignty (he erroneously stated that other nations would be able to dictate America's economy and energy mix). What this narrative glosses over is the fact that America has produced (by far) the largest share of global greenhouse gases since the industrial revolution. It represents only 4 percent of the world's population but consumes almost a fifth of the world's energy. In so doing, it has infringed on other nations' sovereignty, especially those with low-lying coasts being inundated by rising sea levels.

Similarly, we can pin some blame on America's ignominious failure to contain COVID-19 on the fact that many citizens—egged on by President Trump and his gubernatorial acolytes across Middle America—prioritized personal prerogative and profit over the common good. Thousands of people may have died unnecessarily, and schools and businesses have lagged their European counterparts in reopening, in part because many of our politicians and fellow citizens viewed simple public-health precautions like wearing a mask as an infringement on personal liberty. "What they call 'freedom,'" the economist and *New York Times* columnist Paul Krugman bitterly complains, "is actually absence of responsibility."[23] The problem goes deeper than Trump; COVID-19 lockdown protests would most likely have occurred without him in office. Our country's cult of individualism, the almost-proud refusal of so many to prioritize what's best for the community, is entrenched in our politics. To be sure, lots of people sacrificed personal autonomy to protect their compatriots. But too many defected. Most importantly, the federal government, along with many states, refused to enact collectivist policies. Whether to gather mask-free or reopen a theater was often construed as a personal choice. (Our go-it-alone approach to health care and the provision of protective equipment was also catastrophic.)

This is the public/private paradox. When we assert our right to consume a disproportionate share of the world's energy and emit a disproportionate share of the world's greenhouse gases, we seldom acknowledge that exercising that "right" alienates others' rights to liberty and property. And when we assert our right to dine in or barhop during a pandemic, we remain blind to how exercising the "right" to make our own decisions about risk may rob others of their right to life.[24]

Some might argue that, in the case of fracking, the public good that results (e.g., abundant and cheap energy; jobs; royalties) outweighs the individual harms produced by impinging on others' land sovereignty. To be sure, the creation of public goods like highways or parks often requires harm to some. This is the logic of eminent domain. The economist Ronald Coase convincingly made the case that we ought not make polluters liable for damage to others' estates solely on the basis of property rights. What matters most, he contended, is whether greater public utility is produced by allowing versus regulating pollution. In cases of the former, greater societal damage is done if we privilege the property rights of those adjacent to a polluting entity.[25] But the regulatory equation for fracking ought not only weigh the "social costs" and benefits for local property owners. When the aforementioned planetary externalities are accounted for, the social cost of privileging the rights of landowners to lease their properties for drilling is prohibitive. And this is without even calculating the impact of fracking on the well-being and sovereignty of wild animals.[26]

* * *

While it's important that we all recognize our role as metaphorical herdsmen who are contributing to the tragedy of the commons and trespassing on others' civil liberties, we should be wary of the dominant narrative that it's all our fault (by "our" I mean everyday American citizens and, by extension, residents of other wealthy, industrialized countries). As environmental activist Mary Annaise Heglar opines, it's often implied that climate change could have been avoided if "we had all just ordered less takeout, used fewer plastic bags, turned off some more lights, planted a few trees, or driven an electric car." In this individualist and consumerist way of framing the problem, it's easy to dismiss as hypocrites environmentalists like Cindy Bower, who heat their homes with the very energy source they're fighting against and spew greenhouse gases into the atmosphere as they drive or fly to environmental protests. But, Heglar observes, "The belief that this enormous, existential problem could have been fixed if all of us just tweaked our consumptive habits is not only preposterous; it's dangerous."[27] Solutions focused on individual lifestyle changes are "radically out of step with the scale of the crisis."[28] And they deflect attention away from the small handful of powerful corporate actors, and their political enablers, who shoulder outsize responsibility for driving humanity into this ditch.

A mere one hundred companies, many of which are fossil fuel producers, are responsible for over 70 percent of the world's greenhouse gas emissions over the past thirty years.[29] What's more, there's evidence (and a lawsuit) that suggests that Exxon (and likely other petroleum companies) knew for decades that its products were driving climate change. Critics behind the social media campaign #ExxonKnew claim the energy producer "orchestrated a campaign of doubt and deception" to mislead the public and its shareholders about the causes and risks of global warming.[30] The power of the fossil fuel lobby leads political scientist Matto Mildenberger to conclude that the climate crisis is not a tragedy of the commons. Gradual climate policies introduced over the past several decades "could have slowly steered our economy toward gently declining carbon pollution levels" without impacting Americans' lifestyles,

Mildenberger contends. But "that future was stolen from us" by "carbon-polluting interests who blocked policy reforms at every turn to preserve their short-term profits." Mildenberger calls these interest groups' successful efforts to short-circuit climate action the real tragedy, locking individuals into a system of fossil fuel consumption that can only be dismantled through structural—not personal—change.[31]

It's for this reason that Heglar urges us to "stop obsessing over your environmental 'sins'" and "fight the oil and gas industry instead."[32] By pressuring the biggest environmental sinners to clean up their act, with tools like carbon pricing and stringent national targets for reducing greenhouse gas emissions, climatologist Michael Mann argues, we "will reduce everyone's carbon footprint, whether or not they care."[33] If we decarbonize the energy sector, then it hardly matters how much you drive your (electric) car. There are no emissions from the source or tailpipes. It's not a sin to leave the lights on when you step out of the room. The scale of the environmental crisis demands systemic interventions. A personal decision to buy LED lightbulbs won't cut it.

To return to the issue of fracking, it's facile to frame the resource dilemma associated with land leasing in America as unavoidable, or to paint lessors as the bad guys. It's the result of a unique legal and political structure that: (1) constitutionally enshrines—and grants preeminence to—private subsurface mineral ownership, which puts the onus of underground mining decisions on individual property owners; (2) doesn't account for most of the externalities that neighbors—and the planet—must absorb from oil and gas activity on leased land; and (3) strips communities of their traditional autonomy to ensure that private-property rights don't jeopardize the commonwealth. It is this system that makes it so hard for landowners, like most of us, to avoid the public/private paradox.

Like many so-called urban liberals, I support the kind of strict federal regulations and green-energy mandates that most environmental-advocacy organizations agree are needed to make real progress in combating climate change.[34] But my time in Lycoming County has helped me see why this is a nonstarter in many parts of Middle America, where most fracking occurs. Just as Democrats scrambled after 2016 to make sense of how they alienated a constituency that ought to support their economic agenda, environmental advocates would do well to perform their own postmortem. The poorer and more rural a county or state is, the more likely it is to suffer from pollution. This suggests that residents in these areas, by virtue of their vulnerability, should support environmental protection. Maybe. But these are also the reddest regions of the US, where, as sociologist Arlie Hochschild notes, people have rejected environmental regulation. To them, environmentalists' message of more oversight of the oil and gas industry raises the prospect of a paternalistic "nanny state" that brings little but higher taxes, overpaid bureaucrats, and local layoffs. Sociologist Loka Ashwood adds that the usual explanation for antigovernment attitudes in rural America glosses over the history of the state as a dispossessor of people's labor, land, and resources in the name of progress (e.g., the use of eminent domain to construct a nuclear plant). The rural residents in Georgia that are the focus of Ashwood's study were all too aware of this history. Their distrust of the government was born of the belief that profiteering, not the public good, drives state interventions.[35] It's an echo of the critique at the heart of the Sagebrush Rebellion of the 1970s and '80s, which lives on with cattle ranchers like Cliven Bundy who reject the imposition of grazing fees on federal lands they've used freely for generations and who see the creation of public monuments as a land grab.

Like other observers, I found a deep and abiding love for the land among many of the conservative rural landowners I befriended. Their rejection of environmentalism was not a wholesale disavowal of land conservation. It was a circling of the wagons in defense of property rights against the perceived onslaught of urban interests. I think there's room to get rural residents on board with some environmentalist goals, but only if activists *listen* to the concerns of Middle America and emphasize policies that harmonize with so-called rural values like land sovereignty and local control. For lessors, fractivists' alleged "big government" agenda and confrontational politics obscured their shared interests. Commonsense measures like disallowing on-site storage of wastewater or requiring gas companies to repair any tainted water wells within three thousand feet of a drilling accident would have prevented or mitigated many of the worst local impacts. The simple act of requiring gas companies to pipe their water on-site, which a minority of them did voluntarily, would have attenuated what many locals considered the worst blight: tanker truck traffic. Ralph gained traction with landowners by *pragmatically* working to ameliorate quality-of-life issues like these (e.g., by facilitating meetings between lessors and lessees, or informing local representatives of contamination issues) rather than *dogmatically* exhorting them to change (e.g., by framing problems and solutions in explicitly partisan terms).

There's evidence that Ralph's approach has purchase beyond Billtown. Research shows that, as a result of increased political polarization, conservatives often believe that existing regulatory regimes are more restrictive than they really are. Interestingly, one study found that conservatives in Colorado rejected a truly laissez-fair approach to oil and gas drilling. Notwithstanding their stated belief that fracking in the state was overregulated, they supported several policies regarding fracking that were as stringent or more stringent than those actually in place at the time.[36] The implication is a hopeful one: there may be bipartisan support for a variety of rules that could mitigate the worst impacts of fracking and other environmental hazards. In fact, polls show that most Americans support stronger environmental protection. This seems hard to believe, given the chasm between congressional Democrats and Republicans on the issue (which is abetted by organized right-wing climate denialism).[37] The trick is to extricate the particular environmental policies that could enjoy broad support from partisan feuds over the proper role of government in regulating everyday affairs.

* * *

While conservative landowners were cynical about federal, and also state, government institutions like the EPA and the DEP, many immersed themselves in municipal politics. Locals were often on a first-name basis with their state representative or county commissioners. Board of Supervisors meetings were circled on the calendar; residents routinely studied up on the issues and engaged in spirited deliberations about local land use decisions. And, much to my surprise, it was common that locals *did* support various forms of land use restrictions in cases brought before the BOS in the name of protecting scarce public goods like "rural character." The lesson echoes both Tocqueville and Elinor Ostrom. Communities were willing to support policies and instruments (e.g., zoning) that advanced the public interest—even if they effectively limited residents' own property rights—if they were themselves a part of the decision-making process.

Tocqueville argued that self-governance and home rule, which conservatives purport to value more than progressives, invigorated democracy in America. According to the political scientist David Stasavage, the same holds true "across the broad sweep of human history." Citizens are more likely to legitimize, and participate in, democratic governance at the local level.[38] While sociologist Robert Wuthnow considers the combination of faith in self-governance and cynicism toward "big government" to be one of the hallmarks of small-town American life, polls indicate a broader trend: between 2010 and 2020, Americans' trust in the federal government has averaged below 20 percent; over that same decade, their trust in local government has averaged over 70 percent.[39]

Ostrom believed that empowering collective decision-making on the local level could facilitate organic social arrangements that protect the commons. "When interactions enable those who use reciprocity to gain a reputation for trustworthiness, others will be willing to cooperate with them to overcome CPR [common-pool resource] dilemmas." This is the same premise as civic association: familiarity and face-to-face deliberation generates trust and cooperative self-governance. If users of a limited resource are not granted any autonomy to make and enforce their own rules, Ostrom has shown, they are likely to delegitimize efforts to regulate their use of the resource. National and state governments can undermine people's faith in environmental regulation when they assert a monopoly over control of resources and fail to consult with communities, Ostrom and her colleagues have argued.[40]

Regarding fracking, as it stands, private land leasing prevents many community stakeholders from having a say in decisions even though they absorb the externalities. Permit hearings for gas wells are mere performances of local decision-making; the outcome is basically prede-termined. But it is within Pennsylvania's and others states' power to grant towns the right to hold a referendum on whether to allow fracking, or to craft regulations that are tailored to local concerns. Pennsylvania's Supreme Court (in *Robinson Township v. Commonwealth*) actually struck down the preemptive zoning restrictions of Act 13 in December 2013, arguing that they violated the Environmental Rights Amendment to the Pennsylvania Constitution. But the DEP maintains that there's no con-stitutional right to local self-government regarding fracking.[41] Some mu-nicipalities in Pennsylvania and other states have defiantly used home rule arguments to construct community-level mechanisms for managing fracking. Every place I'm aware of that has done this has used increased local control to place greater *restrictions* on fracking, even in conservative areas (in each case, the state, in conjunction with industry, has vigorously pursued lawsuits against the rebel towns). In Lycoming County, it seems that many residents stepped up to stop fracking in Rock Run because they felt that, as public land that they enjoyed and supported through taxes, they were *entitled* to have a say about it. If institutions of commu-nity deliberation were in place that made locals feel entitled to have a say about private leasing, perhaps more residents would support certain re-strictions on freehold property law.

In the end, facilitating greater home rule regarding fracking in Ameri-can communities may do little to reduce greenhouse gas emissions. Fracking is certainly one of those macro environmental problems that, Ostrom acknowledged, are difficult to manage at the scale of a village.[42] But enabling some degree of community-level authority over the oil and gas industry may narrow the gulf that separates conservative, rural com-munities from environmentalism by redefining the parameters of envi-ronmental protection. To the extent that locals I met read environmen-talism as shorthand for greater government control over private property, many viewed it as anathema to their community. But if there were room under the umbrella of environmentalism for greater individ-ual- and community-level control over local land uses, I believe folks like George—who already viewed themselves as land stewards—could be potential allies in the push for greater environmental protections.

The implication of Ostrom's life's work is that they almost certainly would be.

People are more inclined to play the game if they get to be part of crafting the rules. As sociologists Gianpaolo Baiocchi and Ernesto Ganuza have argued about democracy, it is in part people's disconnection from real decision-making that alienates them from the political process.[43] Indeed, what finally got "developing countries" on board with an international climate treaty was the Paris Agreement's balancing of "top-down provisions for strong global emission goals" with a bottom-up structure of nationally determined contributions that assured developing countries that "their priorities for growth and development would be fully respected." Poorer countries literally helped write the Paris rulebook and were promised "flexibility . . . in light of their capacities." In turn, they were willing to endorse a greenhouse gas reduction regime to which they're accountable.[44]

* * *

Where does all this leave the people I befriended in Lycoming County? In preparation for the completion of this book, I went back to Billtown with a photographer to take some additional portraits.[45] Our first stop was Tom and Mary Crawley. In the wake of their settlement with the gas company that contaminated their water, they seemed at ease. New beginnings, they said. To mark the next chapter of their lives, the empty nesters adopted a wily golden retriever, Sadie. They also built a new addition onto the back of their house. It was a cozy den, replete with ceiling beams they salvaged from an old barn on the property and a hearth built from their own fieldstones. And in the garage sat a new Ford Mustang. Tom and Mary had fantasized about buying one as a "Sunday driver" back when the landman first came knocking. The irony wasn't lost on them that their dream came true, but as the result of a settlement, instead. They still couldn't drink their water, but they were trying to make lemonade out of lemons. You can't take your money to the grave, they joked.

Even though gas still leaked from the neighbor's well, the DEP dropped the multimillion-dollar penalty it had imposed on the petroleum firm and reached a new settlement that required no fine (typical of his low-key demeanor, Tom, when I texted him about the settlement, replied simply, "Lol"). Tom had a suspicion that the company might not give up on the well just yet. If the firm did decide to mend and then frac the well, Tom nonchalantly mentioned, they might consider leasing again. He said it would be just their luck to reject a new lease and then learn that it was a productive well that would pay out handsomely. I didn't know what to say. After sitting in silence for about a minute, Mary piped up, 'We're happy, but it's weird. All of our friends are gone.'

The Crawleys were the only ones on Green Valley Road who stayed in place after reaching a settlement. Their next-door neighbors, Doyle and Peggy Bodle, cut bait and moved to Texas to be near their son. Their neighbor across the street who had organized the landowner coalition, Ray Gregoire, moved his family to North Carolina. Donna Gordner, another neighbor, had moved out but was struggling to sell her house. Jim Finkler, who lived down the road, tragically died of cancer before the lawsuit was resolved; he left behind a wife and teenage son. For this once tight-knit group of neighbors, their water wasn't the only casualty of fracking. They lost their community.

When Tristan, the photographer, and I stopped to check in on George Hagemeyer, he was eager to show off his renovated kitchen. At the same time, his current earnings from the gas wells had dipped so low that he opted to start receiving social security at age sixty-three, even though that meant reduced benefits. He also decided to sell the transport van he had splurged on just a few years before, and he was disappointed that it no longer seemed feasible for him to cover the entire cost of his granddaughter's college tuition. He still had what mattered most, "my dad's home," and so he said he was satisfied. But "if people think they are going to get rich from this," George griped, they need to think again. Interestingly, George had also taken to occasionally turning up at Board of Supervisor meetings in neighboring townships to offer testimony if gas-related issues came up. Although he didn't frame it this way,

I saw it as a kind of low-key activism that jibed with his and the community's politics.

As for Ralph Kisberg, he was eager to read a draft of this book as soon as it was available. Not surprisingly, given his vast knowledge of and borderline obsession with the topic, he had lots to say (including a number of suggested corrections and additional sources). Ralph confided his worry that readers might think he is an apologist for fracking. He conceded he had no grand solutions, but he spelled out the logic of his advocacy more explicitly to me in a series of conversations and e-mails than he had before. In an ideal world, he emphasized, there'd be no fracking and we'd be on the fast track to an equitable, job-creating, green-energy future. But Ralph's approach to advocacy was a realist one. Fighting for a ban on fracking in Pennsylvania was a fool's errand. You can't put the genie back in the bottle (e.g., cancel leases or rip out wells and pipelines). Some Democrats were rattling the saber lately about a national fracking ban. Yet Ralph was (rightly) convinced that the best one could hope for is an executive order banning new leasing that would apply only to federal land (a national ban requires an act of Congress). He supported such a ban on principle but worried it could just lead to more drilling on private land to make up the difference.

Being against fracking in heavily drilled places like rural Pennsylvania is "like being against air," Ralph joked. It's just something that's there, "and we have to deal with it and work to make it better." Given this reality, Ralph believed the best strategy was to fight like hell to mitigate the harm caused while trying to stop industry's spread. This was why Ralph was so adamant about fighting for a severance tax, which many fractivists saw as a sorry substitute for a ban. "With the legal property rights the gas industry has in PA," Ralph wrote via e-mail, "a severance tax is the only way for the Commonwealth to control the industry." The tax, he urged, could be set aside to fund the energy transition to renewables. The state could ratchet up the tax annually, Ralph added, which would make an already poor return on investment in shale gas look even worse next to solar and wind power. Gas production would be cut back significantly, "without a long legal fight." Even a severance tax of

100 percent would be "perfectly legal," Ralph argued, and easier to enact than a ban.

The second front of Ralph's war was advocating for bans on fracking in places where it had not yet taken root (e.g., New York, the Delaware River Basin, Maryland). He worried that some of his comrades were too mired in NIMBYism. He thought some of their efforts could be better spent sharing their knowledge of industry malfeasance and activist strategies with legislators and local leaders in unaffected regions, helping convince those communities that they don't want this industry. To Ralph, the argument was simple but powerful. It's not just the ecological risk. Given the glut of oil and gas caused by the fracking boom and the declining cost of renewables, fracking was a bad bet that "was not necessary from any standpoint of national security or energy right now."

The feud between Ralph and some members of the RDA was water under the bridge. The original members were simply too good of friends to stay mad at each other. I might also add that Ralph's wealth of information and wisdom about the issues, and genuine kindness, were too valuable for the group to forgo. But over the last few years, during which Ralph made several extended soul-searching road trips out West (making ends meet by house-sitting, dog-sitting, or painting houses for wealthy friends), he has decided to devote most of his attention to being a part of the transition to clean energy. "Being in at best the last third of my life," he reflected, "I want to focus on solutions to the energy problem rather than continue to fight the same battles over and over with the various clueless politicians, media and businesspeople over the huge disaster that is the gas industry." As this book went to press, Ralph was part of a team trying to build a power plant in the Gulf of California that would be run by energy generated by ocean tides. His role, fittingly, was to make connections that might lead to investors. Ralph was energized by the task, but also demoralized by how "much work and money it will be to transition . . . to a renewable energy economy." All the time he spent, and all the obstacles he encountered, were "just to help get one 500 megawatt project going." A drop in the bucket. He could see why there's still a limited role for methane, and even oil, in the foreseeable future. A complete ban immediately? "Become Amish and then we'll talk," Ralph retorted.

Ralph didn't like ending on a sour note, and so he followed up our back-and-forth with one more e-mail: "There are so many good things going on, so many people out there working hard for the future. It may sound stupid, but I'm optimistic. I doubt I'll live to see a clean energy world, but maybe a clean energy U.S. economy if I can hang around long enough."

*   *   *

As for me, I've come to the conclusion that America's legal and political privileging of individual sovereignty and property rights sanctions the usurping of the commons, frays the fabric of communities, and undermines the social contract. I do entertain some glimmer of optimism that, if more of us recognized that the externalities produced by personal land- and energy-use choices violate others' *human rights*, more people might push for green-energy policies that reign in those externalities in the name of *other* core American principles—namely, fairness and democracy. After all, the idea that *everyone* deserves the same freedoms, and that every community stakeholder should have a say in decisions that affect them, is as American as Little League baseball.

NOTES

Introduction. Land of the Freehold

1. I am deeply indebted to George and the other subjects of this book who let me more or less stalk them for seven years and write about them. All names of people and places herein are real and are used with residents' permission. I use real names because my participants expressed a preference for seeing their own name in print, because it holds me accountable to the public record, and because it allows readers to compare and evaluate my evidence with other forms of data (e.g., census data, newspapers, archives). Along with Alexandra Murphy, I wrote about the issue of naming places and people in ethnography in the article "The Ethical Dilemmas and Social Scientific Trade-offs of Masking in Ethnography," *Sociological Methods and Research* 48, no. 4 (2019): 801–27, https://doi.org/10.1177/0049124117701483.

2. Grace Hood and Jim Hill, "Remember the First Time Colorado Tried Fracking with a Nuclear Bomb?," CPR News, September 6, 2019, https://www.cpr.org/2019/09/06/remember -the-first-time-colorado-tried-fracking-with-a-nuclear-bomb/.

3. A caveat: Pennsylvania's Oil and Gas Conservation Law enables petroleum companies to drill deep beneath a landowner's property even without her consent if enough of her neighbors have leased. But it only applies to wells that tap the Onondaga shale formation, which sits well below the Marcellus and has not yet been targeted for development. See Laura Legere, "Forced Pooling Policies Remain Unclear in Pennsylvania's Shale Plays," *Pittsburgh Post-Gazette*, January 6, 2015, https://www.post-gazette.com/business/powersource/2015/01/06/Forced-pooling -policies-remain-unclear-in-Pennsylvania-s-shale-plays/stories/201412300017.

4. See Joe Massaro, "Wendy Lynne Lee: Activist, Professor, and Now a Fiction Story Teller," Energy in Depth, November 18, 2012, www.energyindepth.org/wendy-lynne-lee-activist -philosophy-professor-and-now-a-fiction-story-teller/.

5. Kai T. Erikson, *Everything in Its Path: Destruction of Community in the Buffalo Creek Flood* (New York: Simon and Schuster, 1976), 72.

6. J. D. Vance, *Hillbilly Elegy: A Memoir of a Family and Culture in Crisis* (New York: Harper, 2016), 4.

7. Kevin D. Williamson, "The White Ghetto," *National Review*, December 16, 2013, https:// www.nationalreview.com/2013/12/white-ghetto-kevin-d-williamson/; Erikson, *Everything in Its Path*, 53.

8. Horace Kephart, *Our Southern Highlanders* (New York: Outing, 1913), 307.

9. See Pennsylvania Environmental Defense Foundation (PEDF), "Highlights of PEDF's Reply Brief," August 26, 2015, www.pedf.org/current-litigation.html.

10. See, e.g., Jessica Smartt Gullion, *Fracking the Neighborhood: Reluctant Activists and Natural Gas Drilling* (Cambridge, MA: MIT Press, 2015); Seamus McGraw, *The End of Country: Dispatches from the Frack Zone* (New York: Random House, 2011).

11. The pro-fracking gadfly Tom Shepstone, a prolific blogger from Pennsylvania, writes often about fractivists as urban elites bent on stripping landowners of their property rights and waging class warfare against them. See, e.g., Tom Shepstone, "If You Believe in Property Rights, Then This Case Matters," *Natural Gas Now* (blog), June 4, 2017, https://naturalgasnow.org/believe -property-rights-case-matters/.

12. Eliza D. Czolowski et al., "Toward Consistent Methodology to Quantify Populations in Proximity to Oil and Gas Development: A National Spatial Analysis and Review," *Environmental Health Perspectives* 125, no. 8 (2017): 086004-1–086004-11, https://doi.org/10.1289/EHP1535; fractracker.org/topics/pipelines/.

13. Adam Mayer and Stephanie Malin, "Keep it Local? Preferences for Federal, State, or Local Unconventional Oil and Gas Regulations," *Energy Research and Social Science* 44 (2018), 336, https://doi.org/10.1016/j.erss.2018.05.028.

14. Office of the Attorney General, Commonwealth of Pennsylvania, *Report 1 of the Forty-Third Statewide Investigating Grand Jury* (Pennsylvania: Office of the Attorney General, 2020), https://www.attorneygeneral.gov/wp-content/uploads/2020/06/FINAL-fracking-report-w .responses-with-page-number-V2.pdf.

15. Marcellus Shale Advisory Commission, *Governor's Marcellus Shale Advisory Commission Report* (Harrisburg, PA: Marcellus Shale Advisory Commission, Office of the Governor, 2011), http://files.dep.state.pa.us/PublicParticipation/MarcellusShaleAdvisoryCommission/Marce llusShaleAdvisoryPortalFiles/MSAC_Final_Report.pdf. For the most up-to-date figures on permitted and drilled gas wells in Pennsylvania, see www.marcellusgas.org.

16. Russell Gold, *The Boom: How Fracking Ignited the American Energy Revolution and Changed the World* (New York: Simon and Schuster, 2014). See also Gary Sernovitz, *The Green and the Black: The Complete Story of the Shale Revolution, the Fight over Fracking, and the Future of Energy* (New York: St. Martin's Press, 2016); Tom Wilber, *Under the Surface: Fracking, Fortunes, and the Fate of the Marcellus Shale* (Ithaca, NY: Cornell University Press, 2012).

17. Emily S. Rueb, "'Freedom Gas,' the Next American Export," *New York Times*, May 29, 2019, https://www.nytimes.com/2019/05/29/us/freedom-gas-energy-department.html.

18. US Department of the Interior, Bureau of Land Management, "About the BLM Oil and Gas Program," accessed August 15, 2020, https://www.blm.gov/programs/energy-and-minerals /oil-and-gas/about.

19. Timothy Fitzgerald, "Importance of Mineral Rights and Royalty Interests for Rural Residents and Landowners," *Choices*, quarter 4, 2014, https://www.choicesmagazine.org/choices -magazine/theme-articles/is-the-natural-gas-revolution-all-its-fracked-up-to-be-for-local -economies/importance-of-mineral-rights-and-royalty-interests-for-rural-residents-and -landowners. See also Kendor P. Jones, John F. (Jeff) Welborn, and Chelsey J. Russell, "Split Estates and Surface Access Issues," in *Landman's Legal Handbook: A Practical Guide to Mineral Leasing*, 5th ed. (Westminster, CO: Rocky Mountain Mineral Law Foundation, 2013).

20. David W. Miller, "The Historical Development of Oil and Gas Laws of the United States," *California Law Review* 51, no. 3 (1963): 505–34, https://doi.org/10.15779/Z38BN2H.

21. Harry S. Sachse, "A Comparison of the Landowner's Rights to Petroleum in France and Louisiana," *Louisiana Law Review* 23, no. 4 (1963): 722–57.

22. John Locke, "Second Treatise of Government (1689)," in *Classics of American Political and Constitutional Thought: Origins through the Civil War*, edited by Scott J. Hammond, Kevin R. Hardwick, and Howard L. Lubert (Indianapolis: Hackett, 2007), 64.

23. "For whoever owns the soil, it is theirs up to Heaven and down to Hell." Though this phrase (in Latin) first appeared in medieval Roman law, it was popularized by English common law and has come the closest to being realized in practice in American property law. See Yehuda Abramovitch, "The Maxim 'Cujus Est Solum Ejus Usque Ad Coelum' as Applied in Aviation," *McGill Law Journal* 8 (1962): 247–69; see also Stuart Banner, *Who Owns the Sky? The Struggle to Control Airspace from the Wright Brothers On* (Cambridge, MA: Harvard University Press, 2008). Another notable caveat to property rights is eminent domain, the contentious clause allowing the state to expropriate private property in special circumstances if it serves the public interest.

24. Jones, Welborn, and Russell, "Split Estates," 182.

25. Claudia Hitaj, Jeremy Weber, and Ken Erickson, *Ownership of Oil and Gas Rights: Implications for U.S. Farm Income and Wealth*, EIB-193, US Department of Agriculture, Economic Research Service, June 2018, https://www.ers.usda.gov/webdocs/publications/89325/eib-193.pdf?v=1911.6. It is not unusual in these states to hear stories of contemporary landowners who were not aware that they didn't own the subsurface and could neither control nor profit from subsurface drilling on their property; see Mayer and Malin, "Keep it Local?"

26. See Stacia S. Ryder and Peter M. Hall, "This Land Is Your Land, Maybe: A Historical Institutionalist Analysis for Contextualizing Split Estate Conflicts in U.S. Unconventional Oil and Gas Development, *Land Use Policy* 63 (2017): 149–59, https://doi.org/10.1016/j.landusepol.2017.01.006. Over 150 years of case law firmly establish the primacy of the mineral estate over the surface estate. The mineral estate owner "has an implied right to use so much of the surface . . . as is reasonably necessary to . . . develop the minerals that exist in the tract." Otherwise the subsurface would be "valueless" (Jones, Welborn, and Russell, "Split Estates," 183). There are no reliable or publicly available datasets that allow us to calculate with confidence the percentage of split estate versus freehold titles. Some analysts estimate, however, that the majority of unconventional oil and gas leases in Texas, Colorado, and North Dakota are split estates. Unless the owner of the mineral estate is the federal or state government, it can be difficult to know much about them (e.g., if they are a descendent of the original freehold title holder, a land tycoon, or a corporation). See Fitzgerald, "Importance of Mineral Rights."

27. A few other Commonwealth nations (former British territories) allow for private mineral ownership, but only in a limited number of instances—e.g., where freehold ownership predates the establishment of the sovereign state. In Canada, for instance, the Crown holds 89 percent of all mineral rights; only the remaining 11 percent is freehold. See Cameron C. Wyatt, "Mineral Rights in Canada," *Pipeline News*, November 10, 2015, https://www.pipelinenews.ca/opinion/columnists/mineral-rights-in-canada-1.2102451#:~:text=In%20Canada%2C%20mineral%20rights%20are,11%20per%20cent%20is%20freehold.

28. Fitzgerald, "Importance of Mineral Rights."

29. Matt Kelso, "Drilled Unconventional Wells in PA by County and Year," FracTracker Alliance, December 31, 2012, https://www.fractracker.org/2012/12/drilled-unconventional-wells-in-pa-by-county-and-year/.

30. See, e.g., Robert W. Howarth, Anthony Ingraffea, and Terry Engelder, "Natural Gas: Should Fracking Stop?," *Nature* 477 (2011): 271–75, https://doi.org/10.1038/477271a; Steven G.

Osborn et al., "Methane Contamination of Drinking Water Accompanying Gas-Well Drilling and Hydraulic Fracturing," *Proceedings of the National Academy of Sciences* 108, no. 20 (2011): 8,172–76, https://doi.org/10.1073/pnas.1100682108.

31. Kaye Burnet, "New Map Shows Fracking on PA State Lands," WESA, March 9, 2015, https://www.wesa.fm/post/new-map-shows-fracking-pa-state-lands#stream/0.

32. Tom Shepstone, "Gentry Class Elites Tell Rural America to Drop Dead," *Natural Gas Now* (blog), May 25, 2017, https://naturalgasnow.org/gentry-class-elites-tell-rural-america-drop-dead/.

33. Eli Pariser coined the term "filter bubble" to describe how social media and search-engine algorithms sift out information that may clash with Internet users' preexisting viewpoints. Eli Pariser, *The Filter Bubble: How the New Personalized Web Is Changing What We Read and How We Think* (New York: Penguin, 2011).

34. See, e.g., Robert D. Bullard, *Dumping in Dixie: Race, Class, and Environmental Quality* (New York: Routledge, 2000); Julie Sze, *Noxious New York: The Racial Politics of Urban Health and Environmental Justice* (Cambridge, MA: MIT Press, 2007); Dorceta E. Taylor, *Toxic Communities: Environmental Racism, Industrial Pollution, and Residential Mobility* (New York: New York University Press, 2014).

35. See Fedor Dokshin, "Whose Backyard and What's at Issue? Spatial and Ideological Dynamics of Local Opposition to Fracking in New York State, 2010 to 2013," *American Sociological Review* 81, no. 5 (2016): 921–48, https://doi.org/10.1177/0003122416663929.

36. Dokshin, "Whose Backyard and What's at Issue?"

37. Jennifer Jacquet et al., "Shame and Honour Drive Cooperation," *Biology Letters* 7, no. 6 (2011): 899–901, https://doi.org/10.1098/rsbl.2011.0367.

38. Alexis de Tocqueville, *Democracy in America*, trans. Delba Winthrop (1835; Chicago: University of Chicago Press, 2002), 484, 482.

39. Colin Woodard, *American Character: A History of the Epic Struggle between Individual Liberty and the Common Good* (New York: Viking Books, 2016), 98.

40. Quoted in Robert D. Putnam, *Bowling Alone: The Collapse and Revival of American Community* (New York: Simon and Schuster, 2000), 48.

41. Woodard, *American Character*, 22.

42. Jedediah Purdy, *This Land Is Our Land: The Struggle for a New Commonwealth* (Princeton, NJ: Princeton University Press, 2019), xii.

43. Putnam, *Bowling Alone*.

44. Robert N. Bellah et al., *Habits of the Heart: Individualism and Commitment in American Life* (Berkeley: University of California Press, 1985), 6.

Chapter 1. Billtown

1. Barbara Griffith Ertel et al., eds., *The West Fourth Street Story* (Williamsport, PA: Junior League of Williamsport, 1975), 6.

2. Ertel et al., *West Fourth Street Story*, 6.

3. Robert H. Larson, Richard J. Morris, and John F. Piper Jr., *Williamsport: Frontier Village to Regional Center* (Woodland Hills, CA: Windsor, 1984), 45.

4. "Peter Herdic (1824–1888) Historical Marker," ExplorePAhistory.com, accessed July 15, 2020, www.explorepahistory.com/hmarker.php?markerId=1-A-334.

5. Robin Van Auken and Louis Hunsinger Jr., *Williamsport: Boomtown on the Susquehanna* (Charleston, SC: Arcadia, 2003), 53–4.

6. Mary Sieminski, "Married to a Magnate: Peter Herdic's Two Wives," *Williamsport Sun-Gazette*, August 11, 2013, https://www.lycoming.edu/lcwhp/PDFs/Herdic's%20Wives.pdf.

7. "Lycoming County History, Facts, and Information," Williamsport.org, accessed July 15, 2020, www.williamsport.org/wp-content/uploads/2019/01/new-school-report-2019.pdf.

8. "The Herdic House Hotel," 800parkplace.com, accessed July 15, 2020, www.800parkplace.com/herdichotel.htm.

9. Federal Writers' Project (PA), *A Picture of Lycoming County* (Williamsport, PA: Commissioners of Lycoming County, Pennsylvania, 1939), 213.

10. "Herdic House Hotel," 800parkplace.com; Ertel et al., *West Fourth Street Story*, 30.

11. Ertel et al., *West Fourth Street Story*, 27

12. Federal Writers' Project, *Picture of Lycoming County*, 216.

13. Federal Writers' Project, *Picture of Lycoming County*, 216.

14. Van Auken and Hunsinger, *Boomtown on the Susquehanna*, 46.

15. John Franklin Meginness, *History of Lycoming County, Pennsylvania* (Chicago: Brown, Runk, 1892), 729.

16. Van Auken and Hunsinger, *Boomtown on the Susquehanna*, 47.

17. Ertel et al., *West Fourth Street Story*, 13; Larson, Morris, and Piper, *Frontier Village to Regional Center*, 56.

18. Larson, Morris, and Piper, *Frontier Village to Regional Center*, 48.

19. Lou Hunsinger Jr., "Ten Hours or No Sawdust: Sawdust War of 1872," accessed July 15, 2020, https://robinvanauken.com/ten-hours-or-no-sawdust-sawdust-war-of-1872/.

20. Laurie Root Harrington, "The Desertmakers: Peter Herdic," accessed August 30, 2020, available at https://www.herdichouse.com/desertmakers.

21. Ertel et al., *West Fourth Street Story*, 32; Van Auken and Hunsinger, *Boomtown on the Susquehanna*, 47; Harrington, "The Desertmakers."

22. Meginness, *History of Lycoming County*, 758–59.

23. Ertel et al., *West Fourth Street Story*, 33.

24. See William R. Freudenberg, "Addictive Economies: Extractive Industries and Vulnerable Localities in a Changing World Economy," *Rural Sociology* 57, no. 3 (1992): 305–32, https://doi.org/10.1111/j.1549-0831.1992.tb00467.x. For a more recent overview, see Stephanie A. Malin, Stacia Ryder, and Mariana Galvão Lyra, "Environmental Justice and Natural Resource Extraction: Intersections of Power, Equity, and Access," *Environmental Sociology* 5, no. 2 (2019): 109–16, https://doi.org/10.1080/23251042.2019.1608420.

25. City of Williamsport, *2015 City of Williamsport Historic Structures Survey* (Williamsport, PA: City of Williamsport), 8, http://www.lyco.org/Portals/1/PlanningCommunityDevelopment/Documents/HeritagePlan/Williamsport%20Historic%20Structures%20Survey.pdf.

26. "Millionaires Row Historic District," LivingPlaces.com, accessed July 15, 2020, https://www.livingplaces.com/PA/Lycoming_County/Williamsport_City/Millionaires_Row_Historic_District.html.

27. "Millionaires Row," LivingPlaces.com; Ertel et al., *West Fourth Street Story*, 30–40; "Herdic House Hotel," 800parkplace.com.

28. "Millionaires' Row," LivingPlaces.com.

29. City of Williamsport, *Historic Structures*, 9.

30. Larson, Morris, and Piper, *Frontier Village to Regional Center*, 94, 102–3.

31. Robin Van Auken and Louis E. Hunsinger Jr., *Williamsport: The Grit Photograph Collection* (Charleston, SC: Arcadia, 2004), 7–8. *Grit* lives on as a bimonthly glossy magazine published in Topeka, Kansas.

32. Van Auken and Hunsinger, *Boomtown on the Susquehanna*, 117.

33. Larson, Morris, and Piper, *Frontier Village to Regional Center*, 186–7.

34. J. D. Vance's despairing *Hillbilly Elegy: A Memoir of a Family and Culture in Crisis* (New York: Harper, 2016), a national best seller, brought these issues to the public consciousness in the heat of the 2016 presidential election.

35. See CensusReporter.org, "Census Tract 4, Lycoming, PA," accessed July 15, 2020, https://censusreporter.org/profiles/14000US42081000400-census-tract-4-lycoming-pa/; Pennsylvania Department of Community and Economic Development, "Qualified Opportunity Zones," accessed July 15, 2020, https://dced.pa.gov/programs-funding/federal-funding-opportunities/qualified-opportunity-zones/. In 2018, my neighborhood was one of three census tracts in Billtown designated by the governor as a "Qualified Opportunity Zone," a classification designed to spur economic development by allowing investors in these areas to defer or eliminate capital-gains taxes.

36. Bongiovi's Downtown menu. The essay closed with a hope that downtown "can regain some of its old glory" and that the restaurant might help encourage its revitalization. It has since gone out of business.

37. Larson, Morris, and Piper, *Frontier Village to Regional Center*, 105, 115; Van Auken and Hunsinger, *Boomtown on the Susquehanna*, 153.

38. Carl Milofsky, *Smallville: Institutionalizing Community in Twenty-First-Century America* (Medford, MA: Tufts University Press, 2008), 40.

39. See Nick Redding, *Methland: The Death and Life of an American Small Town* (New York: Bloomsbury, 2009). For a critical take on "the war on drugs" in rural America, see William Garriott, *Policing Methamphetamine: Narcopolitics in Rural America* (New York: New York University Press, 2011).

40. Carl Milofsky et al., "Small Town in Mass Society: Substance Abuse Treatment and Urban-Rural Migration," *Contemporary Drug Problems* 20, no. 3 (1993): 433–71. Between 1980 and 2015, Lycoming County's Black population rose from 1,789 to 5,640, a trend that many attribute in part to the recovery migration. Though less than 5 percent of the county population, African Americans represent 13 percent of Williamsport's population.

41. See, e.g., John Beauge, "Heroin Ring Leader Found Business Was Good, Less Noticeable in Williamsport: Prosecutor," *Pennsylvania Real-Time News*, December 23, 2016, https://www.pennlive.com/news/2016/12/heroin_ring_leader_found_busin.html.

42. Larson, Morris, and Piper, *Frontier Village to Regional Center*, 131.

43. Vincent Matteo, "Little League World Series: A Yearly Economic Homerun for Williamsport and Lycoming County," accessed July 15, 2020, http://digital.graphcompubs.com/publication/?i=233537&article_id=1859967&view=articleBrowser#{%22issue_id%22:233537,%22view%22:%22articleBrowser%22,%22publication_id%22:%2223403%22,%22article_id%22:%221859967%22}.

44. Jack Brubaker, *Down the Susquehanna to the Chesapeake* (University Park: Pennsylvania State University Press, 2002), 108.

45. Van Auken and Hunsinger, *Boomtown on the Susquehanna*, 51.

46. Center for Rural Pennsylvania, *Establishing a Baseline for Measuring Agricultural Changes Related to Marcellus Shale Development* (Harrisburg, PA: Center for Rural Pennsylvania), accessed July 15, 2020, https://www.rural.palegislature.us/documents/reports/Marcellus-Report -9-Agriculture.pdf.

47. Larson, Morris, and Piper, *Frontier Village to Regional Center*, 131.

48. Milofsky, *Smallville*, 40.

49. Lycoming County is significantly whiter and less poor than Williamsport (92 percent vs. 81 percent white; 14 percent vs. 27 percent poverty rate).

50. Federal Writers' Project, *Picture of Lycoming County*, 36–8.

51. Meginness, *History of Lycoming County*, 92–3.

52. Meginness, *History of Lycoming County*, 197.

53. Colin Woodard, *American Character: A History of the Epic Struggle between Individual Liberty and the Common Good* (New York: Viking Books, 2016), 73–5.

54. See, e.g., Kevin D. Williamson, "The White Ghetto," *National Review*, December 16, 2013, https://www.nationalreview.com/2013/12/white ghetto-kevin-d-williamson/; Vance, *Hillbilly Elegy*.

55. Stephen Wolf, "What If Appalachia Were Its Own State? Trump Dominated the Primaries There, While Clinton Barely Won," *Daily Kos*, May 25, 2016, https://www.dailykos.com /stories/2016/5/75/1577614/-What-if-Appalachia-were-its own state Trump-dominated-the -primaries-there-while-Clinton-barely-won. There is no consensus on the precise boundaries of Appalachia, so estimates of its size differ.

56. Katherine J. Cramer, *The Politics of Resentment: Rural Consciousness in Wisconsin and the Rise of Scott Walker* (Chicago: University of Chicago Press, 2016).

Chapter 2. Boomtown

1. I was not able to find data on the percentage of lessors who hired a lawyer. One law professor claimed that it "often happens" that lessors signed leases "without getting legal advice." See Marie Cusick and Amy Sisk, "Royalties: Why Some Strike It Rich in the Natural Gas Patch, and Others Strike Out," StateImpact Pennsylvania, February 28, 2018, https://stateimpact.npr.org /pennsylvania/2018/02/28/why-some strike-it-rich-in-the-gas-patch-and-others-strike-out/. Some Pennsylvania lessors told the journalist Tom Wilber that landmen would not work with them if they hired a lawyer. See Tom Wilber, *Under the Surface: Fracking, Fortunes, and the Fate of the Marcellus Shale* (Ithaca, NY: Cornell University Press, 2012), 31.

2. For a sobering look at the collateral damage produced by chasing stardom in the NFL, see Robert W. Turner II, *NFL Means Not for Long: The Life and Career of the NFL Athlete* (New York: Oxford University Press, 2018).

3. Anya Litvak, "Drop in Shale Drilling Puts Some Hotels on the Market," *Pittsburgh Post-Gazette*, April 17, 2016, https://www.post-gazette.com/business/powersource/2016/04/17 /Drop-in-shale-drilling-puts-some-hotels-on-the-market-in-Western-Pennsylvania/stories /201604170097.

4. Jim Hamill, "'Pine Square' Replaces Eyesores in Billtown," WNEP, April 20, 2012, https://www.wnep.com/article/news/local/bradford-county/pine-square-replaces-eyesores-in-billtown/523-cocd1fbe-481d-48b4-a8aa-777586feff46.

5. On three occasions, Russ showed me a dozen or more paintings he had just bought from artists or galleries (most costing several hundred dollars each). Luke Yocum, who died at the age of thirty-five, in 2015, told me in 2013 that Russ bought dozens of his paintings in the span of six weeks and commissioned him to paint more.

6. "About Our Lofts" and "Home," 135Flats.com, accessed July 15, 2020, http://135flats.com /about.html, http://www.135flats.com/index.html.

7. After I interviewed Dan in his personal conference room—which felt more like a sports bar, with all the autographed football jerseys and glass-encased baseballs—at Liberty Group's gleaming 85,000-square-foot Montoursville headquarters, he tossed me a camouflage Infinity cap and smirked, 'Wear it when you meet with those anti-frackers.'

8. Joe Massaro, "Williamsport in the International Spotlight Thanks to Natural Gas," Energy in Depth, November 16, 2012, https://www.energyindepth.org/williamsport-in-the-international-spotlight-thanks-to-natural-gas/.

9. See Nikki Krize, "Krize Talks One on One with Cruz," WNEP, April 22, 2016, https://www.wnep.com/article/news/local/lycoming-county/krize-talks-one-on-one-with-cruz/523-f23a9246-4948-423f-9826-67fecb1e7cea.

10. Bloomberg News, "Fracker-Funded Research Pushes Industry Agenda in U.S.," *Financial Post*, July 23, 2012, https://financialpost.com/commodities/energy/fracker-funded-research-pushes-industry-agenda-in-u-s. For an academic assessment, see Anthony E. Ladd, "Priming the Well: 'Frackademia' and the Corporate Pipeline of Oil and Gas Funding into Higher Education," *Humanity and Society* 44, no. 2 (2019): 151–77, https://doi.org/10.1177/0160597619879191.

11. "Community Natural Gas Task Force," Lyco.org, accessed July 15, 2020, http://www.lyco.org/Elected-Officials/Commissioners/Community-Gas-Exploration-Task-Force.

12. See also "What They're Saying: 'Shale Gas Development is a Game-Changer of Huge Proportions,'" Marcellus Shale Coalition, December 28, 2011, http://marcelluscoalition.org/2011/12/what-they%E2%80%99re-saying-%E2%80%9Cshale-gas-development-is-a-game-changer-of-huge-proportions%E2%80%9D/.

13. The unemployment rate fell in forty-six states from 2011 to 2012. See Bureau of Labor Statistics, US Department of Labor, "Regional and State Unemployment—2012 Annual Averages," March 1, 2013, https://www.bls.gov/news.release/archives/srgune_03012013.pdf. On housing, see Jonathan Williamson and Bonita Kolb, *Marcellus Natural Gas Development's Effect on Housing in Pennsylvania* (Williamsport, PA: Center for the Study of Community and the Economy, Lycoming College, 2011).

14. See Shannon Elizabeth Bell, *Fighting King Coal: The Challenges to Micromobilization in Central Appalachia* (Cambridge, MA: MIT Press, 2016); Tony J. Silva and Jessica A. Crowe, "The Hope-Reality Gap: Rural Community Officials' Perceptions of Unconventional Shale Development as a Means to Increase Local Population and Revitalize Resource Extraction," *Community Development* 46, no. 4 (2015): 312–28, https://doi.org/10.1080/15575330.2015.1061678; Adam Mayer and Stephanie Malin, "How Should Unconventional Oil and Gas Be Regulated? The

Role of Natural Resource Dependence and Economic Insecurity," *Journal of Rural Studies* 65 (2019): 79–89, https://doi.org/10.1016/j.jrurstud.2018.11.005.

15. John Schwartz, "Gas Boom County Strives for Economic Afterglow," *New York Times*, November 17, 2012, https://www.nytimes.com/2012/11/18/us/marcellus-shale-county-aims-for-long-term-gain.html.

16. "Well History: Lycoming County, PA," MarcellusGas.org, accessed February 13, 2020, https://www.marcellusgas.org/history/PA-Lycoming. Part of the reason I selected Lycoming County as the site for my research was because of this spike in drilling activity; it was a relative latecomer to fracking compared to counties to the north, giving me a better opportunity to witness the phases of shale gas development.

17. For townships in Pennsylvania, supervisory boards are the primary legislative body; there is no city council, mayor, or comptroller. Impact fees are one-time payments provided by gas companies directly to townships for each well that they drill. A severance tax would instead be paid to the state based on how much gas each well produces over its lifespan. Impact fee figures for Pennsylvania townships can be found in Robert F. Powelson, "Act 13 of 2012 Unconventional Gas Well Impact Fee: Annual Report of Fund Revenue and Disbursements," Commonwealth of Pennsylvania Public Utility Commission, September 30, 2014, http://www.puc.state.pa.us/NaturalGas/pdf/MarcellusShale/Gas_Well_PUC_Rpt_101514.pdf.

Chapter 3. The Fracking Lottery

1. For more on landowner coalitions, see Jeffrey Jacquet and Richard C. Stedman, "Natural Gas Landowner Coalitions in New York State: Emerging Benefits of Collective Natural Resource Management," *Journal of Rural Social Sciences* 26, no. 1 (2011): 62–91. The *New York Times* ran a story in the early days of the "gas rush" that mentions Raymond Gregoire and the landowner coalition he organized: Clifford Krauss, "There's Gas in Those Hills," *New York Times*, April 8, 2008, https://www.nytimes.com/2008/04/08/business/08gas.html.

2. I have excluded the name of the petroleum company at the request of Tom Crawley—though he conceded that it would be easy enough to discover through an Internet search.

3. Garrick Blalock, David R. Just, and Daniel H. Simon, "Hitting the Jackpot or Hitting the Skids: Entertainment, Poverty, and the Demand for State Lotteries," *American Journal of Economics and Sociology* 66, no. 3 (2007): 545–70, https://doi.org/10.1111/j.1536-7150.2007.00526.x.

4. Some of the gas wells that provided royalties to Penn Brook Farm received violations from the state Department of Environmental Protection that the Shaners and their neighbors apparently remained unaware of until a CNN report. "Land Owners in Dark on Fracking Problems," CNN.com, March 14, 2012, http://www.cnn.com/videos/us/2012/03/14/harlow-pa-fracking-violations.cnn.

5. Amy let me examine two binders filled with leases, receipts of payments, lawyer correspondences, and minutes from family meetings. The information described herein was obtained or verified from these sources. Throughout this book, I have attempted to verify subjects' accounts with other forms of information such as archival records, inspection reports, or newspaper articles. I also hired an NYU journalism graduate student, Kimon de Greef, to independently fact-check my claims, facts, figures, and citations. Although he (thankfully) didn't find

any glaring problems, his deep digging did uncover a number of inconsistencies (e.g., misquoting a secondary source or mistaking the decade when petroleum companies began to experiment with horizontal drilling). Kimon's biggest influence on the book was in pushing me to provide more sources, beyond my own observations and interviews, to substantiate some of my major claims. But I am the one ultimately responsible for any remaining errors and omissions. In instances where I must rely solely on my subjects' accounts or hearsay, I try to signal this for the reader by using words such as "reportedly" or "allegedly." To the extent possible, I ground my interpretations and claims in what I was able to directly observe over time and across settings. The thinking behind this is that what people say, on the one hand, and what they actually do in the course of their everyday lives, on the other, are not always consistent. Since I am interested in how people responded to fracking in the "natural setting" of their community, it follows that I should privilege data gathered from my observations of people as they went about their daily routines rather than simply rely on what they told me in an interview.

6. For trends in natural-gas prices, see "Natural Gas Prices—Historical Chart," accessed September 20, 2020, https://www.macrotrends.net/2478/natural-gas-prices-historical-chart.

7. While it is plausible that wealthier and more educated residents were advantaged in negotiating lease and royalty payments, the biggest predictor of whether or not one hired a lawyer was not socioeconomic status but the size of one's property (small landowners surmised that lawyer fees would eat up most of their leasing bonus). Dylan Bugden and Richard Stedman's survey of lessors in northeastern Pennsylvania lends additional support to my claim that socioeconomic status did not play a significant role in determining outcomes in the fracking lottery. They find that "outcomes tend to vary by firm-specific rather than sociostructural factors." See Dylan Bugden and Richard Stedman, "Rural Landowners, Energy Leasing, and Patterns of Risk and Inequality in the Shale Gas Industry," *Rural Sociology* 84, no. 3 (2019): 459–88, https://doi.org/10.1111/ruso.12236.

8. Stephanie A. Malin et al., "The Right to Resist or a Case of Injustice? Meta-Power in the Oil and Gas Fields" *Social Forces* 97, no. 4 (2019): 1811–38, https://doi.org/10.1093/sf/soy094.

9. "Gamble Township, Pennsylvania Housing Data," TownCharts.com, accessed July 15, 2020, https://www.towncharts.com/Pennsylvania/Housing/Gamble-township-PA-Housing-data.html#Figure6.

10. Public data only allow estimates of the total amount of money of leasing bonuses and royalties paid out to lessors by oil and gas companies, not how much each lessor received (see, e.g., Timothy Fitzgerald and Randal R. Rucker, "US Private Oil and Natural Gas Royalties: Estimates and Policy Relevance," *OPEC Energy Review*, 40, no. 1 (2016): 3–25, https://doi.org/10.1111/opec.12052). Anecdotally, few if any journalistic reports of shale communities turn up more than a few local instances of shaleionaires. See, e.g., Tom Wilber, *Under the Surface: Fracking, Fortunes, and the Fate of the Marcellus Shale* (Ithaca, NY: Cornell University Press, 2012); Andrew Maykuth, "Shale Gas Was Going to Make Them Rich. Then the Checks Arrived," *Philadelphia Inquirer*, December 21, 2017, https://www.inquirer.com/philly/business/energy/marcellus-shale-gas-royalty-deductions-anger-disillusioned-landowners-20171221.html.

11. Stephanie Malin, "There's No Real Choice but to Sign: Neoliberalization and Normalization of Hydraulic Fracturing on Pennsylvania Farmland," *Journal of Environmental Studies and Science* 4 (2014): 17–27, https://doi.org/10.1007/s13412-013-0115-2.

Chapter 4. My Land

1. Horace Kephart, *Our Southern Highlanders* (New York: Outing, 1913), 307.

2. Jean-Jacques Rousseau, *A Discourse on Political Economy: Understanding the Economic Basis of Liberty* (West Valley City, UT: Waking Lion Press, 2006), 25.

3. Alexis de Tocqueville, *Democracy in America* (1835; Chicago: University of Chicago Press, 2002).

4. Steven Gillon, "Searching for the American Dream," *Huffington Post*, February 16, 2015, https://www.huffpost.com/entry/searching-for-the-american-dream_b_6314708.

5. Gillon, "American Dream."

6. Jedediah Purdy, *This Land Is Our Land: The Struggle for a New Commonwealth* (Princeton, NJ: Princeton University Press, 2019), viii–ix.

7. Gillon, "American Dream."

8. I could not find sources to verify Scott's claims about the hunting camp and the ruins.

9. Nancy P. Coward, "Our Southern Highlanders: Chapter Summaries," *Horace Kephart: Revealing an Enigma*, accessed July 15, 2020, https://www.wcu.edu/library/digitalcollections/kephart/biography/OSHchapsumm.htm.

10. Kephart, *Our Southern Highlanders*, 320, 313.

11. Colin Woodard, *American Character: A History of the Epic Struggle between Individual Liberty and the Common Good* (New York: Viking Books, 2016), 73–75.

12. Karen I. Vaughn, "John Locke's Theory of Property: Problems of Interpretation," Libertarianism.Org, March 1, 1980, https://www.libertarianism.org/publications/essays/john-lockes-theory-property-problems-interpretation.

13. Gary Fields, *Enclosure: Palestinian Landscapes in a Historical Mirror* (Oakland: University of California Press, 2017), xi. Adam Briggle also writes about the "improvement doctrine" and its relation to fracking; see *A Field Philosopher's Guide to Fracking: How One Texas Town Stood Up to Big Oil and Gas* (New York: Liveright, 2015), 111.

14. Fields, *Enclosure*, xii.

15. Vaughn, "Locke's Theory of Property."

16. Fields, *Enclosure*, xii.

17. John Franklin Meginness, *History of Lycoming County, Pennsylvania* (Chicago: Brown, Runk, 1892), 197.

18. Fields, *Enclosure*, 16.

19. Fields, *Enclosure*, 17. Fields is, in part, quoting William Cronon, *Changes in the Land: Indians, Colonists, and the Ecology of New England* (New York: Hill and Wang, 1983), 128.

20. See Stacia S. Ryder and Peter M. Hall, "This Land Is Your Land, Maybe: A Historical Institutionalist Analysis for Contextualizing Split Estate Conflicts in U.S. Unconventional Oil and Gas Development," *Land Use Policy* 63 (2017): 149–59, https://doi.org/10.1016/j.landusepol.2017.01.006.

21. Stuart Banner, *Who Owns the Sky? The Struggle to Control Airspace from the Wright Brothers On* (Cambridge, MA: Harvard University Press, 2008), 110, 85.

22. Banner, *Who Owns the Sky?*, 13.

23. Vaughn, "Locke's Theory of Property."

24. Isaiah Berlin, "Two Concepts of Liberty," in *Four Essays on Liberty* (Oxford: Oxford University Press, 1969), 121–22.

25. John Locke, "Second Treatise of Government," in *Two Treatises of Government*, ed. Peter Laslett (New York: Cambridge University Press, 1988), 269.

26. Gerald Gaus, Shane D. Courtland, and David Schmidtz, "Liberalism," in *Stanford Encyclopedia of Philosophy*, Stanford University, 1997–, article published November 28, 1996; last modified January 22, 2018, https://plato.stanford.edu/archives/spr2018/entries/liberalism/.

27. Karl Polanyi, *The Great Transformation: The Political and Economic Origins of Our Time* (1944; Boston: Beacon Press, 1957), 3–4. Frank Dobbin, "Review of Fred Block and Margaret R. Somers, *The Power of Market Fundamentalism, Karl Polanyi's Critique*," *American Journal of Sociology* 121, no. 1 (2015): 318–20.

28. Vaughn, "Locke's Theory of Property."

29. Robert Nozick, *Anarchy, State, and Utopia* (New York: Basic Books, 1974), 178.

30. I never was able to speak directly with any members of Poor Shot. The private cabin was empty most of the year. Scott was unable to make introductions—he was barred from interacting with camp members, whom he sued and allegedly threatened.

31. Scott and Betty told me the backstory before he signed the nondisclosure agreement; I rely on my own observations to carry the story into the present.

32. I verified the information for this case by independently obtaining DEP inspection reports and copying lab tests, legal memos, and related documents. At the Crawleys' request, I do not name the company that tainted their water (even though, as Tom conceded, a simple Internet search would reveal its identity). Violations associated with this well can be viewed at "Well: Harman Lewis Unit 1H," StateImpact Pennsylvania, accessed July 15, 2020, http://stateimpact .npr.org/pennsylvania/drilling/wells/081-20292/.

Chapter 5. The Public/Private Paradox

1. Paul Ehrlich, *The Population Bomb* (New York: Ballantine Books, 1968), xi.

2. Bill McKibben, "Rewriting the Tragedy of the Commons," *Yes! Magazine*, January 19, 2011, available at https://truthout.org/articles/rewriting-the-tragedy-of-the-commons/.

3. Garrett Hardin, "The Tragedy of the Commons," *Science* 162, no. 3859 (1968): 1243–48, https://doi.org/10.1126/science.162.3859.1243. As Hardin acknowledges, the problem of the overuse of the commons and the scenario of the herders are both the brainchild of a nineteenth-century "mathematical amateur named William Forster Lloyd" (1244).

4. Hardin, "Tragedy of the Commons," 1244.

5. Garret Hardin, "Lifeboat Ethics: The Case against Helping the Poor," *Psychology Today* (September 1974), available at https://www.garretthardinsociety.org/articles/art_lifeboat _ethics_case_against_helping_poor.html.

6. For a critique, see Lisa Sun-Hee Park and David N. Pellow, *The Slums of Aspen: Immigrants vs. the Environment in America's Eden* (New York: New York University Press, 2011).

7. Carl Safina and Suzanne Iudicello, "Wise Use below the High-Tide Line: Threats and Opportunities," in *Let the People Judge: Wise Use and the Private Property Movement*, ed. John D. Echeverria and Raymond Booth Eby (Washington, DC: Island Press, 1995), 124.

8. "Garret Hardin," Southern Poverty Law Center, accessed July 22, 2020, https://www.splcenter.org/fighting-hate/extremist-files/individual/garrett-hardin.

9. Elinor Ostrom, *Governing the Commons: The Evolution of Institutions for Collective Action* (Cambridge: Cambridge University Press, 1990); Garrett Hardin, "Extensions of 'The Tragedy of the Commons,'" *Science* 280, no. 5364 (1998): 682–83, https://doi.org/10.1126/science.280.5364.682.

10. Hardin, "Tragedy of the Commons," 1245.

11. The quote is from a Marxist-leaning political economist but is a paraphrase of Hardin. See James McCarthy, "Commons as Counterhegemonic Projects," *Capitalism Nature Socialism* 16, no. 1 (2005), 9, https://doi.org/10.1080/1045575052000335348

12. Pennsylvania doesn't have a "forced pooling" law for Marcellus wells, though it does for the untapped Onondaga "horizon" and deeper strata. Other states, like Texas, have embraced it. See, e.g., Adam Briggle, *A Field Philosopher's Guide to Fracking: How One Texas Town Stood Up to Big Oil and Gas* (New York: Liveright, 2015).

13. "Well History: Lycoming County, PA," MarcellusGas.org, accessed February 13, 2020, https://www.marcellusgas.org/history/PA-Lycoming.

14. The state Supreme Court ruled that the state breached its duty as a "trustee" of public resources by depositing bonuses from state forest gas leases into the general fund rather than reinvesting them in public lands. See Pennsylvania Environmental Defense Foundation v. Commonwealth, 161 A.3d 911 (Pa. 2017).

15. New York State Energy Research and Development Authority (NYSERDA), *Patterns and Trends, New York Energy Profiles: 2002–2016* (Albany, NY: NYSERDA, 2019), https://www.nyserda.ny.gov/About/Publications/EA-Reports-and-Studies/Patterns-and-Trends.

16. Michael Sloan, "2016 Propane Market Outlook," Propane Education and Resource Council, accessed September 23, 2020, https://afdc.energy.gov/files/u/publication/2016_propane_market_outlook.pdf.

17. Quoted in Rob Nixon, *Slow Violence and the Environmentalism of the Poor* (Cambridge, MA: Harvard University Press, 2011), 1–2.

18. KJ Dell'Antonia, "Democracy without Politics," *New York Times*, July 2, 2017, https://www.nytimes.com/2017/07/02/opinion/democracy-without-politics.html.

19. Mark Reuther, "Montoursville District Embroiled in More Than Just Building Project," *Williamsport Sun-Gazette*, December 26, 2016, https://www.sungazette.com/news/top-news/2016/12/montoursville-district-embroiled-in-more-than-just-building-project/.

20. See, e.g., Jeff Himler, "State Court's Reversal Blocks Proposed Unity Cellphone Tower," *TribLIVE*, February 19, 2018, https://archive.triblive.com/local/westmoreland/state-courts-reversal-blocks-proposed-unity-cellphone-tower/.

21. Stephanie A. Malin et al., "The Right to Resist or a Case of Injustice? Meta-Power in the Oil and Gas Fields" *Social Forces* 97, no. 4 (2019): 1811–38, https://doi.org/10.1093/sf/soy094.

22. David E. Hess, " PA Superior Court: Taking Natural Gas without Permission from Neighboring Property Is Trespass Overturning Rule of Capture for Unconventional Gas Wells," *PA Environment Digest Blog*, April 3, 2018, http://paenvironmentdaily.blogspot.com/2018/04/pa-superior-court-taking-natural-gas.html.

23. Robert C. Ellickson, *Order without Law: How Neighbors Settle Disputes* (Cambridge, MA: Harvard University Press, 1991).

24. Kai Erikson writes about Appalachians' contradictory leanings toward both individualism and communalism in *Everything in its Path: Destruction of Community in the Buffalo Creek Flood* (New York: Simon and Schuster, 1976).

25. See Robert N. Bellah et al., *Habits of the Heart: Individualism and Commitment in American Life* (Berkeley: University of California Press, 1985).

26. Naomi Oreskes, Dale Jamieson, and Reiner Grundmann, "Climate and Democracy," *Issues in Science and Technology* 32, no. 3 (2016): 9–11, www.jstor.org/stable/24727045.

27. Daniel Victor, "Free of New York's Stinky Sludge Train, an Alabama Town Is Still Steaming," *New York Times*, April 19, 2008, https://www.nytimes.com/2018/04/19/nyregion/poop-train-alabama.html.

28. Hardin, "Tragedy of the Commons," 1245.

29. Robert Paarlberg, *The United States of Excess: Gluttony and the Dark Side of American Exceptionalism* (New York: Oxford University Press, 2015).

30. See Gregory H. Shill. "Should Law Subsidize Driving?" *New York University Law Review* 95, no. 2 (2020): 498–579. Shill argues that the US is car-dependent not only by choice but also by law: government rules "furnish indirect yet extravagant subsidies to driving" that lower the cost of driving by "reassigning its costs to non-drivers and society at large" (498).

31. See, e.g., "Nitrogen and Phosphorous," Chesapeake Bay Foundation, accessed September 23, 2020, https://www.cbf.org/issues/agriculture/nitrogen-phosphorus.html#:~:text=The%20largest%20source%20of%20pollution,the%20Bay%20is%20polluted%20runoff.

32. For a particularly compelling, and harrowing, account of how industrial dumping poisoned an entire community, see Dan Fagin's Pulitzer Prize–winning *Toms River: A Story of Science and Salvation* (New York: Bantam Books, 2013).

33. Hardin, "Tragedy of the Commons," 1244; Paarlberg, *United States of Excess*.

34. Oreskes, Jamieson, and Grundmann, "Climate and Democracy," 10.

Chapter 6. Indentured

1. Lehigh University wrote about the visit on their website: "Fracking," Lehigh University Sustainable Development Program, accessed July 22, 2020, https://sdp.cas2.lehigh.edu/content/fracking.

2. The League has since adopted a skeptical position on fracking: see "Natural Resources," League of Women Voters of Pennsylvania, accessed July 22, 2020, https://www.palwv.org/natural-resources.

3. Anna Driver and Brian Grow, "Big Stakes: The Energy Billionaire's Shrouded Loans," Reuters Special Report, April 18, 2012, https://graphics.thomsonreuters.com/12/04/ChesapeakeMcClendon.pdf.

4. See, e.g., Stephanie A. Malin et al., "The Right to Resist or a Case of Injustice? Meta-Power in the Oil and Gas Fields" *Social Forces* 97, no. 4 (2019): 1811–38, https://doi.org/10.1093/sf/soy094.

5. "Notice is hereby given that on July 8, 2015, Anadarko E&P Onshore LLC has filed a Notice of Intent . . . with the Susquehanna River Basin Commission (SRBC) seeking approval . . . for the consumptive use of water for drilling and development of natural gas well(s) on the George E. Hagemeyer Pad" ("Public Notices," *Williamsport Sun-Gazette*, July 11, 2015).

6. Horace Kephart, *Our Southern Highlanders* (New York: Outing, 1913), 313.

7. Alison L. Bush, "In Pennsylvania, Does 'Production' Really Mean 'Production in Paying Quantities?,'" *PIOGA Press*, June 2014, http://www.pioga.org/publication_file/PIOGA_Press _050_June_2014.pdf.

8. "Creekview Country Cottage Bed and Breakfast," Tripadvisor, accessed March 3, 2020, https://www.tripadvisor.com/Hotel_Review-g53266-d661905-Reviews-Creekview _Country_Cottage_Bed_and_Breakfast-Muncy_Pennsylvania.html.

9. "Gas Companies Penalized Nearly $400K after Methane Seeps into Home Wells," *Times Leader*, September 2, 2015, https://www.timesleader.com/business/379945/gas-companies -penalized-nearly-400k-after-methane-seeps-into-home-wells.

10. Margaret Jane Radin, *Boilerplate: The Fine Print, Vanishing Rights, and the Rule of Law* (Princeton, NJ: Princeton University Press, 2013), 3–4.

11. Radin, *Boilerplate*, 12.

12. Malin et al., "Right to Resist," 1832.

13. The quote about "deleted rights" is from Radin, *Boilerplate*, 16.

14. Radin, *Boilerplate*, 15. On "procedural injustice" in gas leasing, see Stephanie A. Malin and Kathryn Teigen DeMaster, "A Devil's Bargain: Rural Environmental Injustices and Hydraulic Fracturing on Pennsylvania's Farms," *Journal of Rural Studies* 47, part A (2016): 278–90, https://doi.org/10.1016/j.jrurstud.2015.12.015.

15. James S. Coleman, *The Asymmetric Society* (Syracuse, NY: Syracuse University Press, 1982), 22, 89.

16. Dylan Bugden and Richard Stedman's survey of lessors in northeastern Pennsylvania finds many people who think like George: the biggest predictor of whether landowners reported being satisfied with their lease was not the "total amount earned from the lease (as might be assumed), but its perceived procedural equality." "Rural Landowners, Energy Leasing, and Patterns of Risk and Inequality in the Shale Gas Industry," *Rural Sociology* 84, no. 3 (2019): 20, https://doi.org/10.1111/ruso.12236.

17. Michelle Bamberger and Robsert Oswald, *The Real Costs of Fracking: How America's Shale Gas Boom Is Threatening Our Families, Pets, and Food* (Boston: Beacon Press, 2014).

Chapter 7. Unmoored

1. Penn State University, "Private Water Systems FAQs," March 14, 2016, https://extension .psu.edu/private-water-systems-faqs.

2. "Radon in the Home," Pennsylvania Department of Environmental Protection, accessed July 29, 2020, https://www.dep.pa.gov/Business/RadiationProtection/RadonDivision/Pages /Radon-in-the-home.aspx.

3. See "Sustainable Tillage—Beech Grove Farm, Trout Run, PA," University of Vermont Extension 2007, uploaded by PublicResourceOrg, July 4, 2010, YouTube video, 9:25, https:// www.youtube.com/watch?v=A3dEnbKNaUY.

4. . John Schwartz, "Gas Boom County Strives for Economic Afterglow," *New York Times*, November 17, 2012, https://www.nytimes.com/2012/11/18/us/marcellus-shale-county-aims-for -long-term-gain.html.

5. See, e.g., Scott Detrow, "Lycoming County Frack Truck Crash: 3,600 Gallons Spilled," StateImpact Pennsylvania, September 27, 2012, https://stateimpact.npr.org/pennsylvania/2012

/09/27/lycoming-county-frack-truck-crash-3600-gallons-spilled/; Reid Frazier, "Lycoming County Wastewater Spill Tops 63,000 Gallons," StateImpact Pennsylvania, November 16, 2017, https://stateimpact.npr.org/pennsylvania/2017/11/16/lycoming-county-waste-water-spill-tops -63000-gallons/.

6. Rachel Carson, *Silent Spring* (New York: Houghton Mifflin, 1962), 18.

7. Sara Chodosh, "California Needs to Stop Saying Everything Causes Cancer," *Popular Science*, April 4, 2018, https://www.popsci.com/california-coffee-cancer-warning/.

8. See Anthony Giddens, *Consequences of Modernity* (Cambridge: Polity Press, 1990); Ulrich Beck, *Risk Society: Towards a New Modernity*, trans. Mark Ritter (London: Sage, 1992).

9. See, e.g., Robert D. Bullard, *Dumping in Dixie: Race, Class, and Environmental Quality* (New York: Routledge, 2000); Qian Di et al., "Air Pollution and Mortality in the Medicare Population," *New England Journal of Medicine* 376 (2017): 2513–22, https://doi.org/10.1056 /NEJMoa1702747.

10. Eliza D. Czolowski et al., "Toward Consistent Methodology to Quantify Populations in Proximity to Oil and Gas Development: A National Spatial Analysis and Review," *Environmental Health Perspectives* 125, no. 8 (2017): 086004-1–086004-10, https://doi.org/10.1289/EHP1535.

11. Michelle Bamberger and Robert E. Oswald, "Impacts of Gas Drilling on Human and Animal Health," *New Solutions* 22, no. 1 (2012): 52, https://doi.org/10.2190/NS.22.1.e.

12. See, e.g., Bamberger and Oswald, "Impacts of Gas Drilling"; Michael Hill, "Shale Gas Regulation in the UK and Health Implications of Fracking," *Lancet* 383, no. 9936 (2014): 2211–12, https://doi.org/10.1016/S0140-6736(14)60888-6; Lisa M. McKenzie et al., "Human Health Risk Assessment of Air Emissions from Development of Unconventional Natural Gas Resources," *Science of the Total Environment* 424 (2012): 79–87, https://doi.org/10.1016/j.scitotenv.2012.02 .018. For a more recent overview, see Alison M. Bamber et al., "A Systematic Review of the Epidemiologic Literature Assessing Health Outcomes in Populations Living Near Oil and Natural Gas Operations: Study Quality and Future Recommendations," *International Journal of Environmental Research and Public Health* 16, no. 12 (2019): 2123–42, https://www.mdpi.com/1660 -4601/16/12/2123.

13. See Anthony E. Ladd, ed., *Fractured Communities: Risks, Impacts, and Protest against Hydraulic Fracking in U.S. Shale Regions* (New Brunswick: Rutgers University Press, 2018).

14. Natasha Vicens, "With No Health Registry, PA Doesn't Know the Impact of Fracking on Health," *Public Source*, April 30, 2014, https://www.publicsource.org/with-no-health-registry -pa-doesnt-know-the-impact-of-fracking-on-health/.

15. In the heartbreaking, Pulitzer Prize–winning book *Amity and Prosperity*, Eliza Griswold follows a family who became sickened from living next to a "waste pond" in Amity, PA. By the end of the book, the family had signed a nondisclosure agreement as part of a settlement and could no longer discuss the case. See *Amity and Prosperity: One Family and the Fracturing of America* (New York: Farrar, Straus and Giroux, 2018). Reporting like Tom Wilber's *Under the Surface* shows that several families in Dimock, PA, endured a similar plight. See *Under the Surface: Fracking, Fortunes, and the Fate of the Marcellus Shale* (Ithaca, NY: Cornell University Press, 2012).

16. Adam Briggle, *A Field Philosopher's Guide to Fracking: How One Texas Town Stood Up to Big Oil and Gas* (New York: Liveright, 2015), 130.

17. RKR Hess, "Report on the XTO Energy, Inc. Wastewater Contamination Settlement in Lycoming County, PA," accessed July 29, 2020, https://www.rkrhess.com/report-on-the-xto -energy-inc-wastewater-contamination-settlement-in-lycoming-county-pa/.

18. Jameson K. Hirsch et al., "Psychosocial Impact of Fracking: A Review of the Literature on the Mental Health Consequences of Hydraulic Fracturing," *International Journal of Mental Health and Addiction* 16, no. 1 (2018): 1–15, https://doi.org/10.1007/s11469-017-9792-5.

19. Simona L. Perry, "Development, Land Use, and Collective Trauma: The Marcellus Shale Gas Boom in Rural Pennsylvania," *Culture, Agriculture, Food and Environment: The Journal of Culture and Agriculture* 34, no. 1 (2012): 83–88, https://doi.org/10.1111/j.2153-9561.2012.01066.x. See also Debra J. Davidson, "Evaluating the Effects of Living with Contamination from the Lens of Trauma: A Case Study of Fracking Development in Alberta, Canada," *Environmental Sociology* 4, no. 2 (2018): 196–209, https://doi.org/10.1080/23251042.2017.1349638.

20. Kai Erikson, *A New Species of Trouble: The Human Experience of Modern Disasters* (New York: W. W. Norton, 1994), 21.

21. Yi-Fu Tuan, *Topophilia: A Study of Environmental Perceptions, Attitudes, and Values* (1974; New York: Columbia University Press, 1990).

22. Ed Yong, "Nothing to Fear Except Fear Itself—Also Wolves and Bears," *Atlantic*, February 23, 2016, https://www.theatlantic.com/science/archive/2016/02/nothing-to-fear-except -fear-itself-wolves-and-bears/470532/. Yi-Fu Tuan appears to have coined the term in his book *Landscapes of Fear* (New York: Pantheon Books, 1979), though he deployed it in a much more humanistic and expansive way than ecologists. Tuan's interest was in the "diverse manifestations and causes of fear in individuals and societies" (back cover); his use of "landscape" is often more metaphorical than literal, including witches, diseases, famine, and prisons.

23. Seamus McGraw, *The End of Country: Dispatches from the Frack Zone* (New York: Random House, 2011).

Chapter 8. Overruled

1. Because of the poor quality of my audio recording of the hearing, some quotes were reconstructed from my contemporaneous notes and fragments of recordings.

2. Dr. Katz was referring to an ongoing ecosystem study of an "experimental forest" called Hubbard Brook; see https://hubbardbrook.org/.

3. Kate Lao Shaffner, "What Is Home Rule?," WHYY, July 24, 2014, https://whyy.org /articles/what-is-home-rule/.

4. "How Does a Variance Differ from a Conditional Use Permit?," Avallone Law Associates, February 18, 2015, https://www.lawrenceavallone.com/blog/2015/02/how-does-a-variance -differ-from-a-conditional-use-permit.shtml.

5. "Pennsylvania Impact Fee Summary," Range Resources, accessed July 29, 2020, https:// rangeresources.gcs-web.com/static-files/bfa046b5-9853-45dc-96c1-3d1267e41e91.

6. Gorsline v. Board of Supervisors of Fairfield Township, 186 A.3d 375 (Pa. Cmmw. Ct. 2018).

7. Adam Briggle, *A Field Philosopher's Guide to Fracking: How One Texas Town Stood Up to Big Oil and Gas* (New York: Liveright, 2015), 49.

8. Christian C. Hagen-Frederiksen, "Beyond Fracking: How *Robinson Township* Alters Pennsylvania Municipal Zoning Rights," *Journal of Law and Commerce* 34, no. 2 (2016): 383, https://doi.org/10.5195/jlc.2016.101.

9. Briggle, *Field Philosopher's Guide*, 49. Texas's House Bill 40 (2015) created a statewide ban on municipal fracking bans; the Colorado Supreme Court reaffirmed that the state was the sole arbiter of oil and gas regulation in two cases: City of Fort Collins v. Colorado Oil and Gas Association, 2016 CO 28, P.3d (Colo. 2016), and City of Longmont v. Colorado Oil and Gas Association, 2016 CO 29, P.3d (Colo. 2016). For more on how this impacted Colorado communities, see Stephanie A. Malin, Stacia S. Ryder, and Peter M. Hall, "Contested Colorado: Shifting Regulations and Public Responses to Unconventional Oil Production in the Niobrara Shale Region," in *Fractured Communities: Risks, Impacts, and Protest against Hydraulic Fracking in U.S. Shale Regions*, ed. Anthony E. Ladd (New Brunswick, NJ: Rutgers University Press, 2018), 198.

10. Briggle; *Field Philosopher's Guide*, 49.

11. "Water Fight," *Williamsport Sun-Gazette*, May 1, 2013, https://www.sungazette.com/news/top-news/2013/05/water-fight/.

12. "Supervisors Deny Water Withdrawal," *Williamsport Sun-Gazette*, September 26, 2013, https://www.sungazette.com/news/top-news/2013/09/supervisors-deny-water-withdrawal/.

13. "Water Decision Overruled," *Williamsport Sun-Gazette*, May 8, 2014, https://www.sungazette.com/news/top-news/2014/05/water-decision-overruled/.

14. Briggle, *Field Philosopher's Guide*, 137.

15. Hagen-Frederiksen, "Beyond Fracking," 195.

16. Theda Skocpol, "The Tocqueville Problem: Civic Engagement in American Democracy," *Social Science History* 21, no. 4 (1997): 472, https://doi.org/10.2307/1171662.

17. Zachary Roth, *The Great Suppression: Voting Rights, Corporate Cash, and the Conservative Assault on Democracy* (New York: Crown, 2016), 73. See Briggle, *Field Philospher's Guide*, for more on how "fracking is primarily regulated at the state level" (136).

18. Preemption has been wielded by conservative state actors across a range of issues that extend well beyond oil and gas in order to thwart liberal municipalities' ability to pass laws that they abhor, such as gender-neutral bathrooms, plastic bag bans, and mask requirements during the COVID-19 pandemic. See Kriston Capps, "Thwarting Cities in the Trump Era," Bloomberg CityLab, March 30, 2017, https://www.citylab.com/equity/2017/03/thwarting-cities-in-the-trump-era/520398/.

19. See Elinor Ostrom, *Governing the Commons: The Evolution of Institutions for Collective Action* (Cambridge: Cambridge University Press, 1990); Garrett Hardin, "Extensions of 'The Tragedy of the Commons,'" *Science* 280, no. 5364 (1998): 682–83, https://doi.org/10.1126/science.280.5364.682.

20. Monique Coombs, "Lobstering and Common Pool Resource Management in Maine," Grassroots Economic Organizing, May 4, 2011, https://geo.coop/node/654.

21. Cathy Gere, "The Drama of the Commons: A New Script for the Green New Deal," *The Point Magazine*, no. 22, June 12, 2020, https://thepointmag.com/politics/the-drama-of-the-commons/.

22. James Wilson, Liying Yan, and Carl Wilson, "The Precursors of Governance in the Maine Lobster Fishery," *Proceedings of the National Academy of Sciences* 104, no. 39 (2007): 15212–17, https://doi.org/10.1073/pnas.0702241104.

23. "A Lesson in Resources Management from Elinor Ostrom," OECDInsights.org, July 1, 2011, http://oecdinsights.org/2011/07/01/a-lesson-in-resources-management-from-elinor -ostrom/.

24. For a recent analysis of regulatory capture as it pertains to states' energy policy, see Leah Cardamore Stokes, *Short Circuiting Policy: Interest Groups and the Battle over Clean Energy and Climate Policy in the American States* (New York: Oxford University Press, 2020).

25. Laura Olsen, "New DEP Pick Says He Will 'Apply the Law,'" *Pittsburgh Post-Gazette*, March 20, 2011, https://old.post-gazette.com/pg/11079/1133016-454.stm

26. Marie Cusick, "Controversial Head of DEP Leaving Agency to Work on Behalf of Energy Industry," StateImpact Pennsylvania, March 22, 2013, https://stateimpact.npr.org/pennsylvania /2013/03/22/controversial-head-of-dep-leaving-agency-to-work-on-behalf-of-energy-industry/.

27. Robert Jackson and Avner Vengosh, "DEP: Protecting Water or Gas?," *Philadelphia Inquirer*, December 2, 2011, https://www.inquirer.com/philly/opinion/inquirer/20111202_DEP _Protecting_water_or_gas_.html.

28. Cusick, "Controversial Head of DEP Leaving." For more on the lawsuit, see Eliza Griswold, *Amity and Prosperity: One Family and the Fracturing of America* (New York: Farrar, Straus and Giroux, 2018).

29. Sean Kitchen, "Former DEP Secretary Michael Krancer Making Moves in the Utica Shale Play with Silent Majority Strategies," *Raging Chicken Press*, September 11, 2017, https:// ragingchickenpress.org/2017/09/11/former-dep-secretary-michael-krancer-making-moves -utica-shale-play-silent-majority-strategies/.

30. Robert Wuthnow, *The Left Behind: Decline and Rage in Rural America* (Princeton, NJ: Princeton University Press 2018), 98–99.

31. Elinor Ostrom et al., "Revisiting the Commons: Local Lessons, Global Challenges," *Science* 284, no. 5412 (1999): 281, https://doi.org/10.1126/science.284.5412.278.

32. Justin Nobel, "How a Small Town Is Standing Up to Fracking," *Rolling Stone*, May 22, 2017, https://www.rollingstone.com/politics/politics-news/how-a-small-town-is-standing-up -to-fracking-117307/.

33. Whitney Webb, "PA Dept. of Environmental Protection Sues Town over Fracking Ban," *Mint Press News*, April 10, 2017, https://www.mintpressnews.com/pa-dept-environmental -protection-sues-towns-fracking-ban/226672/.

34. Nobel, "How a Small Town."

35. Quoted in Hagen-Frederiksen, "Beyond Fracking," 383.

Chapter 9. Town and Country

1. David Owen, "Economy vs. Environment," *New Yorker*, March 23, 2009, https://www .newyorker.com/magazine/2009/03/30/economy-vs-environment.

2. See, e.g., Allan Schnaiberg and Kenneth Alan Gould, *Environment and Society: The Enduring Conflict* (New York: St. Martin's Press, 1994). For a critique, see William R. Freudenberg, Lisa J. Wilson, and Daniel J. O'Leary, "Forty Years of Spotted Owls? A Longitudinal Analysis of Logging Industry Job Losses," *Sociological Perspectives* 41, no. 1 (1998): 1–26, https://doi.org /10.2307/1389351.

3. Meir Rinde, "Richard Nixon and the Rise of American Environmentalism," Science History Institute, June 2, 2017, https://www.sciencehistory.org/distillations/richard-nixon-and-the-rise-of-american-environmentalism.

4. Peter J. Jacques, Riley E. Dunlap, and Mark Freeman, "The Organisation of Denial: Conservative Think Tanks and Environmental Scepticism," *Environmental Politics* 17, no. 3 (2008): 349, https://doi.org/10.1080/09644010802055576.

5. Ian Carey, "The Great Economy versus Environment Myth," *HuffPost*, June 5, 2010, https://www.huffpost.com/entry/the-great-economy-versus_b_1398439. On the rise of environmental skepticism as a countermovement, see Jacques, Dunlap, and Freeman, "Organisation of Denial."

6. David Remnick, "Ozone Man," *New Yorker*, April 24, 2006, https://www.newyorker.com/magazine/2006/04/24/ozone-man.

7. Riley E. Dunlap, Aaron M. McCright, and Jerrod H. Yarosh, "The Political Divide on Climate Change: Partisan Polarization Widens in the U.S.," *Environment: Science and Policy for Sustainable Development* 58, no. 5 (2016): 4–23, https://doi.org/10.1080/00139157.2016.1208995.

8. Carey, "Economy versus Environment Myth."

9. For a history of climate denialism, and its relationship to Big Tobacco's campaign to discredit the science linking smoking to cancer, see Naomi Oreskes and Erik M. Conway, *Merchants of Doubt: How a Handful of Scientists Obscured the Truth on Issues from Tobacco Smoke to Global Warming* (New York: Bloomsbury Press, 2010).

10. See, e.g., Diane Cardwell and Clifford Krauss, "Frack Quietly, Please: Sage Grouse Is Nesting," *New York Times*, July 19, 2014, https://www.nytimes.com/2014/07/20/business/energy-environment/disparate-interests-unite-to-protect-greater-sage-grouse.html.

11. Colin Harris, "Despite Huge Spike in Jobless Claims, Environmentally Sound Hydraulic Fracturing Continues to Create Tens of Thousands of Jobs," Energy in Depth, May 21, 2010, https://www.energyindepth.org/despite-huge-spike-in-jobless-claims-environmentally-sound-hydraulic-fracturing-continues-to-create-tens-of-thousands-of-jobs/.

12. See, e.g., Clifford Krauss and Tom Zeller Jr., "When a Rig Moves in Next Door," *New York Times*, November 6, 2010, https://www.nytimes.com/2010/11/07/business/energy-environment/07frack.html.

13. See Joe Massaro, "Wendy Lynne Lee: Activist, Professor, and Now a Fiction Story Teller," Energy in Depth, November 18, 2012, https://www.energyindepth.org/wendy-lynne-lee-activist-philosophy-professor-and-now-a-fiction-story-teller/; Wendy Lee, "A Frack-Wolf in Sheep's Clothing: How Pennsylvania Democrats Are Selling Out the Future," *Frack That* (blog), *Raging Chicken Press*, May 23, 2014, https://ragingchickenpress.org/2014/05/23/a-frack-wolf-in-a-sheeps-clothing-how-pennsylvania-democrats-are-selling-out-the-future/.

14. As mentioned in the last chapter, the pro-gas former DEP secretary Michael Krancer cofounded an energy lobbying outfit called Silent Majority Strategies, alluding to the premise that most Pennsylvanians support fracking but don't vocalize their views. Along with Edward Walker, I challenge, in greater depth than I do here, the thesis that economic marginalization explains support for fracking in Colin Jerolmack and Edward T. Walker, "Please in My Backyard: Quiet Mobilization in Support of Fracking in an Appalachian Community," *American Journal of Sociology* 124, no. 2 (2018): 479–516, https://doi.org/10.1086/698215. Similarly, Adam Mayer

and Stephanie Malin's analysis of support for fracking in Colorado finds no connection between local economic conditions and views toward regulating the industry. Perhaps even more surprising given the economic-desperation argument, they found that wealthier people were less likely to endorse restrictive oil and gas regulations. See "How Should Unconventional Oil and Gas Be Regulated? The Role of Natural Resource Dependence and Economic Insecurity," *Journal of Rural Studies* 65 (2019): 79–89, https://doi.org/10.1016/j.jrurstud.2018.11.005.

15. In writing about greater Williamsport in *Smallville: Institutionalizing Community in Twenty-First-Century America* (Medford, MA: Tufts University Press, 2008), sociologist Carl Milofsky identifies two groups of people differentiated not just by class identity and social networks but also by the extent to which their worldviews and lifestyles are either parochial or cosmopolitan. In this typology, RDA members were *cosmopolitans*, who for the most part "do not have deep personal identification with the immediate town they live in or the local commitments anchored in personal and family history" (42) that *locals* (e.g., most rural landowners) have.

16. My use of "style" to describe the contrasting norms of political engagement that typified fractivists versus most lessors draws inspiration from Nina Eliasoph and Paul Lichterman's concept of "group style," which they define as the process of making meaning out of "collective representations" (i.e., ideology and culture) "in a way that usually complements the meaningful, shared ground for interaction" in a given group. See "Culture in Interaction," *American Journal of Sociology* 108, no. 4 (January 2003): 737, https://doi.org/10.1086/367920.

17. Halle Stockton, "Central Pennsylvania Residents Forced to Move after Land Sold to Make Way for Gas Pipeline," *Pittsburgh Post-Gazette*, July 15, 2012, https://www.post-gazette.com/local/marcellusshale/2012/07/15/Central-Pennsylvania-residents-forced-to-move-after-land-sold-to-make-way-for-gas-pipeline/stories/201207150148. The article erroneously states that residents were evicted to make way for a gas pipeline.

18. Andrew Maykuth, "An Artifact of Marcellus Drilling's Disruptive Glory Days," *Philadelphia Inquirer*, May 1, 2016, https://www.inquirer.com/philly/business/20160501_An_artifact_of_Marcellus_drilling_s_disruptive_glory_days.html.

19. Iris Marie Bloom, "Riverdale, Social Justice, and Shale Gas Outrage: Wendy Lee's Remarks," *Protecting Our Waters* (blog), September 30, 2010, https://protectingourwaters.wordpress.com/2012/09/30/riverdale-social-justice-and-shale-gas-outrage-wendy-lees-remarks/.

20. See Sean Kitchen, "PA Rep Garth Everett Bought and Sold by Natty Gas Threatens to Kick Fracktivist Out of the Town Hall Meeting," *Raging Chicken Press*, February 4, 2013, https://ragingchickenpress.org/2013/02/04/pa-rep-garth-bought-and-sold-by-natty-gas-threatens-to-kick-fracktivist-out-of-the-town-hall-meeting-video/.

21. Ralph did, however, point out that Everett's top-five campaign contributors were owners of local companies that benefitted from the gas industry, like Allison Crane & Rigging, when Everett claimed he was unbiased because he didn't take money from the petroleum industry.

22. The Crawleys did eventually agree to speak with the staff attorney for the environmental group PennFuture, Mark Szybist, who connected them with a lawyer willing to represent them pro bono. Tom and Mary seemed to be unaware that Mark also sat on the board of the RDA.

23. Jessica Smartt Gullion, *Fracking the Neighborhood: Reluctant Activists and Natural Gas Drilling* (Cambridge, MA: MIT Press, 2015), 110.

24. Mike Knapp, "Professional Protestors Coming to a Town Near You!," Energy in Depth, July 12, 2012, https://www.energyindepth.org/professional-protesters-coming-to-a-town-near -you/?1222.

25. While clearly relying on caricature, an upstate New York resident's op-ed on what characterized the split between the two "sides" in his town resonates with my observations. On the pro-fracking side: the "Walmart people," many of whom are generational farmers, live "up the backroads," wear "denim and feed caps," work with their hands, and look forward to deer season. On the anti-fracking side: the "LL Bean people," many of whom are newly arrived, live in town, "work with their mouths," and look forward to opera season. See Dick Downey, "Dick Downey of Otego: I Sit with the Walmarts," *NY Shale Gas Now* (blog), May 16, 2011, http://nyshalegasnow .blogspot.com/2011/05/dick-downey-of-otego-i-sit-with.html.

26. The term "green gentry" comes from Joel Kotkin, "Fixing California: The Green Gentry's Class Warfare," *New Geography*, October 27, 2013, https://www.newgeography.com/content /004013-fixing-california-the-green-gentry-s-class-warfare. Tom Shepstone slapped this label on fractivists in Pennsylvania and New York; see Tom Shepstone, "DRBC Action Is Simply Defensive Move in War for Land," *Natural Gas Now* (blog), September 15, 2017, https:// naturalgasnow.org/drbc-action-simply-defensive-move-war-land/.

27. The lawsuit was dismissed in 2020. See Kirkland and Ellis, "6th Circ. Backs Chesapeake Win in Landowners' Royalties Suit," May 21, 2020, https://www.kirkland.com/news/in-the -news/2020/05/6th-circ-chesapeake-win-landowners-royalties-suit.

28. See Melissa A. Troutman, Sierra Shamer, and Joshua Pribanic, "Hidden Data Suggests Fracking Created Widespread, Systemic Impact in Pennsylvania," *Public Herald*, January 23, 2017, https://publicherald.org/hidden-data-suggests-fracking-created-widespread-systemic-impact -in-pennsylvania/. A 2015 EPA draft report trumpeted by the gas industry found "no evidence of widespread, systemic impacts on drinking water" from fracking. However, the EPA later removed that language, stating that "uncertainties prevent the EPA from estimating the national frequency of impacts on drinking water resources" from fracking; see "Questions and Answers about EPA's Hydraulic Fracturing Drinking Water Assessment," US Environmental Protection Agency, accessed August 15, 2020, https://www.epa.gov/hfstudy/questions-and-answers-about -epas-hydraulic-fracturing-drinking-water-assessment#widespread. Pennsylvania's DEP keeps a continuously updated list of cases in which it has determined that "a private water supply was impacted by oil and gas activities." As of September 20, 2020, there were 356 cases. On the one hand, there's reason to believe the actual number is higher, since missing evidence like a predrilling water test would prevent the DEP from making a "positive determination." On the other hand, the DEP notes that some of the impacted water wells have "returned to background conditions," meaning fracking did not permanently impair the water; see "Water Supply Determination Letters," Pennsylvania Department of Environmental Protection, accessed September 20, 2020, http://files.dep.state.pa.us/OilGas/BOGM/BOGMPortalFiles/OilGasReports /Determination_Letters/Regional_Determination_Letters.pdf. In sum, private water wells have been impacted by fracking, even if the overall risk of contamination is relatively low. But there is little evidence of major aquifers being contaminated.

29. In 2019, several public-health researchers did raise the possibility that a cluster of cases of a rare form of cancer—Ewing sarcoma—in southwestern Pennsylvania may be related to

fracking; see David Templeton and Don Hopey, "CDC, State Officials Investigating Multiple Cases of Rare Cancer in Southwestern PA," *Pittsburgh Post-Gazette*, March 28, 2019, https://www.post-gazette.com/news/health/2019/03/28/Ewing-sarcoma-Washington-Westmoreland-cancer-Canon-McMillan-school-cecil-pennsylvania/stories/201903280010.

30. I do not name the cofounder because Ralph forwarded me the e-mail in confidence.

31. Erica Brown et al., "The National Surveys on Energy and Environment Public Opinion of Fracking: Perspectives from Michigan and Pennsylvania," Center for Local, State, and Urban Policy, University of Michigan, May 2013, available at https://papers.ssrn.com/sol3/papers.cfm?abstract_id=2313276.

32. Maryland banned fracking in 2017; New York's moratorium became a ban in 2014.

33. "The Shale Justice First Year Anniversary: One of the Most Important Environmental and Human Rights Issues of Our Times—Unconventional Fossil Fuel Extraction Must Be Banned," *The Wrench* (blog), January 20, 2014, http://thewrenchphilosleft.blogspot.com/2014/01/the-shale-justice-first-year.html.

34. Because Ralph shared these e-mails with me without the permission of the other parties involved, I don't name his critics.

35. See Wendy Lee, "Of Aristotle and Anadarko: Why 'Better Laws' Will Never Be Enough," *Frack That* (blog), *Raging Chicken Press*, July 16, 2013, https://ragingchickenpress.org/2013/07/16/of-aristotle-and-anadarko-why-better-laws-will-never-be-enough/.

36. Frances Fox Piven, *Challenging Authority: How Ordinary People Change America* (Lanham, MD: Rowman and Littlefield, 2006), 21.

37. See Doug McAdam, John D. McCarthy, and Mayer N. Zald, "Social Movements," in *Hand book of Sociology*, ed. N. J. Smelser (New York: Sage, 1988); Herbert H. Haines, *Black Radicals and the Civil Rights Mainstream, 1954–1970* (Knoxville: University of Tennessee Press, 1988).

38. The phrase "repertoires of contention" comes from Charles Tilly, *The Contentious French* (Cambridge, MA: Harvard University Press, 1986).

39. Mary Esch, "Fervent Foes Devote Their Lives to Fracking Fight," *Democrat and Chronicle*, July 7, 2013, https://www.democratandchronicle.com/story/news/local/2013/07/07/fervent-foes-devote-their-lives-to-fracking-fight/2496569/.

40. Fedor A. Dokshin, "Whose Backyard and What's at Issue? Spatial and Ideological Dynamics of Local Opposition to Hydraulic Fracturing in New York, 2010 to 2013," *American Sociological Review* 81, no. 5 (2016): 921–48, https://doi.org/10.1177/0003122416663929; Ian Bogdan Vasi et al., "'No Fracking Way!' Documentary Film, Discursive Opportunity, and Local Opposition against Hydraulic Fracturing in the United States, 2010 to 2013," *American Sociological Review* 80, no. 5 (2015): 934–59, https://doi.org/10.1177/0003122415598534.

41. Richard C. Stedman et al., "Marcellus Shale Gas Development and New Boomtown Research: Views of New York and Pennsylvania Residents," *Environmental Practice* 14, no. 4 (2012): 382–93, https://doi.org/10.1017/S1466046612000403; Jeffrey B. Jacquet, "Landowner Attitudes toward Natural Gas and Wind Farm Development in Northern Pennsylvania," *Energy Policy* 50 (2012): 677–88, https://doi.org/10.1016/j.enpol.2012.08.011.

42. Fedor A. Dokshin and Amanda Buday, "Not in Your Backyard! Organizational Structure, Partisanship, and the Mobilization of Nonbeneficiary Constituents against 'Fracking' in Illinois, 2013–2014," *Socius* 4 (2018): 1–17, https://doi.org/10.1177/2378023118783476.

43. Paul H. Tice, "It's Not Too Late for New York to Start Fracking," *Wall Street Journal*, July 12, 2019, https://www.wsj.com/articles/its-not-too-late-for-new-york-to-start-fracking-11562970236.

44. The state had already agreed to allow drilling in the prior decade, while New York instituted an indefinite moratorium before wells were spudded. Would petroleum companies and lessors really abide the billions of dollars in stranded assets that would result from a ban? What's more, pro-industry Republicans from rural and suburban districts maintained a stranglehold on Pennsylvania's house and senate. Any hope for an executive order banning fracking, which Governor Cuomo signed in New York, also seemed far-fetched. The Republican governor at the time, Tom Corbett, was enamored of the industry. So was his Democratic predecessor, Ed Rendell, who opened up the state for drilling. The Democrat who bested Corbett in 2014, Tom Wolf, merely campaigned on enacting a severance tax (he didn't). If a ban was ever even possible, it seemed that ship had sailed politically.

45. On "astroturf" politics (i.e., elite- and industry-backed mobilization disguised as grassroots activism), see Edward Walker, *Grassroots for Hire: Public Affairs Consultants in American Democracy* (Cambridge: Cambridge University Press, 2014).

46. Dokshin, "Whose Backyard and What's at Issue?," 924.

47. Fedor A. Dokshin, "NIMBYs and Partisans: How Material Interests and Partisanship Shape Public Response to Shale Gas Development." *Environmental Politics* 29, no. 3 (2020): 395, https://doi.org/10.1080/09644016.2019.1611020.

48. Adam Mayer and Stephanie Malin, "How Should Unconventional Oil and Gas Be Regulated? The Role of Natural Resource Dependence and Economic Insecurity," *Journal of Rural Studies* 65 (2019): 80, https://doi.org/10.1016/j.jrurstud.2018.11.005. The study Mayer and Malin cite to support this claim is William R. Freudenburg and Debra J. Davidson, "Nuclear Families and Nuclear Risks," *Rural Sociology* 72, no. 2 (2009): 215–43, https://doi.org/10.1526/003601107781170017. Similarly, Shannon Bell and Richard York argue that many West Virginia residents uncritically supported coal mining even when the economic benefits they personally received were minimal, because they believed that coal was of central economic, social, and cultural importance to the community. The authors refer to this as "community economic identity" and suggest, in this case, that it was a narrative largely constructed by industry and political elites. See "Community Economic Identity: The Coal Industry and Ideology Construction in West Virginia," *Rural Sociology* 75, no. 1 (2010): 111–43, https://doi.org/10.1111/j.1549-0831.2009.00004.x

49. Similarly, Stephanie Malin and Becky Alexis-Martin found that a community they studied framed its support for uranium mining as an environmental-justice issue; residents viewed environmentalists seeking to halt the mining as trying to trample on residents' right to self-determination. Stephanie A. Malin and Becky Alexis-Martin, "Embedding the Atom: Pro-neoliberal Activism, Polanyi, and Sites of Acceptance in American Uranium Communities," *Extractive Industries and Society* 7, no. 2 (2020): 535–43, https://doi.org/10.1016/j.exis.2018.12.004.

50. See Shepstone, "DRBC Action."

51. Adam Mayer and Tara O'Connor Shelley, "The Dual Importance of Political Identity in Environmental Governance," *Society and Natural Resources* 31, no. 11 (2018): 1239.

52. Ben Casselman and Jim Tankersley, "Would You Go to a Movie Right Now? Republicans Say Yes. Few Others Do," *New York Times*, July 24, 2020, https://www.nytimes.com/2020/07 /24/business/economy/republicans-democrats-coronavirus-survey.html.

53. In *Strangers in Their Own Land: Anger and Mourning on the American Right* (New York: New Press, 2016), Arlie Hochschild notes a similar dynamic in a conservative Louisiana community she studied. Many of her interviewees identified as Tea Party members who had a "visceral hate" for the government (151) and expressed faith in the private sector. Even after their backyards were poisoned by local petrochemical companies that were able to flout the state's lax regulatory apparatus, many residents "renounced the desire to remediate" the damage "because that would call for more dreaded government" (177). Echoing Katherine Cramer' s "politics of resentment" thesis (see *The Politics of Resentment: Rural Consciousness in Wisconsin and the Rise of Scott Walker* [Chicago: University of Chicago Press, 2016]), Hochschild implies that locals' support of industry was shaped by "cultural values" and emotional "feeling rules" that unfolded from their conservative political identities (15), which bred a distrust of politicians and of any policies that appeared to threaten personal sovereignty. Regarding fracking, sociologist Anthony Ladd observed an implicit social contract between Louisianans and the oil and gas industry, in which conservative residents, grateful for the economic growth associated with fracking, trusted the industry to self-regulate more than they trusted the state to regulate the industry. See "Environmental Disputes and Opportunity-Threat Impacts Surrounding Natural Gas Fracking in Louisiana," *Social Currents* 1, no. 3 (2014): 293–311, https://doi.org/10.1177 /2329496514540132.

Chapter 10. Our Land

1. See Ad Crable, "Outdoors: Rock Run, Prettiest Stream in Pennsylvania?," August 25, 2013, updated October 3, 2013, *Lancaster Online*, https://lancasteronline.com/news/outdoors-rock -run-prettiest-stream-in-pennsylvania/article_2a8ab20d-bf06-5acb-9f99-0b55c756e7df.html.

2. According to Crable, "Outdoors: Rock Run."

3. Karl Blankenship, "Conservationists Fight to Save One of PA's Gem Streams," January 7, 2013, updated June 25, 2020, *Bay Journal*, https://www.bayjournal.com/news/growth _conservation/conservationists-fight-to-save-one-of-pas-gem-streams/article_1a75b921-0f17 -58e7-91f4-0b2f68f3817b.html.

4. "Natural Gas Management," Pennsylvania Department of Conservation and Natural Resources, accessed August 9, 2020, https://www.dcnr.pa.gov/Conservation/ForestsAndTrees /NaturalGasDrillingImpact/Pages/default.aspx. Almost all DCNR-managed land was at one time privately held. Sellers were often reluctant to relinquish the mineral rights; in those cases, the DCNR was only able to purchase the surface rights. Mineral rights trump surface rights in Pennsylvania (and elsewhere); thus, the surface owner (in this case, the DCNR) must allow subsurface access (e.g., gas drilling) if someone else holds the mineral rights.

5. See "Natural Gas Development and State Forests: Shale Gas Leasing Statistical Summary," Pennsylvania Department of Conservation and Natural Resources (DCNR), May 2017, http:// www.docs.dcnr.pa.gov/cs/groups/public/documents/document/dcnr_20029363.pdf; see also Marie Cusick, "Forest Drilling to Generate $80 Million this Year," StateImpact Pennsylvania,

February 24, 2017, https://stateimpact.npr.org/pennsylvania/2017/02/24/forest-drilling-to -generate-80-million-this-year/; *Shale Gas Monitoring Report*, Pennsylvania Department of Conservation and Natural Resources (DCNR), July 2018, http://www.docs.dcnr.pa.gov/cs /groups/public/documents/document/dcnr_20033642.pdf.

6. DCNR, "Natural Gas Development and State Forests." Most portions of public land now managed by the DCNR have a long history of resource extraction. Edwin Drake drilled America's first oil well near Titusville, Pennsylvania, in 1859, around the time that the Williamsport area was becoming known as the lumber capital of the world. Subterranean orphan wells and abandoned mine shafts are evidence of the state's legacy of oil, gas, and coal mining. Yet most mining operations were shuttered decades ago, because they were small-scale and inefficient, and the lumber industry collapsed before the turn of the twentieth century, after denuding the entire state. Since then, millions of acres of second-growth woodlands have swallowed up almost all traces of this extractive history and been turned into protected public commons that collectively "represent one of the largest expanses of wildland in the eastern United States." See DCNR, "DCNR's Bureau of Forestry Celebrates 125 years of Conserving Penn's Woods," August 5, 2020, https://www.dcnr.pa.gov/GoodNatured/Pages/Article.aspx?post=136.

7. "About the Pennsylvania Wilds," Pennsylvania Wilds, accessed June 13 2013, https:// pawilds.com/about/.

8. DCNR, *Shale Gas Monitoring Report* (2018), 67.

9. In 2017, the DCNR reduced the size of one well pad by two acres and planted native trees and shrubs on portions of five pipeline corridors. However, "to date, no gas infrastructure sites have reached the final restoration stage"—i.e., returned to a natural state). See DCNR, *Shale Gas Monitoring Report* (2018), 70.

10. *Shale Gas Monitoring Report*, Pennsylvania Department of Conservation and Natural Resources (DCNR), April 2014, http://www.docs.dcnr.pa.gov/cs/groups/public/documents /document/dcnr_20029147.pdf; DNCR, *Shale Gas Monitoring Report* (2018).

11. Relatedly, the gas industry advocated the controversial "Endangered Species Coordination Act," which would limit the ability of Pennsylvania state agencies to designate endangered species. See Natasha Lindstrom, "Controversial Endangered Species Bill Clears Committee," *The Times*, November 14, 2013, https://www.timesonline.com/article/20131114/News/311149810.

12. See the following time-lapse satellite imagery of the park, beginning in the year 2007: https://earthengine.google.com/timelapse/#v=41.31621,-77.31539,11,latLng&t=19840101&et =%2020181231&startDwell=0&endDwell=0.

13. DCNR, *Shale Gas Monitoring Report* (2018), 147.

14. "About the Pennsylvania Wilds," Pennsylvania Wilds, accessed September 20, 2020, https://pawilds.com/about/.

15. In an online survey conducted by the DCNR, 29 percent of respondents said that "Marcellus activity" had altered the way they *used* Tiadaghton (e.g., where they go; what they do); 35 percent said that fracking changed the way they *experienced* the forest (e.g., how it feels to them). Of those who said gas drilling changed how they used the forest, most emphasized the "displacement" of nature and closed roads. What's more, the plurality of respondents (35 percent) believed that energy development in the forest was being managed poorly or very poorly (22 percent said that it was being managed well or very well). The DCNR also analyzed comment cards left by visi-

tors in the Tiadaghton and other forests. It reports that the most common theme was concerns about truck traffic, dust, noise, litter, and the presence of gas workers in the forest. The second-most-common theme was categorical opposition to the very idea of shale gas development in state forests, followed closely by remarks expressing concern over the loss of natural scenery and the forest's wild character. See DCNR, *Shale Gas Monitoring Report* (2018), 185–86.

16. DCNR, *Shale Gas Monitoring Report* (2018), 157–60.

17. See Marie Cusick, "On Public Land, a Gas Company Takes Private Control," StateImpact Pennsylvania, August 11, 2014, https://stateimpact.npr.org/pennsylvania/2014/08/11/on-public-land-a-gas-company-takes-private-control/.

18. William Cronon, "The Trouble with Wilderness; or, Getting Back to the Wrong Nature," *Environmental History* 1, no. 1 (1996): 13, https://doi.org/10.2307/3985059.

19. Henry D. Thoreau, *Walden*, ed. J. Lyndon Shanley (1854; Princeton, NJ: Princeton University Press, 2004).

20. Henry David Thoreau, "Walking," *Atlantic Monthly*, June 1862, https://www.theatlantic.com/magazine/archive/1862/06/walking/304674/.

21. Thoreau had argued that taxes supported government-sponsored injustices like slavery and the war with Mexico. See Rebecca Beatrice Brooks, "Henry David Thoreau Arrested for Nonpayment of Poll Tax," *History of Massachusetts Blog*, July 14, 2010, https://historyofmassachusetts.org/henry-david-thoreau-arrested-for-nonpayment-of-poll-tax/.

22. The most (in)famous version of this argument is Frederick Jackson Turner's "frontier thesis." *The Frontier in American History* (1920; Midland, NJ: Pinnacle Press, 2017).

23. Edward Abbey, "Freedom and Wilderness, Wilderness and Freedom," in *The Journey Home: Some Words in Defense of the American West* (1977; New York: Plume, 1991), 235.

24. J. Drew Lanham, "With Liberty, Justice, and Wildness for All: A Plea to My Country," *Sierra*, July 19, 2020, https://www.sierraclub.org/sierra/liberty-justice-and-wildness-for-all.

25. DCNR, *Shale Gas Monitoring Report* (2014), 43.

26. This interpretation from Mark Szybist comes from his response to a comment on the FracTracker Alliance website. See Mark Szybist, "Controversy in the Loyalsock," FracTracker Alliance, May 29, 2013, https://www.fractracker.org/2013/05/clarence-moore/.

27. Clarence W. Moore v. Commonwealth of Pennsylvania, Department of Environmental Resources, 566 A.2d 905 (Pa. Cmmw. Ct. 1989).

28. For details and video clips of the event, see RDA, "Lost & Found in the Loyalsock," September 27, 2012, http://keepitwildblog.blogspot.com/2012/09/.

29. Jim Hamill, "Invite-Only Gas Drilling Meeting Excludes Public, Media," WNEP, April 4, 2013, https://www.wnep.com/article/news/local/lycoming-county/invite-only-gas-drilling-meeting-excludes-public-media/523-b9ea9a24-8dcd-4a96-b6d7-41fe0db7289f.

30. Secretary: 'Muddled' Rights Delay Decisions," *Williamsport Sun-Gazette*, May 30, 2013, https://www.sungazette.com/news/top-news/2013/05/secretary-muddled-rights-delay-decisions/.

31. Marie Cusick and Susan Phillips, "Corbett Forces Out DCNR Secretary Richard Allan," StateImpact Pennsylvania, June 13, 2013, https://stateimpact.npr.org/pennsylvania/2013/06/13/corbett-forces-out-dcnr-secretary-richard-allan/; Dennis Owens, "DCNR Secretary Allan Forced to Resign over an Email," *Sentinel*, June 13, 2013, https://cumberlink.com/news/local

/govt-and-politics/dcnr-secretary-allan-forced-to-resign-over-an-email/article_d18966b0
-d434-11e2-b22a-001a4bcf887a.html.

32. Marie Cusick, "Public Will Get to Weigh In on Loyalsock Forest Drilling Plans," StateImpact Pennsylvania, July 30, 2014, https://stateimpact.npr.org/pennsylvania/2014/07/30/public
-will-get-to-weigh-in-on-loyalsock-forest-drilling-plans/.

33. Ralph told me he believed they had collected about 19,000 signatures; however, 12,000
is the number PennEnvironment reported to the media. "12,000 Pennsylvanians Demand: 'Protect Loyalsock from Fracking,'" PennEnvironment, August 22, 2013, https://pennenvironment
.org/news/pae/12000-pennsylvanians-demand-%E2%80%9Cprotect-loyalsock
-fracking%E2%80%9D.

34. Cusick, "Public Will Get to Weigh In."

35. Responsible Drilling Alliance, "Five Alarm Fire," RDA Newsletter, July 31, 2014, http://
responsibledrillingalliance.org/wp-content/uploads/2017/01/Five-Alarm-Fire.pdf.

36. Mirabito lost his reelection bid to a Republican before he could introduce the bill. Vitali's
resolution never reached a floor vote in the Republican-controlled House, but it did garner
seven conservative cosponsors.

37. Andrew Maykuth, "Wolf Being Pressured to Restrict Gas Drilling," Pittsburgh Post-Gazette, February 8, 2015, https://www.post-gazette.com/business/powersource/2015/02/08
/Wolf-being-pressured-to-restrict-gas-drilling/stories/201502080179.

38. See Edward McAllister, "America's Biggest Gas Field Finally Succumbs to Downturn,"
Reuters, December 2, 2015, https://www.reuters.com/article/us-usa-marcellus-decline-insight
-idUSKBN0TL0CY20151202.

39. "Anadarko Sells All Marcellus Assets for $1.24B to Alta Resources," Marcellus Drilling
News, December 22, 2016, https://marcellusdrilling.com/2016/12/anadarko-sells-all-marcellus
-assets-for-1-24b-to-alta-resources/.

40. Responsible Drilling Alliance, "11,700 More Acres of Lycoming County Public Land
Bites The Dust . . . ," RDA e-Newsletter, February 2013, v. 5, https://myemail.constantcontact
.com/RDA-Newsletter--What-Moxie-.html?soid=1108623850811&aid=fffmNoyqEYc.

41. Stacia S. Ryder and Peter M. Hall, "This Land Is Your Land, Maybe: A Historical Institutionalist Analysis for Contextualizing Split Estate Conflicts in U.S. Unconventional Oil and
Gas Development," Land Use Policy 63 (2017): 149–59, https://doi.org/10.1016/j.landusepol
.2017.01.006.

42. US Department of the Interior, Bureau of Land Management, "About the BLM Oil and
Gas Program," accessed August 15, 2020, https://www.blm.gov/programs/energy-and-minerals
/oil-and-gas/about.

43. US Department of the Interior, "8 Things You Didn't Know about the Bureau of Land
Management," blog, July 13, 2017, https://www.doi.gov/blog/8-things-you-didnt-know-about
-bureau-land-management.

44. Ryder and Hall, "This Land Is Your Land," 152. One telling fact about the landmark Great
American Outdoors Act (2020), a bipartisan bill that finally provides a permanent source of
revenue for preserving chronically underfunded national parks and is widely seen as a major
environmental win: the funding comes from royalties generated by oil and gas drilling on federal lands.

45. Christopher Ketcham, "This Land Was Your Land," *New York Times*, July 13, 2019, https://www.nytimes.com/2019/07/13/opinion/sunday/conservation-mining-west.html.

46. Coral Davenport, "Trump Drilling Plan Threatens 9 Million Acres of Sage Grouse Habitat," *New York Times*, December 6, 2018, https://www.nytimes.com/2018/12/06/climate/trump-sage-grouse-oil.html.

47. Eric Lipton and Hiroko Tabuchi, "Driven by Trump Policy Changes, Fracking Booms on Public Lands," *New York Times*, October 27, 2018, https://www.nytimes.com/2018/10/27/climate/trump-fracking-drilling-oil-gas.html.

48. Ketcham, "This Land Was Your Land."

Conclusion. Bust and Beyond

1. Andrew Maykuth, "Williamsport, Booming Gas-Drilling City, Stays Optimistic as Drilling Slows," *Pennsylvania Real-Time News*, November 25, 2013, updated January 5, 2019, https://www.pennlive.com/midstate/2013/11/williamsport_booming_gas-drill.html.

2. Sarah Buynovsky, "Keeping Hope Alive for NuWeld Workers in Williamsport," WNEP, May 4, 2016, https://www.wnep.com/article/news/local/lycoming-county/nuweld-inc-in-williamsport-closing/523-6b926a64-5c09-42b1-9b66-d657713e8c34.

3. Candy Woodall, "Pa. Rig Count Lower than Before the Marcellus Shale Boom," *PennLive Patriot-News*, January 5, 2019, https://www.pennlive.com/news/2016/02/pa_rig_count_lower_than_before.html#:~:text=There%20are%20now%20fewer%20drilling,the%20century%2C%20falling%20to%20571; Joseph Hammond, "After the Boom: How the Marcellus Shale Changed Life in Pennsylvania," *Daily Caller*, July 11, 2016, https://dailycaller.com/2016/07/11/after-the-boom-how-the-marcellus-shale-changed-life-in-pennsylvania/.

4. Matt Goldman and Mike Byhoff, "How Fracking Became America's Money Pit," Bloomberg QuickTake Originals, July 2, 2020, YouTube video, 16:49, https://www.youtube.com/watch?v=jFWIIxZpF9rc&feature=youtu.be.

5. Christopher Helman, "Itemizing the Oil Bust: 75,000 Layoffs and Counting," *Forbes*, March 16, 2015, updated March 18, 2015, https://www.forbes.com/sites/christopherhelman/2015/03/16/oil-layoffs-itemized-75000-and-counting/#494acbdb7582.

6. Clifford Krauss, "Natural Gas Boom Fizzles as U.S. Glut Sinks Profit," *New York Times*, December 11, 2019, https://www.nytimes.com/2019/12/11/business/energy-environment/natural-gas-shale-chevron.html.

7. Joe Carroll et al., "Shale Drillers are Staring Down the Barrel of the Worst Oil Bust Yet," *Pittsburgh Post-Gazette*, March 10, 2020, https://www.post-gazette.com/business/powersource/2020/03/10/shale-oil-drillers-bust-2020-price-war-OPEC-Russia-crude-US-prices/stories/202003100019.

8. Jillian Ambrose, "Shell Reports $18bn Loss as Global Oil and Gas Prices Collapse," *Guardian*, July 30, 2020, https://www.theguardian.com/business/2020/jul/30/shell-reports-18bn-financial-loss-amid-covid-19-collapse-in-global-oil-and-gas-prices.

9. For an overview, see Adam Mayer, Shawn K. Olson-Hazboun, and Stephanie Malin, "Fracking Fortunes: Economic Well-Being and Oil and Gas Development along the Urban-Rural Continuum," *Rural Sociology* 83, no. 3 (2017): 532–67, https://doi.org/10.1111/ruso.12198.

10. Emily S. Rueb, "'Freedom Gas,' the Next American Export," *New York Times*, May 29, 2019, https://www.nytimes.com/2019/05/29/us/freedom-gas-energy-department.html.

11. "Natural Gas Explained: Natural Gas Imports and Exports," US Energy Information Administration, accessed August 15, 2020, https://www.eia.gov/energyexplained/natural-gas/imports-and-exports.php.

12. The Environmental Defense Fund supports transitioning to "truly clean, renewable sources of electricity . . . as quickly as possible." Although it claims not to endorse the concept of natural gas a "bridge fuel," it said that "natural gas can help provide an exit ramp" from the "carbon highway." See Eric Pooley, "What InsideClimate Got Right and Wrong about EDF's Methane Work," *EDF Voices* (blog), Environmental Defense Fund, April 13, 2015, https://www.edf.org/blog/2015/04/13/what-insideclimate-got-right-and-wrong-about-edfs-methane-work.

13. John Broderick and Kevin Anderson, "Has US Shale Gas Reduced CO_2 Emissions? Examining Recent Changes in Emissions from the US Power Sector and Traded Fossil Fuels," Tyndall Centre at the University of Manchester, October 2012, https://tyndall.ac.uk/sites/default/files/publications/broderick_and_anderson_2012_impact_of_shale_gas_on_us_energy_and_emissions_exec_summary_0.pdf.

14. John C. Dernbach and James R. May, "Can Shale Gas Help Accelerate the Transition to Sustainability?," *Environment: Science and Policy for Sustainable Development* 57, no. 1 (2015): 12, https://doi.org/10.1080/00139157.2015.983835.

15. Adam R. Brandt et al., "Methane Leaks from North American Natural Gas Systems," *Science* 343, no. 6172 (2014): 733–35, https://doi.org/10.1126/science.1247045; Ramón A. Alvarez et al., "Assessment of Methane Emissions From the U.S. Oil and Gas Supply Chain," *Science* 361, no. 6398 (2018): 186–88, https://doi.org/10.1126/science.aar7204.

16. Hiroko Tabuchi, "Despite Their Promises, Giant Energy Companies Burn Away Vast Amounts of Natural Gas," *New York Times*, October 16, 2019, https://www.nytimes.com/2019/10/16/climate/natural-gas-flaring-exxon-bp.html.

17. See Lawrence E. Culleen et al., "Hydraulic Fracturing Legal Update—November 2016," Arnold & Porter, November 8, 2016, https://www.arnoldporter.com/en/perspectives/publications/2016/11/hydraulic-fracturing-legal-update.

18. Johan Rockström et al., "A Safe Operating Space for Humanity," *Nature* 461 (2009): 472–75, https://doi.org/10.1038/461472a.

19. Dominic Dudley, "Renewable Energy Costs Take Another Tumble, Making Fossil Fuels Look More Expensive Than Ever," *Forbes*, May 29, 2019, https://www.forbes.com/sites/dominicdudley/2019/05/29/renewable-energy-costs-tumble/#155fef9ee8ce.

20. Amol Phadke et al., "2035, the Report: Plummeting Solar, Wind, and Battery Costs Can Accelerate Our Clean Energy Future," Goldman School of Public Policy, University of California, Berkeley, June 2020, http://www.2035report.com/wp-content/uploads/2020/06/2035-Report.pdf?hsCtaTracking=8a85e9ea-4ed3-4ec0-b4c6-906934306ddb%7Cc68c2ac2-1db0-4d1c-82a1-65ef4daaf6c1

21. Christopher Helman, "President Obama Gets It: Fracking Is Awesome," *Forbes*, February 12, 2013, https://www.forbes.com/sites/christopherhelman/2013/02/12/president-obama-gets-it-fracking-is-awesome/#2da412d8425d; Clifford Krauss and Ivan Penn, "Oil and Gas Groups See 'Some Common Ground' in Biden Energy Plan," *New York Times*, July 28, 2020,

https://www.nytimes.com/2020/07/28/business/energy-environment/joe-biden-oil-gas
-energy.html?searchResultPosition=4.

22. Krishna Savani, Nicole M. Stephens, and Hazel Rose Markus, "The Unanticipated Interpersonal and Societal Consequences of Personal Choice: Victim Blaming and Reduced Support for Public Good," *Psychological Science* 22, no. 6 (2011): 795–802, https://doi.org/10.1177/0956797611407928.

23. Paul Krugman, "The Cult of Selfishness Is Killing America," *New York Times*, July 27, 2020, https://www.nytimes.com/2020/07/27/opinion/us-republicans-coronavirus.html.

24. On the connection between the reopening of bars and restaurants and the rise of COVID-19 cases, see Jennifer Steinhauer, "The Nation Wanted to Eat Out Again. Everyone Has Paid the Price," *New York Times*, August 12, 2020, https://www.nytimes.com/2020/08/12/health/Covid-restaurants-bars.html.

25. Ronald H. Coase, "The Problem of Social Cost," *Journal of Law and Economics* 3 (1960): 1–44.

26. See Cameron T. Whitley, "Exploring the Place of Animals and Human-Animal Relationships in Hydraulic Fracturing Discourse," *Social Sciences* 8, no. 2 (2019): 61–80, https://doi.org/10.3390/socsci8020061. On "wild animal sovereignty," see Sue Donaldson and Will Kymlicka, *Zoopolis: A Political Theory of Animal Rights* (Oxford: Oxford University Press, 2011).

27. Mary Annaise Heglar, "I Work in the Environmental Movement. I Don't Care If You Recycle," *Vox*, June 4, 2019, https://www.vox.com/the-highlight/2019/5/28/18629833/climate-change-2019-green-new-deal.

28. Sami Grover, "How 'Environmentalism' Became a Lifestyle Experiment," *Noteworthy—The Journal Blog*, October 24, 2019, https://blog.usejournal.com/how-environmentalism-became-a-lifestyle-experiment-d6f8a027d897.

29. Tess Riley, "Just 100 Companies Responsible for 71% of Global Emissions, Study Says," *Guardian*, July 10, 2017, https://www.theguardian.com/sustainable-business/2017/jul/10/100-fossil-fuel-companies-investors-responsible-71-global-emissions-cdp-study-climate-change.

30. ExxonKnew.org, accessed August 15, 2020, https://exxonknew.org/.

31. Matto Mildenberger, "The Tragedy of the *Tragedy of the Commons*," *Voices* (blog), *Scientific American*, April 23, 2019, https://blogs.scientificamerican.com/voices/the-tragedy-of-the-tragedy-of-the-commons/.

32. Heglar, "I Work in the Environmental Movement."

33. Michael E. Mann, "Lifestyle Changes Aren't Enough to Save the Planet. Here's What Could," *Time*, September 12, 2019, https://time.com/5669071/lifestyle-changes-climate-change/.

34. See Kate Aronoff et al., *A Planet to Win: Why We Need a Green New Deal* (New York: Verso, 2019).

35. Arlie Hochschild, *Strangers in Their Own Land: Anger and Mourning on the American Right* (New York: New Press, 2016); Loka Ashwood, *For-Profit Democracy: Why the Government Is Losing the Trust of Rural America* (New Haven, CT: Yale University Press, 2018).

36. Adam Mayer, "Political Identity and Paradox in Oil and Gas Policy: A Study of Regulatory Exaggeration in Colorado, US," *Energy Policy* 109 (2017): 452–59, https://doi.org/10.1016/j.enpol.2017.07.023.

37. Peter J. Jacques, Riley E. Dunlap, and Mark Freeman, "The Organisation of Denial: Conservative Think Tanks and Environmental Scepticism," *Environmental Politics* 17, no. 3 (2008): 349, https://doi.org/10.1080/09644010802055576.

38. David Stasavage, "Covid-19 Has Exposed the Weakness of America's Federal Government," CNN, July 1, 2020, https://www.cnn.com/2020/07/01/opinions/covid-19-america-federal-government-stasavage/index.html. See also David Stasavage, *The Decline and Rise of Democracy: A Global History from Antiquity to Today* (Princeton, NJ: Princeton University Press, 2020).

39. "Public Trust in Government: 1958–2019," Pew Research Center, April 11, 2019, https://www.pewresearch.org/politics/2019/04/11/public-trust-in-government-1958-2019/; Justin McCarthy, "Americans Still More Trusting of Local Than State Government," Gallup, October 8, 2018, https://news.gallup.com/poll/243563/americans-trusting-local-state-government.aspx.

40. Elinor Ostrom et al., "Revisiting the Commons: Local Lessons, Global Challenges," *Science* 284, no. 5412 (1999): 279–81, https://doi.org/10.1126/science.284.5412.278.

41. Whitney Webb, "PA Dept. of Environmental Protection Sues Town over Fracking Ban," *Mint Press News*, April 10, 2017, https://www.mintpressnews.com/pa-dept-environmental-protection-sues-towns-fracking-ban/226672/.

42. Ostrom et al., "Revisiting the Commons," 278.

43. Gianpaolo Baiocchi and Ernesto Ganuza, *Popular Democracy: The Paradox of Participation* (Stanford, CA: Stanford University Press, 2017).

44. Todd Stern, "Report: The Paris Agreement and Its Future," Brookings, October 2018, https://www.brookings.edu/research/the-paris-agreement-and-its-future/.

45. Although I have stayed in regular contact with most of the people mentioned in this book, my in-person visits admittedly became much less frequent after the births of my beloved sons, Kai and Roman.

INDEX

Note: Illustrations are indicated with *italic* page numbers.

A NOTE ON THE TYPE

This book has been composed in Arno, an Old-style serif typeface in the classic Venetian tradition, designed by Robert Slimbach at Adobe.